D0045193

ARCO

Triple Your Reading Speed

by WADE E. CUTLER

THOMSON
★
PETERSON'S

Australia • Canada • Mexico • Singapore • Spain • United Kingdom • United States

An ARCO Book
ARCO is a registered trademark of Thomson Learning, Inc., and is used herein under license by Thomson Peterson's.

About Thomson Peterson's
Thomson Peterson's (www.petersons.com) is a leading provider of education information and advice, with books and online resources focusing on education search, test preparation, and financial aid. Its Web site offers searchable databases and interactive tools for contacting educational institutions, online practice tests and instruction, and planning tools for securing financial aid. Thomson Peterson's serves 110 million education consumers annually.

> **Petersons.com/publishing**
> Check out our Web site at www.petersons.com/publishing to see if there is any new information regarding the test and any revisions or corrections to the content of this book. We've made sure the information in this book is accurate and up-to-date; however, the test format or content may have changed since the time of publication.

For more information, contact Thomson Peterson's, 2000 Lenox Drive, Lawrenceville, NJ 08648; 800-338-3282; or find us on the World Wide Web at www.petersons.com/about.

2005 © Thomson Peterson's, a part of The Thomson Corporation Thomson Learning™ is a trademark used herein under license.

Previous editions © 1970, 1988, 1993, 2002 and 2003 by Wade E. Cutler,

ISBN 0-7689-0903-1

Printed in Canada

9 8 7 6 5   06 05 04

Fourth Edition

Contents

Before You Start To Read . . .

To get the greatest benefit from this or any book, *do not* start to read on the first page of the text (Part I). Get acquainted with the whole book first.

1. Thoroughly read the outside. (Check the title, the author's name, and read all comments on the covers.)

2. Note any information given about the author, his qualifications, experience, etc.

3. Check the publisher's name and the copyright/revision/printing dates on the back of the main title page.

4. Carefully read the introduction and preface to the revised edition.

5. Study the contents pages.

6. Thumb through the entire book. (Note the layout.)

7. Peruse the information contained in the appendices.

Only now are you ready to turn to Part I for serious reading. You know a lot about this book—the subject, the author, the treatment of the topic, the typography, etc. This book has its own individuality that sets it apart from all others; the same is true of all other books with different titles. If you take a few minutes to preview any book, you will get much more from your study. More will be explained about previewing in Part II.

Go now to Part I with the confidence that you are prepared to begin meaningful study.

Preface to the Fourth Edition

Triple Your Reading Speed has been in print continuously since 1970, and has undergone three previous revisions. While this type of self-help book course seldom, if ever, becomes a "best-seller," this book has been in consistent demand for over 30 years, and now is approaching one million copies in print.

In this newly-revised fourth edition, numerous improvements and additions have been incorporated—including additional book-length assignments with tests to measure your reading speed and comprehension. Also included are additional explanations and new easy-to-do-anywhere exercises to help you become a faster and more effective reader in the shortest time possible.

Still, however, it is only fair to caution that a pronounced desire to succeed and a willingness to practice as required are necessary if you aspire to become an outstanding Acccele*reader*. No one will become an effective faster reader overnight.

Triple Your Reading Speed is a complete how-to course; everything you require to learn and succeed is here, but you will need to do the work necessary to assure that the techniques work for you.

In Appendix 1, you can learn the tested and proven techniques for making your study time easier, more successful, and more productive.

In Appendix 2, you will discover rock-solid ways to prepare yourself psychologically and otherwise to score higher on all types of tests: true and false, multiple choice, and even essay tests.

Appendix 3 explains clearly and logically how the Acccele*read* Method works.

Introduction

From the mid-sixties to the early seventies, the Cutler Accele*read* Method was taught successfully in classrooms to over 10,000 persons—both students and adults—primarily in the Southwest.

In-residence classes conducted for relatively small study groups developed dramatic improvements in individual reading rates and comprehension scores. Accelerated Education Schools, the name under which the Accele*read* Course was marketed exclusively, operated for the most part in Texas, New Mexico, Oklahoma, Louisiana, and Mississippi.

The schools guaranteed that all graduates of the program would be able to read 1,000 words-per-minute or three times the pre-course tested rate (whichever was greater), with improved comprehension. Records prove the average rate increase for graduates of the closely-supervised, individualized course ranged from seven to twelve times—depending upon the individual student's basic ability, the type of material being read, the purpose for which it was read, and other factors.

Comprehension, as measured by objective tests, typically improved an average of 13 percent. However, overall understanding of what was read improved markedly—usually far more than that which could be measured solely by objective testing. An integral part of the outstanding success of this reading method was the intensive, specialized training and practice in developing previewing techniques, better study habits, and improved test-taking skills.

This book course contains all the necessary theory, explanations, drills, study, and practice exercises to enable a motivated, "average" reader to at least *triple* his or her present reading rate, and improve overall comprehension—if the program outlined here is closely followed.

This is a tested and proven method; it is in no way experimental. You can put the techniques that are described here to valuable use by applying them to improve your personal/business success and educational prowess. Remember: reading is the basis of all education.

PART I

Learn About Reading and Yourself

In this section you will learn...

📖 that you definitely can read faster, much faster—and comprehend more of what you read

📖 how to measure your present reading rate and comprehension with two inventory reading exercises and tests

📖 how you actually were taught and, consequently, learned to read slowly

📖 the important role eye movements play in determining your reading speed

📖 some of the many actual rewards of accelerated (speed) reading

You Can Read Much Faster

If you can read these words easily, you can read faster. You probably have some doubts or reservations. You might say that it just is not possible, that you can only read so fast and that is it. Not true! It is now possible for all readers (possessing at least average abilities) who apply themselves to the guides and materials in this book-course to at least triple their present words-per-minute rate, and improve overall comprehension of what is required or chosen reading.

What does this mean to you personally?

It means you will be able to read *three* similar books in the time you now require to read only one—and you will understand what you read much better.

- You will reduce normal reading fatigue by as much as two-thirds.

- You will be able to keep up with the required reading of your profession or professional pursuit—the paper backlog that seems to get bigger with each passing day.

- You will be able to read daily newspapers, magazines, reports, and letters in much less time.

- You will also have time to read a few of the current bestsellers so you can discuss them intelligently with friends. (It does get to be embarrassing to always have to say no when an acquaintance asks if you have read such and such book!)

- You might even be able to have a lot more leisure- and fun-time when you become an Accelerated Reader.

These are just a few of the many advantages of successful faster reading. You will no doubt be able to add to this limited list.

Interested?

Wonderful! Read on.

A strong *desire* to improve reading speed and comprehension is absolutely necessary before a marked change for the better is to be either expected or actually noted—know this from the outset. If you honestly desire improvement, you will drill, practice, and read with the regularity and determination that will assure you achieve your reading speed and comprehension goals sooner.

Perhaps you still question your innate ability to succeed with tripling your reading rate *and* improving comprehension. If so, contemplate the following statement: Psychologists have estimated that the average individual uses only about 10 percent of his or her mental abilities. Ten percent! What a pity to waste some 90 percent! If you are reading at say 100 to 300 words per minute now—using 10 percent of your reading ability—how fast could you read if you used 20, 30, 40 percent or more?

A primary purpose of *Triple Your Reading Speed* is to assist you to search out, perfect, and more fully utilize the wonderful skills you already possess. After you learn to exploit this innate "genius potential" for faster reading with better comprehension, you certainly should be able to make reading and study time a more meaningful, valuable, productive, and enjoyable experience.

When you learn to triple your reading speed, you will confront two pleasant scenarios: (1) you will be able to reduce markedly the time you now require to do necessary reading; and (2) you will be able to get much more done in the same amount of time. Either way *you* are the winner!

Measure Present Reading Rate/ Comprehension

Before beginning serious study and practice for becoming an Accelerated Reader, you must take an "inventory" to determine your present reading rate of words-per-minute and comprehensive ability.

The purpose for the two selections that follow is to get a most-accurate-as-possible measure of both your reading speed and comprehension. Therefore, you are urged to read each at your normal rate. Following each selection is a thorough multiple-choice test to measure comprehension. Read for understanding and details.

In order to time yourself, you will need a watch or clock with a second hand. Do not read the timepiece from an angle, which could result in an inaccurate computation of actual reading rate.

It is best, if possible, to adjust the clock so that the minute and second hands are synchronized. If a timer or stopwatch is available, all the better.

Select a starting time in advance and note it on the lines below.

Starting Time: MINUTES_____ SECONDS_____

As the second (and minute) hands reach the time you have written down, begin reading.

INVENTORY SELECTION 1

Radio Communications and the Sun

by Wade E. Cutler

Through the years, man has become more and more critical about carefree and undistorted radio communications, but frequently he finds reception poor or totally impossible. What is the principal reason?

Radio interference, often the major reason for poor long-distance communication, can be widely classified into two groups: (1) that caused by man; and (2) that caused by nature. The disturbances caused by man and man-made machines are numerous; but, overall, they are not as important regarding radio communications as are those caused by nature. It is not the purpose of this article to discuss the numerous man-made interferences with which most radio users are already quite familiar, but to discuss the greatest hamperer of radio communication over great distances—the sun and the role it plays.

The sun is looked to for many things; in fact, all life is dependent on it for survival. However, it is unlikely that many radio users are aware of the dominant influence the sun exercises on radio-wave transmission and reception. Therefore, an explanation of what happens to a radio wave after transmission seems appropriate at this point.

All signaling by means of radio occurs as the result of waves that travel from a transmitter to a receiver. These waves, which are electromagnetic in character, arise from the presence of rapidly alternating currents in the antenna of the transmitter. From the antenna, these waves spread out in all (or specifically engineered) directions with the velocity of light—186,000 miles per second. The distant receiving antenna intercepts only a very small amount of the wave energy that is radiated by the transmitter's antenna. In most instances, this tiny amount of energy is quite adequate for satisfactory communication levels.

The carrier waves that are sent out by the radio station's antenna may be divided into two categories: First, the ground wave; and second, the sky wave. The distance of ground-wave travel is limited and, therefore, is seldom of importance for communication over distances of more than a few hundred miles. The sky wave is relied upon for long-range communications.

When the receiver is far from the transmitter—say, well around the curve of the earth—transmission and reception would be impossible were it not for the presence of several layers of electricity high above the surface of the earth at altitudes of 60 to 250 miles. These layers act as "mirrors," reflecting back to earth radio waves that otherwise would be lost in interplanetary space. This upper region of the atmosphere consists of electrically charged particles originally emitted by the sun, and molecules and atoms whose electrons have been torn from them as the result of ultraviolet radiation. The charged particles are commonly referred to as ions; hence, the reflecting layers are usually referred to as the ionosphere.

Considering the above, it is evident that the sun is instrumental in forming this complex layer known as the ionosphere. Although the ionosphere has been referred to as a sort of mirror, it might more accurately be compared to a "sieve." This ionospheric sieve that encloses the entire spherical earth is not at all uniform. Over that portion of the earth where the sun's rays strike nearly vertically, the sieve openings are small. This characteristic arises from the fact that in the vertical striking area solar radiation produces the greatest electrification.

The conclusion that radio waves are literally bounced off this mirror is a very accurate one. Then it is easy to see that a radio wave, which, instead of bouncing off this electrical field goes through it, would be lost and could not be picked up by the antenna of any earth-based receiver. Most of the time the "mesh" of this sieve remains fairly constant; radio experts have been able to set frequencies of the correct size and length so that they normally bounce as they are intended to do. But at times they do not reflect or bounce and go right through enlarged sieve openings to become lost in interplanetary space forever. Why do these openings or "holes" in the ionospheric layers vary in size? Why do they tend to change somewhat even from minute to minute? For the answer, the radio user must look to the sun and its habits.

As has been stated earlier, the sun is responsible for the creation of this electrical ionosphere—its ultraviolet light shines upon molecules of oxygen and nitrogen, partly decomposing them and knocking off tiny electrons from the atoms, which creates the so-called ions.

Radio engineers and scientists have ascertained this layer's presence and can measure its altitude by sending up radio pulses through the stratosphere until they hit the radio ceiling, bounce back, and are caught in a receiving apparatus. The time it takes the waves to go to the ionosphere and return is carefully noted by computing the rate of travel at the velocity of light.

On the side of the earth turned toward the sun, where the ionosphere is exposed directly to the sun's rays, the ceiling is much lower than on the side of the earth away from the sun. This accounts for the great difference in the way in which radio waves travel in daytime as compared to nighttime. The shorter waves—higher frequencies—are better for daytime transmission, while longer or lower frequencies are better for nighttime transmission.

Just as there is a day and night effect on transmission, there is also a seasonal effect. In the northern hemisphere, the top of the atmosphere is much more heavily ionized during the long summer months, than during the shorter days of the winter season. The radio ceiling, therefore, is lower in summer than in winter; regular radio users are probably aware that long-distance transmission and reception are usually much better in winter than in the long, hot days of summer. This is due mainly to a higher, more stable, more reflective radio ceiling, or ionosphere.

If the sun's atmospheric influence remained constant, it would be quite simple to work out charts, frequencies, and plans to overcome most of the common difficulties and failures related to radio-wave transmission and reception. But unfortunately, the sun, like all things, is changing constantly. The most noticeable change is the appearance of sunspots.

Sunspots are the darker areas at times visible on the sun's surface, thought to be tornado-like solar storms. Their average duration is about two weeks, and they usually occur in eleven-year cycles. In reality, sunspots are storm areas within the solar atmosphere. Like similar cyclonic low-pressure disturbances on the earth's surface, they are cooler than their surroundings. While the sun's radiating surface appears to have a temperature of about 6,000 degrees centigrade, the temperature of sunspots is about 2,000 degrees lower, which is why they appear relatively darker by contrast.

Exactly how do sunspots affect radio? When, during sunspot maxima, solar activity results, as it generally does, in a greater output of ultraviolet light, the ionosphere is more heavily ionized than during the years of sunspot minima. This results in long undulations of the radio ceiling as it rises and falls over a cyclical eleven-year period. Further, when a sunspot is formed suddenly or a violent eruption takes place in the atmosphere of the sun, there is a burst of energy sent toward the earth which, upon hitting the ionosphere, may create all sorts of electromagnetic disturbances.

Thus, in view of the fact that long-range transmission and reception depend upon the radio sky wave being reflected back to earth from the ionosphere, it is easy to see that radio communications and the sun are intimately linked. However, this link and its inherent problems are becoming less of an issue since, in many cases, man-made satellites in space are performing well as artificial ionospheres.

Finishing Time: MINUTES_____SECONDS_____

HOW TO FIGURE READING RATE

To determine your words-per-minute (wpm) reading rate, do this: (1) subtract your starting time from your finishing time; (2) convert whole minutes into seconds by multiplying by 60; (3) now add to this any extra seconds; (4) divide total seconds into 1,306 (the number of words in this selection). Carry only to the largest single decimal place. Your answer will be something like 2.7, or 3.4, etc. This is the words-per-second rate; (5) finally, multiply the words-per-second rate by 60 to determine the words-per-minute rate. Record the result below.

Selection 1: Reading Rate:_____wpm

Now answer the following 25 questions covering the selection by circling the letter before the answer which seems most nearly correct. Read each question and each possible answer carefully. (Careful reading of this and all tests can result in better scores.)

If a question stumps you, skip it and return to it later. Do not leave any question unanswered since you are graded on the number of correct answers.

An answer left blank will count as an incorrect response.

NOTE: All questions are to be answered totally from recall. Do not look back for an answer until after you have checked and scored the test.

INVENTORY COMPREHENSION TEST 1

1. In radio communication, man-made disturbances are

    (A) important.
    (B) unimportant.
    (C) numerous.
    (D) not as important as are nature's.
    (E) both (C) and (D).

2. In order to be effective, all radio waves must travel

    (A) from a receiver to a transmitter.
    (B) from antenna to antenna.
    (C) through the sky.
    (D) from a transmitter to a receiver.
    (E) directly through the ground.

3. Radio waves are said to be

    (A) static.
    (B) non-static.
    (C) electromagnetic.
    (D) ion free.
    (E) weak.

4. Radio waves arise from the presence of rapidly alternating

    (A) currents in the transmitter.
    (B) currents in the transmitter's antenna.
    (C) currents in the receiver.
    (D) currents in the receiver's antenna.
    (E) ion particles in the atmosphere.

5. Radio waves travel at

    (A) 186,000 miles per hour.
    (B) 186,000 miles per second.
    (C) the speed of light.
    (D) Both (A) and (C).
    (E) Both (B) and (C).

6. The layers of "electricity" high above the earth vary in altitude from

    (A) 600 to 1,000 miles.
    (B) 300 to 750 miles.
    (C) 60 to 250 miles.
    (D) 600,000 to 750,000 feet.
    (E) 40 to 300 miles.

7. According to the article, long-range communications rely upon

    (A)   good telephone service.
    (B)   better connectors.
    (C)   the sky wave.
    (D)   the ground wave.
    (E)   non-jamming practices.

8. The upper region of the atmosphere consists of electrically charged particles

    (A)   originally emitted by the sun.
    (B)   having like poles.
    (C)   visible only rarely.
    (D)   originally part of the moon.
    (E)   originally part of the planet Mars.

9. The aforementioned charged particles are called

    (A)   strata-fibers.
    (B)   stardust.
    (C)   atoms.
    (D)   "mirrors."
    (E)   ions.

10. The ionosphere might most accurately be compared to

    (A)   a sort of mirror.
    (B)   a sieve.
    (C)   a grate.
    (D)   a fence.
    (E)   an umbrella.

11. Over that portion of the earth where the sun's rays strike nearly vertically, openings in the ionosphere are

    (A)   large.
    (B)   small.
    (C)   nonexistent.
    (D)   enlarged.
    (E)   pear-shaped.

12. "Radio waves are literally bounced off this 'mirror'." This statement is

    (A)   not accurate.
    (B)   accurate.
    (C)   partially true.
    (D)   very accurate.
    (E)   a half-truth.

13. When radio waves are not reflected, they

    (A) go through large openings.
    (B) become weakened.
    (C) are lost in space.
    (D) gain power.
    (E) pass through the mesh and are lost in space.

14. Openings in the electrical field in the ionosphere

    (A) never vary in size.
    (B) change in size frequently.
    (C) are all pear-shaped.
    (D) are constant in size and in form.
    (E) change even from minute to minute.

15. The electrical ionosphere is created by

    (A) the solar-plexus.
    (B) the solar time-year.
    (C) photostatic activity.
    (D) the sun.
    (E) the moon.

16. Engineers have ascertained the ionosphere's presence by

    (A) "dead-reckoning."
    (B) electromagnets.
    (C) studying charts.
    (D) sending up radio pulses.
    (E) measuring light intensity.

17. On the side of the earth exposed to the sun, the radio ceiling is

    (A) much lower.
    (B) much higher.
    (C) average.
    (D) twice as high as on the dark side.
    (E) somewhat higher.

18. For nighttime radio transmission, which frequencies are best?

    (A) the higher ones.
    (B) the lower ones.
    (C) the medium ones.
    (D) the very high ones.
    (E) the ultra-high ones.

19. Long-distance radio reception usually is better in the

    (A) summer.
    (B) spring.
    (C) fall.
    (D) winter.
    (E) in between seasons.

20. The sun is described as

    (A) never changing.
    (B) "a golden ball."
    (C) changing seasonally.
    (D) seldom changing.
    (E) constantly changing.

21. The dark areas on the sun's surface commonly are called

    (A) dark spots.
    (B) cyclonic disturbances.
    (C) volcanos.
    (D) sunspots.
    (E) storm clouds.

22. The estimated temperature of the "dark spots" is

    (A) 60,000 degrees centigrade.
    (B) 16,000 degrees centigrade.
    (C) 4,000 degrees centigrade.
    (D) 2,000 degrees centigrade.
    (E) 6,000 degrees Fahrenheit.

23. The "dark spots" are believed to be

    (A) storm areas.
    (B) cooler than others.
    (C) optical illusions.
    (D) cyclonic low pressure areas.
    (E) (A), (B), and (D).

24. Their duration is normally

    (A) eleven years.
    (B) fourteen days.
    (C) two years.
    (D) two months.
    (E) one week.

25. The sun's effect on radio communications affects mainly

    (A)   FM radio.
    (B)   television.
    (C)   AM radio.
    (D)   long-range reception.
    (E)   short-range reception.

Check back to make certain you attempted an answer for all 25 questions, then check your answers with the key for "Inventory Test 1" below. Deduct 4 points for each incorrect answer and for each omitted answer, then record your comprehension score.

Correct Answers for Inventory Test 1

(Value: 4 points each) 1,306 words

1.   The correct answer is (E).

2.   The correct answer is (D).

3.   The correct answer is (C).

4.   The correct answer is (B).

5.   The correct answer is (E).

6.   The correct answer is (C).

7.   The correct answer is (C).

8.   The correct answer is (A).

9.   The correct answer is (E).

10. The correct answer is (B).

11. The correct answer is (B).

12. The correct answer is (D).

13. The correct answer is (E).

14. The correct answer is (E).

15. The correct answer is (D).

16. The correct answer is (D).

17. The correct answer is (A).

18. The correct answer is (B).

19. The correct answer is (D).

20. The correct answer is (E).

21. The correct answer is (D).

22. The correct answer is (C).

23. The correct answer is (E).

24. The correct answer is (B).

25. The correct answer is (D).

Inventory Test 1:_____**% (Comprehension Score)**

Selection 2 is to be read following the same procedure as that used for Selection 1. (If necessary, go back and reread instructions.)

Select a starting time and write it below.

Starting Time: Minutes_____**Seconds**_____

As the second (and minute) hands reach the time you have written down, begin reading.

INVENTORY SELECTION 2

Narrative of A. Gordon Pym

by Edgar Allan Poe

Chapter 23

(Excerpt)

During the six or seven days immediately following we remained in our hiding place upon the hill, going out only occasionally, and then with the greatest precaution, for water and filberts. We had made a kind of penthouse on the platform, furnishing it with a bed of dry leaves, and placing in it three large flat stones, which served us for both fireplace and table. We kindled a fire without difficulty by rubbing two pieces of dry wood together, the one soft, the other hard. The bird we had taken in such good season proved excellent eating, although somewhat tough. It was not an oceanic fowl, but a species of bittern, with jet black and grizzly plumage, and diminutive wings in proportion to its bulk. We afterward saw three of the same kind in the vicinity of the ravine, apparently seeking for the one we had captured; but, as they never alighted, we had no opportunity of catching them.

As long as this fowl lasted we suffered nothing from our situation, but it was now entirely consumed, and it became absolutely necessary that we should look out for provision. The filberts would not satisfy the cravings of hunger, afflicting us, too, with severe gripings of the bowels, and, if freely indulged in, with violent headache. We had seen several large tortoises near the sea-shore to the eastward of the hill, and perceived they might be easily taken, if we could get at them without the observation of the natives. It was resolved, therefore, to make an attempt at descending.

We commenced by going down the southern declivity, which seemed to offer the fewest difficulties, but had not proceeded a hundred yards before (as we had anticipated from appearances on the hilltop) our progress was entirely arrested by a branch of the gorge in which our companions had perished. We now passed along the edge of this for about a quarter of a mile, when we were again stopped by a precipice of immense depth, and, not being able to make our way along the brink of it, we were forced to retrace our steps by the main ravine.

We now pushed over to the eastward, but with precisely similar fortune. After an hour's scramble, at the risk of breaking our necks, we discovered that we had merely descended into a vast pit of black granite, with fine dust at the bottom, and whence the only egress was by the rugged path in which we had come down. Toiling again up this path, we now tried the northern edge of the hill. Here we were obliged to use the greatest possible caution in our manoeuvres, as the least indiscretion would expose us to the full view of the savages in the village. We crawled along, therefore, on our hands and knees, and, occasionally, were even forced to throw ourselves at full length, dragging our bodies along by means of the shrubbery. In this careful manner we had proceeded but a little way, when we arrived at a chasm far deeper than any we had yet seen, and leading directly into the main gorge. Thus our fears were fully confirmed, we found ourselves cut off entirely from access to the world below. Thoroughly exhausted by our exertions, we made the best of our way back to the platform, and, throwing ourselves upon the bed of leaves, slept sweetly and soundly for some hours.

For several days after this fruitless search we were occupied in exploring every part of the summit of the hill, in order to inform ourselves of its actual resources. We found that it would afford us no food, with the exception of the unwholesome filberts, and a rank species of scurvy-grass, which grew in a little patch of not more than four rods square, and would soon be exhausted. On the fifteenth of February, as near as I can remember, there was not a blade of this left, and the nuts were growing scarce; our situation, therefore, could hardly be more lamentable. On the sixteenth we again went round the walls of our prison, in hope of finding some avenue of escape; but to no purpose. We also descended the chasm in which we had been overwhelmed, with the faint expectation of discovering, through this channel, some opening to the main ravine. Here, too, we were disappointed, although we found and brought up with us a musket.

On the seventeenth we set out with the determination of examining more thoroughly the chasm of black granite into which we had made our way in the first search. We remembered that one of the fissures in the sides of this pit had been but partially looked into, and we were anxious to explore it, although with no expectation of discovering here any opening.

We found no great difficulty in reaching the bottom of the hollow as before, and were now sufficiently calm to survey it with some attention. It was, indeed, one of the most singular-looking places imaginable, and we could scarcely bring ourselves to believe it altogether the work of nature. The pit, from its eastern to its western extremity, was about five hundred yards in length, when all its windings were threaded; the distance from east to west in a straight line not being more (I should suppose, having no means of accurate examination) than forty or fifty yards. Upon first descending into the chasm—that is to say, for a hundred feet downward from the summit of the hill, the sides of the abyss bore little resemblance to each other, and, apparently, had at no time been connected, the one surface being of the soapstone, and the other of marl, granulated with some metallic matter. The average breadth or interval between the two cliffs was probably here sixty feet, but there seemed to be no regularity of formation. Passing down, however, beyond the limit spoken of, the interval rapidly contracted, and the sides began to run parallel, although, for some distance farther, they were still dissimilar in their material and form of surface. Upon arriving within fifty feet of the bottom, a perfect regularity commenced. The sides were now entirely uniform in substance, in color, and in lateral direction, the material being a very black and shining granite, and the distance between the two sides, at all points, facing each other, exactly twenty yards. The precise formation of the chasm will be best understood by means of a delineation taken upon the spot; for I had luckily with me a pocket-book and pencil, which I preserved with great care through a long series of subsequent adventures, and to which I am indebted for memoranda of many subjects which would otherwise have been crowded from my remembrance.

Finishing Time: MINUTES_____ SECONDS_____

Compute your reading rate of words-per-minute and write in below. This selection contains 1,140 words. (If necessary, see instructions given in "How To Figure Rate" at the end of the first reading selection.)

Selection 2:_____**wpm**

Take the test, circling the letter before the most nearly correct answer. (Remember: Work from recall only.)

INVENTORY COMPREHENSION TEST 2

1. From their hiding place on the hill, Pym and his companion went out for

    (A) water and wood.
    (B) water and fish.
    (C) fish and wood.
    (D) water and meat.
    (E) water and filberts.

2. The platform on which they hid was referred to as

    (A) a stone cliff.
    (B) a treehouse.
    (C) a jungle den.
    (D) a penthouse.
    (E) a magic carpet.

3. They kindled a fire by

    (A) striking wet matches.
    (B) striking two stones together.
    (C) rubbing two pieces of dry wood together.
    (D) rubbing a stone firmly on dry wood.
    (E) rubbing two hard sticks together.

4. The bird that they ate was

    (A) a raven.
    (B) a species of bittern.
    (C) a species of hawk.
    (D) a type of bat.
    (E) one of a group of long-legged cranes.

5. The filberts, if freely eaten, caused

    (A) a loss of vision.
    (B) intense indigestion.
    (C) great thirst.
    (D) extreme dizziness.
    (E) violent headaches.

6. The men left their hiding place later in search of

    (A) water.
    (B) snails.
    (C) tortoises.
    (D) birds that were to be cooked for food.
    (E) seagull eggs.

7. They were hiding from

   (A) the storms of life.
   (B) themselves.
   (C) savages in the village.
   (D) the sheriff.
   (E) the truant officer from their school.

8. To avoid being seen, they

   (A) crawled on hands and knees.
   (B) planted a decoy.
   (C) took off their shirts.
   (D) decided not to move.
   (E) waited for nightfall before moving.

9. Returning to their starting point, they threw themselves upon

   (A) the mercy of the court.
   (B) a bed of straw.
   (C) a pile of stones.
   (D) a bed of ants.
   (E) a bed of leaves.

10. This search is described as

    (A) rewarding.
    (B) fruitless.
    (C) tiring.
    (D) partly successful.
    (E) ending early.

11. The hilltop afforded food only in the form of filberts and

    (A) Johnson grass.
    (B) scurvy-grass.
    (C) tomatoes.
    (D) Bermuda grass.
    (E) summer grass.

12. The aforementioned food was soon

    (A) killed.
    (B) spoiled.
    (C) frozen.
    (D) totally eaten.
    (E) stolen.

13. While examining the chasm, they found

    (A)   fresh berries.
    (B)   a cannon ball.
    (C)   a brown bear.
    (D)   a sword.
    (E)   a musket.

14. The pit, from east to west, was about

    (A)   200 feet long.
    (B)   200 yards long.
    (C)   500 feet long.
    (D)   1,000 yards long.
    (E)   500 yards long.

15. The pit is described by Pym as the

    (A)   darkest place on earth.
    (B)   coldest place he'd seen.
    (C)   deepest hole on earth.
    (D)   most singular-looking place imaginable.
    (E)   hottest place on earth.

16. The chasm was

    (A)   100 yards deep.
    (B)   500 feet deep.
    (C)   1,000 feet deep.
    (D)   some depth not stated.
    (E)   20 yards deep.

17. One to the other, the sides of the chasm bore

    (A)   little resemblance.
    (B)   a most striking resemblance.
    (C)   a remote resemblance.
    (D)   a most strange resemblance.
    (E)   no resemblance.

18. The sides of the abyss, apparently, had

    (A)   been once connected.
    (B)   at no time been connected.
    (C)   been severely eroded.
    (D)   encrusted large diamonds and other stones.
    (E)   the same texture.

19. Within fifty feet of the bottom,

    (A)   the walls grew colder.
    (B)   the walls grew warmer.

(C) the walls grew darker.
(D) a perfect regularity commenced.
(E) Pym grew ill.

20. Pym had with him

(A) a pocket-book.
(B) a fountain pen.
(C) a yardstick.
(D) a pencil.
(E) a pocket-book and pencil.

21. The adventurers were apparently having

(A) a lot of fun.
(B) a party.
(C) no difficulties.
(D) great hardships.
(E) a vacation.

22. The author of the story is

(A) Pope.
(B) Allen.
(C) Poe.
(D) Pugh.
(E) Edgars.

23. Pym's whole name was

(A) A. Glenn Pym.
(B) Gordon A. Pymm.
(C) A. Pym Gordon.
(D) A. Gordon Pymm.
(E) A. Gordon Pym.

24. The story's title identifies it as

(A) a short story.
(B) a narrative.
(C) a thriller.
(D) a prose work.
(E) both a thriller and a prose work.

25. This reading is an excerpt from Chapter

(A) 25.
(B) 26.
(C) 28.
(D) 23.
(E) 22.

Make certain you attempted an answer for all 25 questions, then check your answers with the key for "Inventory Test 2" below. Deduct 4 points for each incorrect answer and for each omitted answer, then record your comprehension score.

Correct Answers for Inventory Test 2

(Value: 4 points each) 1,140 words

1. The correct answer is (E).
2. The correct answer is (D).
3. The correct answer is (C).
4. The correct answer is (B).
5. The correct answer is (E).
6. The correct answer is (C).
7. The correct answer is (C).
8. The correct answer is (A).
9. The correct answer is (E).
10. The correct answer is (B).
11. The correct answer is (B).
12. The correct answer is (D).
13. The correct answer is (E).
14. The correct answer is (E).
15. The correct answer is (D).
16. The correct answer is (D).
17. The correct answer is (A).
18. The correct answer is (B).
19. The correct answer is (D).
20. The correct answer is (E).
21. The correct answer is (D).
22. The correct answer is (C).
23. The correct answer is (E).
24. The correct answer is (B).
25. The correct answer is (D).

Inventory Test 2:_____**% (Comprehension Score)**

INVENTORY RESULTS: WHERE YOU ARE, WHERE YOU ARE GOING

In this inventory, you have been offered two selections on different difficulty levels—one on science, another on fiction—so that you might get a more accurate idea of your present reading efficiency, both in speed and comprehension.

Now, obtain an average speed for the two reading selections.

Selection 1:_____**wpm**

Selection 2:_____**wpm**

Add and divide by 2. Present Rate:_____wpm

Next, obtain your average comprehension score.

Selection 1:_____**%**

Selection 2:_____**%**

Add and divide by 2. Present Comprehension:_____%

To become an Accelerated Reader, you must *at least* triple your reading rate, and improve comprehension. To determine the *minimum* goals you must achieve, multiply as below.

3 _____ (Present wpm) =_____ (GOAL)

Comprehension better than_____% (GOAL)

However, feel free to set higher goals or to increase the above as you progress if you wish. Be careful not to set goals at this point that are so unrealistic they may defeat you psychologically.

At this point you have a good idea where you stand with respect to rate and comprehension, as well as the minimum goals you are striving to attain. You can and will attain these goals with a conscientious application of the techniques and practice drills in Part III, but do not skip what follows in Part I and Part II.

(*Special Note*: You have been given instructions for using a watch or clock for timing the two Inventory selections. You may continue to keep time in this manner or prepare a tape to assist you. For instruction, see Appendix 4—How to Prepare a "Time-Tape.")

How You Learned to Read Slowly

Each individual reads mainly at the basic rate he or she has been taught. This statement is most important in understanding why the so-called "average" reader can seldom achieve a rate far in excess of his or her speech rate, which is somewhere in the neighborhood of 150 wpm.

On the average, English-speaking persons talk at the rate of 125 to 150 words per minute. Franklin D. Roosevelt spoke at the rate of approximately 135 wpm in his famous "fireside chats" on radio. Sixty-second radio and television commercials usually contain 100 to a maximum of 150 words, depending on whether they are "soft-" or "hard-sell."

Speech rates are fairly well fixed by practice and custom. Unfortunately, the same is often true of basic reading rates. Most "untrained" readers read between 125 and 250 wpm. Some individuals have increased their reading rates to 350 wpm through intensive practice, but is unlikely that they ever will read faster unless they deliberately work at it.

Why are reading and speech rates so closely linked? For the answer, we have to see how children are taught to read in school.

Traditionally, a student is first taught to recognize letters of the alphabet. How does a teacher check each student's progress? The only way possible (or logical). *Orally*. Each student is required to respond aloud. At this point the student cannot be expected to prove his or her progress by taking a written examination!

Then, as the instruction proceeds, the youngster learns words, simple expressions, phrases, and sentences. Still, all the reading response is, of necessity, oral.

When the student reaches a certain degree of word recognition proficiency, he is told to "read to himself." And this he must do even if the teacher has to hold a hand over his mouth to keep the frustrated student from uttering continuous audible sounds.

With most students, the transition is finally made—to one degree or another. The student is reading silently . . . and at the same slow pace he used to read aloud. Everything basically is fine so far, but the sad truth is that the student may not be given even the slightest hint that now it is all right to increase the reading speed. Now the student should start looking for word "pictures" and ideas rather than just continuing with conditioned, slow word-hunting. Ideas and information are the important benefits to be gained from silent reading—not the words themselves.

Generally speaking, when a student starts "reading to himself" satisfactorily, he receives little if any further help or instruction with reading. Indeed, the student well may finish elementary, junior high, and high school—maybe even college—and still read only slightly faster than the snail's pace assumed when the transition from oral to silent reading was made. What a shame, what an unnecessary waste of mental, educational, and human potential!

If this is the unfortunate concept you have been limited by all your life, it is time you understood that you can break away from these restrictions. There is no plausible reason why you cannot read faster.

READING SPEED—THE EYES DETERMINE IT

What really determines your words-per-minute reading rate?

You may be surprised to learn that reading speed is intimately related to eye movements—the fewer, the faster; the greater, the slower. Or, putting it technically: Reading rate is controlled primarily by the deviations of fixations made per line of print.

Studies show (and logic supports) that the slower the reader, the more his eyes move as he struggles over the printed page. Very poor (slow) readers may make as many or more visual stops per line as there are letters in the words on that line. Good (faster) readers may stop (fixate) only once every two or three words, taking larger visual "bites" as they move forward. Excellent (fast) readers seldom stop (visually fixate) more than twice per line, and only once on the shorter line-lengths.

Then it would follow that the quickest and one of the most effective ways to increase reading rate would be to reduce the amount of eye movement. This will be discussed at length later. But first, how much do you know and understand about the function of your eyes during silent reading?

Eyes Are Living Cameras

The best way to understand the role of the eyes relative to reading is to compare them to a camera. As you know, in photography the object to be captured on film must be caught perfectly still when the camera's shutter is open or the unfortunate result will be a blur on the film. Therefore, if you want distortion-free images, both the subject and camera must be completely still at the instant the shutter snaps. (Of course, high-speed cameras and improved film and tape now make it possible to photograph objects in motion, but still a blur will manifest if both the equipment and film are not right for the job.)

The case or principle is the same with reading. The eyes can see well enough to read with accuracy and certainty only when they are absolutely still (fixated). When the eyes are in motion across the printed line, all letters and words are blurred and no actual reading can take place. In fact, as far as productive reading is concerned, *all* eye movement is a total waste—a waste of time, energy, and comprehension. When you read, you function much the same as a photographer who, in order to capture on film an expansive panorama (letters, words, phrases, sentences, paragraphs, pages, chapters, books), must move his camera (eyes), determine the subject, snap the picture, and then repeat the process again and again.

Which "Reader-Photographer" Are You?

Look at the examples following and study the patterns of the fixations or "eye-stops" of four very different types of readers.

Each stop is numbered above the letter, word, or phrase. At this point, where would you place yourself as a reader-photographer?

The very poor (slow) reader:

1 2 3 4	5 6 7	8 9 10 11	12 13 14 15	16 17
W h e n	y o u	r e a d	w o r d	b y

18 19 20 21	22 23 24	25 26 27 28 29	30 31 32 33 34 35 36 37
w o r d	y o u	w a s t e	v a l u a b l e

38 39 40 41
t i m e.

The slow word-by-word reader:

1	2	3	4	5	6	7	8
When	you	read	word	by	word	you	waste

9	10
valuable	time.

The better-than-average reader:

1	2	3	4
When you read	word by word	you waste	valuable time.

The Accelerated Reader:

1	2
When you read word by word	you waste valuable time.

It is not difficult to see how much longer it would take the very poor reader to cover the same material as the slow word-by-word reader, and so on.

It makes good sense that when you drive, you hope to catch all the traffic lights green. If you do, all other conditions being equal, you will arrive at your destination more refreshed and much sooner than if many or most lights were red. The same principle applies almost exactly to reading. Make fewer stops and you get through sooner—and with better understanding of what you have read and less fatigue and frustration.

Check Your Visual "Bite"

In the five following specially printed exercises (from Edgar Allan Poe's *Narrative of A. Gordon Pym*), see which is *least* uncomfortable or frustrating to read and understand.

If you already were an Accelerated Reader, you no doubt would find the first the most difficult (slowest) and the last the easiest (fastest) to get through and understand.

In any event, read each, pause, and mentally evaluate (self-test) your comprehension. The single one that seems most comfortable and understandable will tend to indicate the size of your visual "bite" at present and the "rhythm" of your visual reading pattern.

As you study to become an Accelerated Reader, you may wish to check your progress by repeating these exercises from time to time.

Narrative of A. Gordon Pym, Part 1

My name is Arthur Gordon Pym. My father was a respectable trader in sea-stores at Nantucket, where I was born. My maternal grandfather was an attorney in good practice. He was fortunate in every thing, and had speculated very successfully in stocks of the Edgarton New Bank, as it was formerly called. By these and other means he had managed to lay by a tolerable sum of money. He was more attached to myself, I believe, than to any person in the world, and I expected to inherit the most of his property at his death. He sent me, at six years of age, to the school of old Mr. Ricketts, a gentleman with only one arm, and of eccentric manners— he is well known to almost every person who has visited New Bedford. I stayed at his school until I was sixteen, when I left him for Mr. E. Ronald's academy on the hill. Here I became intimate with the son of Mr. Barnard, a sea-captain, who generally sailed in the employ of Lloyd and Vredenburgh— Mr. Barnard is also very well known in New Bedford, and has many relations, I am certain, in Edgarton. His son was named Augustus, and he was nearly two years older than myself. He had been on a whaling voyage with his father in the John Donaldson, and was always talking to me of his adventures in the South Pacific Ocean. I used frequently to go home with him, and remain all day, and sometimes all night. We occupied the same bed, and he would be sure to keep me awake until almost light, telling me stories of the natives of the Island of Tinian, and other places he had visited in his travels. At last I could not help being interested in what he said, and by degrees I felt the greatest desire to go to sea. I owned a sail boat called the Ariel, and worth about seventy-five dollars. She had a half deck or cuddy, and was rigged sloop fashion—I forget her tonnage, but she would hold ten persons without much crowding. In this boat we were in the habit of going on some of the maddest freaks in the world; and, when I now think of them, it appears to me a thousand wonders that I am alive today.

Narrative of A. Gordon Pym, Part 2

I will   relate one   of these   adventures by   way of introduction to   a longer   and more   momentous narrative. One night   there was   a party   at Mr.   Barnard's, and both Augustus   and myself   were not   a little   intoxicated toward   the close   of it.   As usual,   in such   cases, I   took   part of   his bed   in preference   to going home.   He went   to sleep,   as I   thought, very   quietly (it being   near one   when the   party broke   up), and without saying   a word   on his   favorite topic.   It might have been   half an   hour from   the time   of our   getting in   bed, and   I was   just about   falling into   a doze, when he   suddenly started   up, and   swore with   a terrible oath that   he would   not go   to sleep   for any   Arthur Pym   in Christendom,   when there   was so   glorious a breeze from   the southwest.   I never   was so   astonished in my life,   not knowing   what he   intended, and   thinking that   the wines   and liquors   he had   drunk had   set him entirely beside   himself. He   proceeded   to talk   very coolly, however, saying   he knew   that I   supposed him   intoxicated, but   that he   was never   more sober   in his   life. He was only   tired, he   added, of   lying in   bed on   such a fine night   like a   dog, and   was determined   to get   up and   dress, and   go out   on a   frolic with   the boat. I can   hardly tell   what possessed   me, but   the words were no   sooner out   of his   mouth than   I felt   a thrill of the   greatest excitement   and pleasure,   and thought   his mad   idea one   of the   most delightful   and most   reasonable things in   the world.   It was   blowing almost   a gale, and the   weather was   very cold—   it being   late in October. I   sprang out   of bed,   nevertheless,   in a   kind of ecstasy, and   told him   I was   quite as   brave as   himself, and   quite as   tired as   he was   of lying   in bed   like a dog, and   quite as   ready for   any fun   or frolic   as any Augustus Barnard   in Nantucket. We lost   no time   in getting   on our   clothes and hurrying down   to the   boat. She   was lying   at the old decayed   wharf by   the lumber-yard   of Pankey   & Co., and almost   thumping her   side out   against the   rough logs. Augustus got   into her   and bailed   her, for   she was nearly   half full   of water.   This being   done, we   hoisted jib   and mainsail,   kept full   and started   boldly out   to sea.

frolic

Narrative of A. Gordon Pym, Part 3

The wind, as   I before said,   blew freshly from   the southwest. The   night was very   clear and cold.   Augustus had taken   the helm, and   I stationed myself   by the mast,   on the deck   of the cuddy.   We flew along   at a great   rate—neither of   us having said   a word since   casting loose from   the wharf. I   now asked my   companion what course   he intended to steer, and what   time he thought   it probable that   we should get   back. He whistled   for a few   minutes, and then said crustily: "I   am going to   sea—you may   go home if you think proper."   Turning my eyes   upon him, I   perceived at once   that in spite   of his assumed   nonchalance, he was greatly agitated. I   could see him   distinctly by the   light of the   moon—his face   was paler than   any marble, and   his hand shook   so excessively that   he could scarcely   retain hold of the tiller. I   felt that something   had gone wrong,   and became seriously   alarmed. At this   period, I knew   little about the management of a   boat, and was   now depending entirely upon the nautical   skill of my   friend. The wind   too, had suddenly   increased, and we   were fast getting   out of lee   of the land—   still I was   ashamed to betray   any trepidation, and for almost half   an hour maintained   a resolute silence.   I could stand   it no longer,   however, and spoke   to Augustus about the propriety of   turning back. As   before, it was   nearly a minute   before he made   answer, or took   any notice of   my suggestion. "By   and by," said   he at length—   "time enough— home   by and by."   I had expected   such a reply,   but there was   something in the   tone of these   words which filled   me with an   indescribable feeling of   dread. I again   looked at the speaker attentively. His   lips were perfectly   livid, and his knees shook so   violently together that   he seemed scarcely able to stand.   "For God's sake,   Augustus," I screamed, now heartily frightened,   "what ails you—   what is the matter?—what are   you going to   do?" "Matter!" he   stammered, in the   greatest apparent surprise,   letting go to the   tiller at the   moment, and falling   forward into the   bottom of the boat—"matter—why   nothing is the   matter—going home d-d-don't   you see?"The   whole truth now   flashed upon me.   I flew to   him and raised   him up. He   was drunk— beastly   drunk—he could   no longer either   stand, speak, or see. His eyes   were perfectly glazed;   and as I   let him go in the extremity   of my despair,   he rolled like   a mere log   into the bilgewater,   from which I   had lifted him.   It was evident   that, during the   evening, he had   drunk far more than I suspected,   and that his   conduct in bed   had been the   result of a   highly-concentrated state   of intoxication.

Narrative of A. Gordon Pym, Part 4

It is hardly possible   to conceive the extremity   of my terror. The   fumes of the wine   lately taken had evaporated, leaving me doubly timid   and resolute. I knew   that I was altogether   incapable of managing the   boat, and that a fierce wind and strong   ebb-tide were hurrying   us to destruction. A   storm was evidently gathering   behind us; we had   neither compass nor provisions;   and it was clear   that, if we held our present course, we   should be out of   sight of land before daybreak. These thoughts, with   a crowd of others,   equally fearful, flashed through   my mind with a   bewildering rapidity, and for   some moments paralyzed me   beyond the possibility of making any exertion. The   boat was going through   the water at a   terrific rate—full before   the wind—no reef   in either jib or   mainsail—running her bow   completely under the foam. It was a thousand   wonders she did not   broach to—Augustus having   let go the tiller,   as I said before,   and I being too much agitated to think   of taking it myself.   By good luck, however,   she kept steady, and   gradually I recovered some degree of presence of   mind. Still the wind   was increasing fearfully; and   whenever we rose from   a plunge forward, the sea behind fell combing   over our counter, and   deluged us with water.   I was so utterly   benumbed, too, in every   limb, as to be   nearly unconscious of sensation.   At length I summoned up the resolutions of   despair, and rushing to   the mainsail, let it   go by the run.   As might have been   expected, it flew over   the bows, and, getting   drenched with water, carried away the mast, short   off by the board.   This latter accident alone   saved me from instant   destruction. Under the jib only, I now boomed   along before the wind.   Shipping heavy seas occasionally,   but relieved from the   terror of immediate death. I took the helm,   and breathed with greater   freedom, as I found that there yet remained   to us a chance   of ultimate escape. Augustus still lay senseless in   the bottom of the   boat; and as there   was imminent danger of   his drowning (the water   being nearly a foot   deep just where he   fell), I contrived to   raise him partially up,   and keep him in   a sitting position, by passing a rope around   his waist, and lashing   it to a ring-bolt in the deck of   the cuddy. Having thus   arranged every thing as well as I could   in my chilled and   agitated condition, I recommended myself to God, and   made up my mind   to bear whatever might   happen with all the   fortitude in my power.

Narrative of A. Gordon Pym, Part 5

Hardly had I come to this resolution,   when suddenly,   a
loud and long scream or yell,   as if from the throats of a thousand
demons,   seemed to pervade the whole atmosphere   around and above
the boat.   Never while I live   shall I forget the intense agony of
terror   I experienced that moment.   My hair stood erect on my
head—   I felt the blood congealing in my veins—   my heart ceased
utterly to beat,   and without having once raised my eyes   to learn
the source of my alarm,   I tumbled headlong and insensible   upon
the body of my companion.
I found myself, upon reviving,   in the cabin of a large whaling-ship
(the Penguin)   bound to Nantucket.   Several persons were standing
over me,   and Augustus, paler than death,   was busily occupied in
chafing my hands.   Upon seeing me open my eyes,   his exclamations
of gratitude and joy   excited alternate laughter and tears   from the
rough-looking personages   who were present.   The mystery of our being
in existence   was now soon explained.   We had been run down
by the whaling ship,   which was close-hauled,   beating up to Nantucket
with every sail she could venture to set,   and consequently
running almost at right angles   to our course.   Several men were on
the lookout forward,   but did not perceive our boat   until it was an
impossibility   to avoid coming in contact—   their shouts of warning
upon seeing us   were what so terribly alarmed me.   The huge ship, I
was told,   rode immediately over us   with as much ease as our own
little vessel   would have passed over a feather,   and without the least
perceptible impediment   to her progress.   Not a scream arose   from
the deck of the victim—   there was a slight grating sound   to be
heard mingling   with the roar   of wind and water,   as the frail bark
which was swallowed up,   rubbed for a moment   along the keel   of
her destroyer—   but this was all.   Thinking our boat   (which it
will be remembered was dismasted)   some mere shell cut adrift as useless,
the captain   (Captain E. T. V. Block   of New London)   was for
proceeding on his course   without troubling himself further   about the
matter.   Luckily, there were two   of the lookout   who swore
positively   to having seen some person   at our helm,   and represented
the possibility   of yet saving him.   A discussion ensued,
when Block grew angry,   and after a while said   "it was no business
of his   to be eternally watching for eggshells;   that the ship should
not put about   for any such nonsense;   and if there was a man run
down,   it was nobody's fault but his own—   He might be drowned
and be d—d,"   or some language to that effect.

The Rewards of Accelerated Reading

IMPROVED READING COMPREHENSION

When you learn to read noticeably faster, you will better understand the meaning of what you read—both objectively and subjectively.

But, as a member of a slogan-conscious society, you may be somewhat skeptical of such a statement, having heard such often repeated sayings as, "Haste makes waste," and/or "Slow but steady wins the race." If you do tend to adhere to such maxims, now is the time to take a meaningful step toward reading progress—forget them! The fact, proven again and again, is that when individuals learn to read faster, they have a better, more complete understanding of what they read. Let's see why this is true.

Do you think you would really enjoy or appreciate seeing 15 minutes of a good movie today, leaving at the end of a scene, returning another day for 15 minutes of viewing the next scene, and repeating the process until you had seen the entire film? After viewing the final segment—say, one or two weeks later—would you have understood the whole story, theme, and meaning of the film? Not likely. Yet your reading is probably done in much the same impractical, intermittent manner. Often you may feel let down, confused, or uncertain about the plot and characters and the purpose of the book after a drawn-out, read-as-time-permits attempt.

Why might you stretch out reading over such extended periods? Mainly because you may not have too many days when you can devote several hours just to reading; secondly, because it simply may become too fatiguing—even boring—to read more than an hour or so at a single sitting. In addition, whether you think about it or not, you do have a "one-track" mind—and this is no joke or any mark of lack of intelligence.

Humans have a spatial concept of time—60 seconds to the minute, 60 minutes to the hour, 24 hours to the day, and so on. The conscious mind runs along this track and thinks about only one thing at the time—that is, if anything is being thought about in an orderly and constructive manner. Indeed, it is not possible to think successfully about two or more things simultaneously.

To read effectively, your mind must be on what is being read; if the mind wanders, you are, at that moment, thinking about something else—and you cannot remember or comprehend what you have covered visually while your one-track mind was elsewhere.

Did you ever hear someone who drank too much the night before comment the morning after that he cannot remember what was said to him, or what went on? The reason is not that he cannot remember, but that his mind was in no condition to be impressed with what he heard or saw. In other words, it was elsewhere; few if any memorable impressions were able to penetrate his consciousness.

Do you too often have to reread relatively easy paragraphs, pages, or even entire chapters to get much meaning from them? If so, the only conclusion to draw is that your mind was not on what you were covering visually (reading) the first time. Blame your one-track mind, but know that it is your responsibility to keep it on the right track.

Why is the mind so often inclined to wander? A dozen or more good reasons might be listed, but most of them would, in the final analysis, equal *boredom*—boredom resulting from slow, poorly-motivated readers. Slow reading hinders your natural ability to grasp the concept of what is being expounded. As you read, you may be trying fervently to fit the pieces together—bits from yesterday's reading, the day before, and maybe even a few pieces from last week's reading. It can be exceedingly frustrating. Just to illustrate, suppose you are reading a long mystery novel in which you confront a minor character, Aunt Mary, in the first chapter. But she does not reappear until the final chapter, which you read several days later. To your chagrin, you discover that she holds an important key to the mystery's solution—and you do not remember that such a character appeared in the story at any point. Such unfortunate and frustrating problems can become a thing of the past when you learn to become a successful Accelerated Reader.

A novel such as the one mentioned above normally can be read by an Accelerated Reader in one hour or less—certainly at one sitting. If you had "met" Aunt Mary only an hour or so ago, you would have a much better chance of remembering her vividly, and be able to fit her into the plot to get a more accurate and complete understanding of the entire book.

Undoubtedly, developing the potential for completing most reading tasks in one or two sittings (or hours) will improve your overall understanding and completeness of thought.

REDUCED FATIGUE

At present, how long does it take you to read a 100,000-word novel? If you read at the rate of 200 wpm, it takes approximately 8½ hours. For most "regular" readers, serious reading is nearly as fatiguing as manual labor. How exhausted would you be after reading straight for 8½ hours? Your eyes would ache, your neck would be stiff, your back might feel broken—you might be about ready for some sort of special therapy! Then it is no wonder that slower readers may tend to dread reading and shun doing any more of it than is absolutely necessary. Not many would have either the patience or time to attempt reading such a novel at one sitting; therefore, the reading time would be stretched out over several days, even weeks.

When you learn to triple your reading rate, you will be able to read that 100,000 word tome in one third the time, reducing 8½ hours to about two hours and 45 minutes—that is, approximately a 5½ hour saving! If you normally read about ten such books a year, you can actually save over 50 hours of reading time—well over a full workweek! This sort of economy is worth some effort on your part.

Faster reading gets the job done sooner, resulting in a major reduction of both physical and mental fatigue. Overall comprehension is improved because, among other important factors, you can concentrate more on what you are reading and less on the physical aches and pains that can accompany extended periods of little physical activity, as well as the normal stresses and tensions associated with prolonged reading.

PART II

Identify and Overcome Your Blocks to Better Reading

In this section you will learn...

- how to preview chapters, books, reports, letters, memos, newspaper and magazine articles as a valid aid to being a faster, more effective reader

- how to overcome wasted eye movement: regressions, progressions, distractions, and others

- why vision span is so important to faster, more effective reading—and why improving it is so essential

- how vocalization and subvocalization while reading "silently" hinder reading speed (and comprehension)—and techniques for overcoming these non-productive negative habits

- ways to eliminate other miscellaneous blocks to faster reading and better comprehension

Block 1— Failure to Preview

In a nutshell, to read faster you must identify and overcome slow, ineffective reading habits and practices. Just to identify and overcome them, however, is not enough; they must be replaced with faster, more effective habits and practices.

Slow reading and less-than-fully-effective reading are caused by five "blocks." While you may not be hindered by all of these blocks, you should know what they are, and how to remove those which might stand between you and your goal to become an Accelerated Reader.

It is unlikely that you would start on a motor trip to an unknown place without a road map, or that you would dive headfirst into a pool without knowing the water's depth, or that you would attempt to cook a totally new dish without a recipe.

But, would you be guilty of starting serious reading of a book, chapter, or report without a preview, preparation, or forethought? If you answer in the negative, you may be fooling yourself. Unless you are the exception, you, like most beginners of the Cutler Acceleread Method, dive right into the business of reading with little if any preparation for, or idea of, what you are supposed to get from the reading experience.

At the beginning of one Cutler course, each student was given a history book and told that he had been assigned Chapter 10 for the next day's class and to begin the assignment immediately.

Five minutes later he was told to close the book, and was then given a test that asked:

1. What is the chapter's title?

2. What is the author's name?

3. How many pages in the chapter?

4. How much time will you require to study this assignment?

5. Are there subheadings in the chapter?

6. Are there any graphics?

7. Is there a formal summary or conclusion?

8. Are there study questions at the end?

Ninety-eight percent of the students failed this simple test. Eight out of ten could answer only two or three questions accurately! In brief, the results were catastrophic. Conclusion: Most individuals (both students and adults) either do not know or fail to use the few simple steps of preview (prereading) which would enable them to get much greater benefit from the time spent actually reading the text material.

Therefore, it may be well worth your time now to study the simple but effective steps necessary to properly preview different types of reading matter. Prereading can tend to reduce your actual reading load by helping to determine quickly whether what you have before you is worth spending time to read in depth.

HOW TO PREVIEW A NONFICTION BOOK

This essentially is the same procedure you were asked to follow before you began serious reading of this book.

1. Examine the outside—front and back. (Study title, illustrations; read the "blurbs" or comments on the jacket or cover; study the messages on the end flaps, if any.)

2. Note the author's name; read any biographical information about him. (What are his qualifications?)

3. Check the publisher's name and the copyright date. (Dates are of utmost importance in many areas of study. The book, if unrevised, could be very outdated. Study the

publishing history—number of copies; dates of reprints, revisions, etc. This information normally is found on the back of the title page.)

4. Read the front matter—Introduction, Preface, Foreword, etc. (A quick check of this information will give a good indication of what the writer sets out to do in the book.)

5. Carefully look over the Table of Contents. (This is the skeletal outline for the entire book. It will indicate the writer's approach and general treatment of the subject and the number of chapters and their approximate length and structure. It will also list back matter—Indexes, Bibliographies, Glossaries, etc.)

6. Thumb through the book. (Stop briefly to note layout and typography. Note any graphics—photographic inclusions, maps, diagrams, cartoons, foldouts, etc.)

7. If there is an overall Summary or Conclusion, read it carefully.

8. Peruse Indexes, Bibliographies, or Glossaries if any are included.

9. From the preview, evaluate the book's value for your purpose. (If it lacks what you need or want, select another title and repeat this preview process.)

At first, this may seem to be a lot of time-consuming work and effort. On the contrary, with a little practice and experience, it will take but a few minutes of your time—a relative few minutes that could well be among the most important of the total time spent studying and reading the book.

HOW TO PREVIEW A BOOK OF FICTION

Since one of the major motivators for reading fiction is to discover the outcome of a story, previewing a book of fiction normally should not include an attempt to find out in advance how it ends. However, a preview should include finding out as much about the book and its author as possible before you begin to read. Study all information printed on the outside; find out what you can about the author; check the publisher and the copyright date; read any front matter; look over the Table of Contents; thumb through the book, note typography and illustrations; check the back matter (if any); then, determine whether you wish to read it (if it is not required reading) or select another title.

HOW TO PREVIEW A CHAPTER

Most reading tasks necessary to succeed in work, school, or college involve the study and reading of portions—chapters, sections, parts—of books and other publications. The procedure for previewing parts of longer reading matter is essentially the same as previewing entire books, with a few variations.

1. Study the title. (In nonfiction it usually states with one or very few words what is to be covered in the chapter.)

2. Question the title:

    a. What do I already know about this subject?

    b. Will this be mainly review, or will it contain a lot of new or unfamiliar information?

    c. What are the logical points to look for as I read?

    d. What will be the writer's attitude and approach?

    e. Does the title seem to suggest his final conclusions?

    (This questioning technique helps to get your thoughts subject-oriented. It, in effect, prepares the mental "soil" for the "seeds" the writer has ready for planting in your "field" of knowledge.)

3. Note the number of pages assigned. (Make it a practice always to know the approximate length of whatever you are going to read. You will be able to budget reading and study time better.)

4. Read the first paragraph or so. (These usually introduce the chapter's content.)

5. Read the last paragraph or so. (If there is no formal summary, these can be most helpful in determining the conclusions the author has reached.)

6. If there is a summary or conclusion, read it carefully. (It will clue you in on the major points to look for when you actually read the text.)

7. Look over any study questions, tests, or problems at the end. (They will aid in guiding your study of the chapter.)

8. Page through the entire chapter. (Stop briefly to check all subheadings and any graphics.)

9. Take a few moments to reflect upon what you have learned already (you may be surprised), and what in addition you expect to gain from a careful reading of the chapter.

10. You are now ready to read and study with a purpose. Consider yourself better prepared to understand what you read.

Again, this may seem like a lot of effort to expend before actual reading, but rest assured the rewards in comprehension will prove to be worth much more than the few minutes required for an adequate preview of a chapter.

HOW TO PREVIEW REPORTS

Your desk or work area may be piled high with reports that you would like to get out of the way quickly. If you utilize a method of previewing (prereading) them similar to that already outlined, you will be able to expedite them much faster and easier. Of course, modifications may be necessary for certain exceptional reports, but generally you should practice the following steps:

1. Check the title. (What is the report about?)

2. Note the writer/preparer/compiler, his company, department, etc. (Who put it together? Where is it from?)

3. Check the date—preparation, delivery.

4. Note carefully for whom it was prepared or sent— person, company, department, etc.

5. Read and understand the purposes and reasons for its preparation and dispatch. (What is it supposed to show or prove?)

6. Study its Table of Contents, or equivalent. (What is covered in the total report?)

7. Read the Abstract or Summary carefully. (What are the final conclusions and proposals, if any?)

8. Peruse all front and back matter. (What are the sources for information contained in the report, etc.?)

9. Thumb through for subheadings, organization, typography. (Study all graphs, charts, etc.)

10. Read in depth as necessary.

HOW TO PREVIEW LETTERS (AND MEMOS)

You may be required to read many more letters (and memos) each year than you would care either to enumerate or remember. In many cases, you may find that prereading may suffice for a number of the more routine letters and other such communications that you may be inclined to labor over. Preview letters (and memos) with the following three steps in mind—and *in the suggested order*.

1. Check the *top*. (Letterhead, date, salutation.)

2. Check the *bottom*. (Writer's name and title.)

3. Check the *middle* for the main idea(s). (In most letters and memos, you will find the "meat" in or near the visual center. The first paragraph or so are generally routine introductory comments and polite remarks. The last paragraph or so, more likely than not, contain formalities.)

HOW TO PREVIEW MAGAZINE ARTICLES

In a rapidly changing world, magazines and other periodicals provide a convenient vehicle for informing us of what is happening in research and development. Consequently, the well-read, motivated individual may need to read several publications on a regular basis. Time-saving help is available to anyone who heeds the following simple steps:

1. Read the article's title and any subheadings. (You will get the overall idea of the subject and its treatment.)

2. Note the writer's name; read any biographical notes about him.

3. Carefully examine all graphics—photographs, tables, charts, illustrations, etc.

4. Read the first few paragraphs for the theme, etc.

5. Next, read the first, or topic sentence of all succeeding paragraphs.

6. Near the end of the article, start reading more carefully when you sense the writer is giving his conclusions, or a summary.

After this brief preview time, you will know if the article is worth a more thorough and careful reading. If so, the good skeletal framework you have built in your mind will make any further reading easier, faster, and more meaningful.

Previewing or prereading is not only wise, it is necessary if you want to enhance your chances for professional, academic, or social success. It certainly is to your advantage to find out all you can about anything you might feel you should read before you invest a lot of valuable time. A good preview often will indicate that many of the things you now spend a lot of time laboring through may not deserve a careful, in-depth reading—some may contain no new information, others may be only cleverly disguised sales promotions, and still others might need to be directed to another's attention.

While previewing is not rapid reading per se, the practice can help to save enough time to cause you to feel you are close to being an Accelerated Reader already.

Practice using previewing with *everything* you read, or think you should read.

Block 2— Wasted Eye Movement

Have you ever observed the average reader's eyes as he reads? If so, you would notice they tend to move across the line of print in a series of short jerks, stopping approximately once for each word. If you watched long enough, you would notice this jerky movement frequently is interrupted by glances above, below, to the far left and far right, and perhaps even totally away from the page. These unnecessary movements are known respectively as *regressions* (looking back, or above), *progressions* (looking ahead, or below), and *distractions* (looking left-right, or away from the page).

You might also note the eyes travel to the last printed word on the right (or into the right margin), and then snap back to the first printed word of the next line (or into the left margin).

Observing the Accelerated Reader, however, you would see marked differences in the number and types of eye-stops and movements. First, you would note there are markedly fewer jerks. The eyes move across the line with only two or three stops. (Remember: Reading rate is, to a large degree, determined by the number of stops or fixations the eyes make while reading each line. The fewer the stops, the faster the rate.)

Further, you would find that the left-right swing of the eyes would limit travel to only about one-half the total line length, and this half includes the middle half—the second and third quarters. The eyes do not move over the first or fourth quarters of the line. Also, you would note few if any regressions, progressions, and certainly a bare minimum of visual distractions. However, you would notice that pages were being turned quite frequently.

MINIMIZING VISUAL REGRESSIONS

The most effective means for overcoming the wasteful habit of looking back to see what was missed the first time is simply to stop doing it. It will help very much if you realize that the benefits gained by visual regressions are seldom, if ever, worth the time and energy required.

Strive to develop this attitude: If I do miss some minor point the first time, I will get it straight and in proper order when I read through the material again. Senseless? Not at all. When you learn to preview thoroughly, and practice so that you are reading at least three times faster than before, you will have *created* more than enough time for a quick review or two. In other words, you can, if necessary, read the material *three* times in the same amount of time once required to read it through, more or less effectively, once. In addition, when you reread, you can employ spatial (intermittent) study, which many educators recommend for deep learning. This means you can read (review) the material again later in the day, tomorrow, or the next day. It is the same general process you might use to prepare for examinations.

When reading, the only profitable direction for the eyes to move is forward—basically down the page. To aid at first with minimizing and overcoming visual regressions, try sliding a blank card or piece of paper down the page, covering each line as it is read.

Using the card is only a temporary practice; it should not be employed for more than a few days at most. During effective rapid reading, the entire page must be exposed to both the eyes and the mind at all times. Furthermore, the mechanics of covering portions of the printed page would be too cumbersome and time-consuming if continued for extended periods of reading.

In Part III, you will encounter drills and exercises to help further with minimizing wasteful visual regressions.

MINIMIZING VISUAL PROGRESSIONS

The reader who constantly is noting the number at the bottom of the page, checking out upcoming unusual words or strange visual patterns caused by certain combinations of printed letters

on the page, or even flipping forward a page or so to determine how many more have to be waded through, simply is not thinking very effectively about what he is supposed to be reading.

When this type of inattention and impatience becomes too great, it is best to simply put the book aside until such time as you are psychologically prepared to devote the attention that reading demands and deserves for any type of satisfactory comprehension.

At the risk of seeming overly simplistic, the best way to overcome time- and comprehension-wasting progressions is just to stop; keep your eyes focused where they are, not where they are going.

Minimizing the useless practice of looking ahead will be helped by adequately previewing the material. During the preview stage, you will check through the whole assignment before you begin intensive study. You will know *in advance* the approximate amount of time to set aside for reading and what charts, graphs, maps, etc., are included in the reading passage. So, you will not have to interrupt reading to expectantly flip through the pages ahead. Moreover, the preview, if properly done, will serve to stimulate interest. Thus, it will be much easier to keep your mind on the subject in general and, specifically, on the words being read at any moment. In short, your best defense against wasteful, time-consuming visual progressions is to preview thoroughly—as explained in detail earlier in this section. (See *Block 1.*)

MINIMIZING VISUAL DISTRACTIONS

When the eyes are moved totally off the page or to the left or right without purpose, it is natural to assume the reader's mind (concentration) is, for the moment, directed away from the subject matter on that page.

Generally, what has been said about minimizing regressions and progressions applies as well to distractions. Maintain a constant vigil to ensure you make serious business of reading when that is what you are supposed to be doing; save the distractions for a time when you can enjoy them without concern that they might be robbing you of an acceptable level of reading comprehension.

The negative effects of visual distractions can be minimized markedly if you adhere to a few commonsense rules and practices relative to the "how and why" of studying. Before you begin to read, make definite preparations. Go to your "reading place"—a desk, your room, the kitchen table—a specific place where you can be reasonably comfortable. Get away from the television set, the stereo, the radio; remove yourself from the mainstream of activity. Clear the area of all reading and study materials except those you actually require at the moment. Concentrate adequate light on the desk or book; if possible, have another soft light on in the room. Make sure the area is not too warm or you might become drowsy. Do not read or study until you are exhausted; take an occasional short break.

When should you take a break? Indulge yourself with a "breather" as soon as you find it actually difficult to keep full attention on what you are reading. When you break, get both physically and mentally away from reading and study materials. You might take a leisurely walk through the house or office, get a cup of coffee, or a light snack. In a few minutes, you should be able to return and resume effective reading and study. (See also *Appendix 1*.)

The "average" reader tends to move his eyes across the printed line in a series of short jerks, stopping approximately once per word. To read noticeably and productively faster, the number of visual fixations or eye-stops made per line must be reduced. Any reduction, however minor, will tend to increase reading rate. And with a marked increase in rate, better comprehension can be expected to follow as practice at the accelerated rate is gained.

To reduce the number of stops, it is necessary to train the eyes to pay conscious attention to (see) a larger area of the page each time they stop (fixate). Training involves drill and practice designed to "develop" the peripheral vision—the side-to-side and up-and-down areas. Without specialized training, most readers pay adequate conscious attention to only five to ten percent of the total visual area—that closest to the centermost point of focus. While it is unrealistic to think that the total vision area can be developed to the point of complete usefulness for the reading of normal print, it is a realistic goal to attempt to enlarge the area so that more of it can be utilized for normal reading.

With practice, it definitely is possible for individuals with normal vision to increase the vision span, to develop and utilize more of the so-called "side vision" so that the eyes, when reading, take larger visual "bites" with each fixation. Consider the good basketball player who, after much practice on the court, develops the ability to see what is happening all around him with a minimal amount of eye and/or head movement. Being able to see a wide area at all times is necessary if he is to plan his moves in the midst of the frenzied action and excitement. With practice and patience, your eyes will adjust surprisingly well to the need to see a larger area of the printed page each time they fixate (stop).

Block 4— Vocalization and Subvocalization

Vocalization when reading is, of course, reading aloud; subvocalization might be defined as reading aloud silently—to one degree or another. Reading aloud too fast would present problems mainly for the reader's listeners, but subvocalizing can present serious problems for the person who wishes to read noticeably faster than he normally speaks. If you wish to become an Accelerated Reader, you must overcome subvocalization completely; failure to do so will forever bond your silent reading rate to your speech rate of about 150 wpm.

How do you know if you are subvocalizing? Look at the reading rate that you determined earlier in this book. The closer it is to 150 (or below), the stronger the evidence that you are reading aloud to yourself.

This carry-over from primary reading training and practice must be minimized and, as soon as possible, eliminated entirely. "But," the average reader may complain, "I cannot understand what I read unless I say the words in my mind as I read them." This argument may sound rational, but under a bit of examination proves false.

Recall your most recent shopping trip. Did you speak silently or aloud to yourself as you looked at all the merchandise, checked the prices, made selections?

When you walk through a new home, is it not possible to observe with much accuracy the furnishings and floor plan without speaking word-for-word to your "inner ear"? The visual images go directly into your memory; later, if desired, you can review these images to answer almost any question concerning that house. Indeed, you do go about constantly making visual observations from which you make critical decisions and perform numerous acts, all without uttering a single word, either aloud or silently. Driving would be a problem if you lacked this ability!

With practice, most persons can learn to do the same with their reading. It should be mentioned, however, that the English language's 26 different alphabetic symbols (letters) and 10 numerals can be arranged to present an infinite number of visual patterns. Consequently, it takes a systematic method of observation to recognize the various combinations which represent different words, word-pictures, ideas, thoughts, etc. Thus, the potential Accelerated Reader must develop an orderly method for complete visual coverage of the printed page, but at a much faster rate than normal. This technique will be presented in Part III, "The Two-Stop Method."

A silent reading rate near the speech rate—150 wpm—is not the only indicator or symptom of subvocalization (and/or vocalization). There are five other culprits, some humorously termed, that are indicators of subvocalization (and/or vocalization). These are: *lipping, tongue warbling, jawing, Adam's appling,* and *diaphragming.* Read and test to determine if any of them stand in the way of your becoming an Accelerated Reader.

LIPPING

Slow-to-average readers *always* demonstrate excessive eye movement. In addition, most slow readers "lip-read" on one or more of three movement levels. Some fluctuate from one level to another.

First, there is the slowest reader who speaks most words aloud. Not only is lip movement quite obvious, but there is ongoing vocalized sound as well. No problem spotting him.

Second, there is the whisperer. He rarely utters vocalized sounds but limits himself to the more or less audible whisper.

The above two "lippers" are easy to detect. And you will have no difficulty with recognizing these time-consuming and limiting practices or habits if you utilize them at either level—even occasionally.

Number three, the "lip-sync-er" is more difficult to spot because he seldom if ever makes any type of audible sound while reading; however, his lips are just as busy forming syllables and words as if he were reading aloud.

Do you "lip-sync"? To find out, place a finger lightly on the lips as you read, or ask a friend to observe while you read for a few minutes. You may be surprised to find how much your lips are involved with silent reading.

In all the cases explained above, the reader's rate is literally anchored fast to his speech rate. The only way the dyed-in-the-wool "lipper" will ever increase reading rate is to learn to talk faster. And this has its drawbacks since he might then have some difficulty with being understood, not to mention the added lip and facial muscle fatigue.

"Lipping" habits can be overcome quickly and with relative ease if you are aware of their presence, and apply the following techniques until you succeed.

1. Cup both hands behind the ears as you read. If you hear any sounds or whispers at all, concentrate on maintaining silence, and listen as necessary until you break the habit.

2. Read with a pencil held lightly between the lips. Any movement of the lips will be illustrated and exaggerated by the pencil's actions. Practice until the pencil remains still.

3. In severe or extreme cases, the mouth can be sealed temporarily with plastic tape.

In most cases, a relatively short regimen of practice utilizing the techniques above and/or others you might think of should eliminate "lipping" completely, and move you up an important step on the ladder toward becoming an Accelerated Reader. Good luck!

TONGUE WARBLING

Birds may warble and utter sweet sounds, but effective readers should not. The "tongue warbler" is a near-master at concealing this tiring and limiting practice. You would no doubt have to watch his throat carefully to catch him because his lips may be as steady as those of the very best ventriloquist's; however, inside the mouth and throat, the tongue is busily engaged with forming each and every sound as he reads.

As you read this short paragraph, are you aware of even the slightest movement of the tongue not associated with breathing? If so, no matter however slight, you must overcome it.

Excellent results with stopping "tongue warbling" may be obtained by first ascertaining that it is going on and (if it is), applying the following techniques.

1. Read with a pencil gripped midway back in the mouth, with the tongue held underneath.

2. Read with chewing gum held between the top of the tongue and the roof of the mouth.

3. Hold fingers beneath the jaws to detect tongue movement.

JAWING

The "jawer" does exactly what the term suggests; his jaw tends to "keep time" with his reading. It may appear that he is chewing. If you need to check for and/or overcome this habit, try the following.

1. Read with your chin resting solidly on a clinched fist. (The elbow is planted firmly on a desk or table.)

2. Read while chewing gum; however, make certain to avoid chewing in rhythm with your reading.

3. Practice reading with a pencil clinched firmly between the front teeth.

ADAM'S APPLING

The reader here has ostensibly succeeded with cutting out or concealing practically all external and internal movement relative to the head and has, instead, substituted what amounts to throat "exercises."

As he reads silently, he unconsciously puts the voice box and vocal cords through all or most of the intricate movements and changes necessary for normal speech. Inaudibly, he raises and lowers pitch as he experiences the action of the words being read. If a very sensitive microphone were attached to the throat, he might be surprised to learn how much inarticulated "speaking" is going on beneath the normal hearing level.

Check yourself now. Place fingers lightly on both the sides and front of the Adam's apple—voice box. Is there any vibration or movement there except that necessary for breathing and swallowing? If so, you are "Adam's Appling." You can put a stop to it by utilizing these hints.

1. Consciously and deliberately relax the entire throat and neck area. Stop occasionally to roll and turn the head; breathe deeply, comfortably.

2. Continue to read with fingers on the voice box. Any vibration or movement will alert you to relax further.

DIAPHRAGMING

The "diaphragmer" adds action to silent reading by regulating respiration to correspond with words, phrases, and sentences as he reads. He is unconsciously "projecting" his unverbalized speech. Aside from slowing reading rate, he may well find extended periods of reading quite exhausting.

To test yourself for this weakness, first place a finger beneath the nostrils to ascertain any erratic movement of air; next, put the other hand on the stomach area (beneath the ribs) to feel if the rhythm of the diaphragm corresponds at all with that of your reading.

It is relatively easy to eliminate this practice by reading with hands placed as has been suggested until you succeed with divorcing action of the diaphragm totally from silent reading. While breathing is necessary to life and health, it should have no connection with reading to yourself.

Block 5—
Miscellaneous
Weaknesses

There are three other blocks to faster, more effective reading. While they might seem rather insignificant, they should nonetheless be identified and eliminated if they hamper your progress.

POINTING/MARKING

Pointing out or marking your place with a finger, hand, pencil, ruler, card, sheet of paper, or any other object or device is both an unnecessary and a time- and energy-wasting practice. The entire page should be open and exposed to your eyes when you are reading. If you find it difficult to resist pointing/marking, place all such devices out of reach so you will not pick them up unthinkingly. If fingers persist with returning to the page to point and mark your "place," literally sit on your hands until you learn to rely on the eyes to do the job for you.

HAND SCANNING

Hand scanning, recommended by some exponents of rapid reading, is the second miscellaneous weakness to avoid. Any physical covering (concealing) of the page, for whatever purpose, limits the reader's chances for a more complete understanding of the material printed on that page. Any movement of a hand or finger either down or across a page is not only distracting, it is unnecessary. Hand scanning is, in fact, a "crutch" and has no positive purpose for inclusion in your program to increase reading rate and improve comprehension.

SLOW PAGE TURNING

You may think the third of these lesser blocks to rapid reading is trivial. Observations of thousands of readers of all types confirmed conclusively that many ineffective readers may take an average of four seconds just to turn a page and resume reading. This is nearly as much time as some faster readers require to *read* a whole page! At four seconds per page, the reading of a 400-page book would consume some 13 minutes of wasted time on page turning alone.

Ideally, all books should be printed on a continuous sheet; but since there are no 500 foot bookshelves at the local library, these sheets are chopped into more convenient-to-use sections called pages. Therefore, the writer's thought does not necessarily end at the bottom of a page, but more often than not continues on the page following, which should be presented to the eye and mind as quickly as possible for maximum comprehension.

To assure greater efficiency and time economy with page turning, read with the book flat on the surface of a desk or table. The moment the eyes begin reading the left-hand page, you should "feel out" with the thumb and forefinger of the right hand the next single sheet. Doing so will assure avoidance of the frustrating mistake of turning more than one sheet at a time. As soon as you finish reading the right-hand page, flip the paper quickly, and if necessary, use the fingertips of the left hand—near the bottom—to hold down the newly turned page. Repeat the "feel out" process immediately.

If the pages resist lying flat as often is the case with paperback titles, it might be best to "break" the book's back. This is accomplished by holding the book in both hands and bending it forcibly and repeatedly all the way back so that the front and back covers meet totally. "Breaking" should be done again about every 10 or 15 pages. This process relaxes the binding and, if properly done, allows the pages to lie flat without the necessity for holding them down with the hand. (note: It may not be appreciated by others if you do this to books that do not belong to you. Rest assured that booksellers will disapprove most strongly. Therefore, break the backs only of those books that you own. Hardback books, it is worth adding, will not require this process since they will lie flat on their own.)

PART III

Become An Accelerated Reader

In this section you will learn...

📖 how the Acceleread program's specifically designed and proven drills can aid you to become the accelerated reader you want to be

📖 how to develop eye control and increase your eye span (visual awareness/field of view)

📖 to employ and benefit from pacing and block reading

📖 how to master and use the very important two-stop method for faster reading—and reduction of physical and mental fatigue

📖 to apply and further hone your Acceleread techniques with seven real-practice reading selections in this book, including tests to measure your comprehension

Develop Eye Control and Expand Vision

If you skipped the reading and study of even one page prior to this one, believing you could become an Accelerated Reader sooner, you have only shortchanged yourself. Go back to the beginning and start over. You will win if you do and lose if you do not.

Now that you have studied the theory and explanations, and are on your way to overcoming negative reading practices, it is time to reveal the secrets that will enable you to triple your current reading speed and improve your reading comprehension.

In Part III, you will be shown how to become the rapid reader you desire to be. However, the fact that you are given all the vagaries of the Cutler Accele*read* Method is no guarantee that you will give the drills and exercises the necessary attention and time required to achieve your reading speed and comprehension goals. A physician can prescribe medicine to a patient, but cannot make the patient take the pills. In the final analysis, it is up to the individual to successfully reach his or her goals.

Tripling your reading rate is worth whatever amount of time and practice it may require. You will have mountains of reading to do in the future; why not prepare yourself now to handle this imposing stack of reading material—before it overwhelms you?

In the sections that follow, you will learn to develop eye control, increase vision span, master the Two-Stop Method, and attempt to make your newly acquired improved skills more useful. Before starting the eye drills on the pages following, please take time to read and understand the explanation and clarification here.

Realistically, you cannot expand your vision (field of view) to any great degree—but you absolutely can, through deliberate effort and practice, condition and train your brain (mind) to make fuller use of the field of view (vision span) you already possess.

For persons with normal sight, the field of view ranges from 220 to 240 degrees in the horizontal (side to side) direction. That is an impressive percentage of 360 degrees (a full circle). Naturally the best visual acuity is right in the center of the field of view—the normal area used for close examination and detailed study of objects, including printed words.

The question that needs to be asked of those who desire to read much faster is: Are you reading to study/examine individual words or to gain comprehension (useful understanding) of the content of the material to be covered visually? If you answer that you want to mainly study/examine the individual words, your reading speed and comprehension are not likely to improve to a noticeable degree unless you redefine your purpose for reading.

Therefore, for some of you who desire to excel in both reading speed and comprehension, some modification of the thinking about the real purpose for reading might need to be made.

Simply stated, the real purpose for most necessary and required reading for education and career is not to examine words themselves but to get and understand what the words used together in phrases, sentences, paragraphs and pages convey in the form of thoughts, ideas, and concepts. These are "pictures" that you should garner as the result of covering the material visually and mentally.

When you speed read effectively, the proper goal is to get a valid and useful understanding of what you read without getting "tripped-up" by the words themselves. Yes, it will take time, practice, and patience to get the hang of it but it certainly is worth the effort when you realize how much reading awaits you—both short and long-term.

IMPORTANT

During eye drill practice, instructors of Acceleread classroom courses pair students to work and help each other.

Seated across from one another, one student practices a drill while the other closely monitors and cautions aloud or taps the desk when any unwanted eye movement is detected. In time, the roles are reversed. Each class session begins with at least 10 minutes of eye drills, followed by other reading activities.

You are encouraged to **work with a partner** if at all possible. It will ensure that your progress will be more rapid and your reading speed goals will be realized in less time. Ask someone to help who may also be interested in improving his or her reading speed and comprehension. It can be an enjoyable and rewarding experience for both you and your partner.

Easy-To-Do-Anywhere Exercises

While dutifully practicing the printed eye drills that follow is absolutely essential to your success, there are other exercises you can do just about anywhere—and any time. They can be done for several seconds or more extended periods of time.

While watching television, fix your focus on the center of the screen. Then without physically moving your eyes up, down, left or right, concentrate on becoming more mentally aware of ascertaining (making out) more and more detail surrounding the fixed-point focus. With a little practice and patience, you will soon start to realize that you can actually "see" a lot more than you expect—including objects surrounding the television set itself.

While riding in or driving a vehicle, visually fixate on the road ahead and work on paying conscious "attention" to a broader area than normal. (If driving by yourself, don't disregard safety!) As you deliberately train and condition your mind (brain) to take in and notice more and more of what your eyes perceive routinely, you may be surprised at how much you can distinguish with one bite.

Similar exercises can be done almost anywhere in your home, office, and outdoors—just about anywhere.

In the exercises that follow, focus your eyes on the *center* letter of each line. Then, without eye movement either to the left or right, read aloud or silently vocalize each letter in this order: *center* letter, *left* letter, *right* letter.

Then, move the eyes straight down to the next horizontal line and repeat the process through the entire drill.

DRILL A

F	M	E
W	K	G
Q	J	N
S	V	B
P	G	J
A	E	N
R	G	Y
C	W	J
L	Q	C
V	R	Y
B	M	V
S	G	J
B	O	K
Q	T	L
X	U	I
S	K	D
M	P	E
K	J	G
C	T	L
E	J	G
A	K	M
W	U	P
M	U	G
B	H	G
S	C	K
V	K	E
W	J	M
O	T	J
J	A	L
E	M	V

The width of Drill A is about 1¼ inches—the area the average untrained reader can see well enough to read with a minimum of effort.

If you experienced any difficulty the first time through (or even if you did not), repeat Drill A several times. Pay close attention to your eyes so that you start to become consciously and keenly aware of undesired left-right movement.

In repeating Drill A, and the drills that follow, you will find the letters easier to see and read if you focus just slightly *above* each center letter rather than in the vertical center of the letter itself. You will find this practice valuable in regular reading as well. The white spaces between words can be compared to pickets on a fence; they tend to "catch" the eyes and may interrupt their smooth transition to the next fixation (stop). When you focus slightly above the tops of the printed letters/words, the eyes will be moving in smooth, uncluttered space.

Do not force or strain to see while practicing. *Relax*. Realize that at this point—and for some time—you will make numerous mistakes while attempting to call letters correctly. This is normal for the present. Now, your main purpose is to train your eyes to look only where you direct them rather than where habit would have them look. Remember, you are in charge. Your accuracy will improve as your vision span increases with patient practice.

Only after you master Drill A should you begin work on Drill B. Practice Drill B aloud and/or silently, calling the letters in this order: *center, immediate* left, *immediate* right, *far* left, *far* right.

DRILL B

L	CSB	K
M	YPD	V
E	PGL	M
X	GMI	P
C	RKG	L
W	CYH	P
E	DNL	Q
A	DJM	L
B	SKH	L
V	TKF	M
C	MRI	D
B	MRC	T
O	SLO	V
T	AMG	Y
O	PVB	J
W	MGI	L
B	KCD	W
K	GBN	R
B	AKT	J
V	MTO	L
W	GDI	X
R	UVD	Y
B	RPL	M
D	YFO	Z
T	NFI	U
J	LDN	M
E	OFN	P
D	IVN	D
W	KTP	B
P	IMV	Q

NOTE: You will find it much more productive and far less fatiguing if you practice frequently for short periods of time instead of in a few long sessions. It is perfectly normal for the eyes to feel a little "strange" or tire quickly at first, but these minor problems will diminish entirely after a few practice sessions of reasonable length.

After Drill B is mastered, go on to Drills C, D, and then E, mastering each before going on to the next. Each time you begin a new practice session, start with Drill A and work up to your level of mastery. All drills may be repeated as many times as necessary now, as well as from time to time throughout your reading improvement program—and even afterward. Going through these drills is an excellent "warm-up" for future reading assignments.

When you get to Drill E, note that it has an overall width of about 3¼ inches—the typical column width of most paperbacks. When you can read Drill E well, you should then be able to read straight down the center of such a page without moving your eyes either left or right. However, most would-be Accelerated Readers are reluctant to spend the practice time necessary with these drills to acquire such outstanding peripheral development and, though highly desirable, it is not required of the reader who wishes to at least triple his reading speed. (This will be explained in more detail when you study the Two-Stop Method.)

DRILL C

T	J	M	G	E
P	S	B	N	R
C	E	L	Y	K
X	D	W	A	Z
L	Y	V	D	C
K	P	W	A	X
X	G	W	K	M
Z	Y	I	P	M
W	D	X	B	M
Z	T	I	L	B
A	U	T	K	Y
V	M	S	R	K
K	T	D	X	C
Q	G	J	I	L
A	J	E	I	R
B	D	X	L	C
S	G	U	R	K
C	H	T	D	L
G	L	I	P	K
N	R	D	H	I
W	G	Q	K	P
J	Y	K	M	N
O	L	G	P	D
T	K	I	L	P
Z	D	T	U	L
Y	K	N	W	Z
U	M	D	S	C
S	H	K	T	L
B	D	R	F	E
H	I	L	M	P
Z	B	X	N	A
X	G	B	B	U
W	T	V	D	W
D	R	Z	S	Y
M	C	C	P	I
K	M	A	Q	D
C	R	U	E	W
M	O	Q	F	Y
M	M	W	T	R
X	V	C	B	T
A	E	T	I	O
G	U	O	R	A

DRILL D

V	U	SBN	E	L
S	I	CKR	S	L
X	R	DLT	C	Y
P	G	RKY	V	J
B	F	LDI	P	H
O	Y	SJR	J	T
I	G	LRI	D	P
F	G	SYT	J	W
R	T	RTL	C	S
Z	F	GLT	B	R
Q	D	GKY	L	G
Z	P	TIL	V	M
L	M	VYT	K	E
W	A	FKY	N	C
A	S	MSL	W	Z
Q	D	GKI	Z	B
N	I	OSD	L	W
P	L	WLT	D	F
T	G	BMN	S	T
B	R	BCN	X	K
P	J	SCB	W	L
S	G	YTR	I	H
K	H	YGT	G	V
I	H	RJF	H	B
X	G	UKV	F	H
A	X	BJT	T	U
D	B	RKT	V	S
M	B	FKR	K	L
O	C	VIJ	F	Y
S	K	TLY	C	Z
X	B	CUW	A	L
Q	A	XNK	C	P
I	X	TSP	D	M
P	A	ROT	W	S
E	T	ATU	X	O
L	P	CWB	X	Z
A	X	VML	B	O
Q	Y	NOP	N	M
X	B	MTN	K	L
I	V	OUA	M	V
T	V	NXM	C	P
N	A	BXY	N	O

DRILL E

H	F	D	BAC	E	G	I
C	S	P	URL	N	B	N
M	D	R	TYH	B	M	S
L	S	K	DTB	X	J	W
L	A	D	RYM	C	K	E
P	A	F	GTW	Q	M	D
T	K	F	EXB	U	M	W
T	N	D	RWS	C	I	A
R	J	E	PQT	X	P	M
L	E	G	JWQ	U	I	N
S	J	D	VBN	Z	Q	T
M	E	O	IUK	L	A	P
L	B	W	SAI	F	B	C
F	T	Q	HLS	C	V	M
C	M	E	SBC	D	H	E
M	R	W	QUM	L	D	J
A	D	Q	GXB	M	K	L
R	E	S	SCN	F	S	D
L	B	D	TYZ	V	S	L
B	R	S	QUI	E	P	W
W	L	T	HKX	A	T	H
K	L	T	BZS	W	W	L
C	B	S	NBC	A	B	C
K	L	R	UZA	M	F	E
H	P	U	QUT	V	E	B
C	T	G	BMD	R	M	A
E	X	B	CDJ	F	H	Q
B	N	J	FWQ	T	P	M
M	S	F	ACH	R	M	S
P	Q	K	LSG	A	W	E

Practical Application

Newspaper and magazine columns provide excellent material for practicing the eye control and vision expansion that you have been developing.

Before starting to practice news-type columnar reading exercises, use a ruler or other straightedge to trace a thin line down the vertical center of several columns. Then make your eyes follow the line downward as you attempt to see all words on either side of the center—without left-right movement. Repeat each column several times, and note that comprehension tends to improve with each repetition. It must be emphasized that neither speed nor good comprehension is the main objective of this practice; further development of eye control and increased vision span are the main goals here. At first, your eyes will have a tendency to scan both left and right, a tendency that you must resist. Remember that you are in control! With continued practice, the left-right movement will be minimized more and more and eventually overcome completely.

In time, you should begin practice on narrow columns without a line drawn down the middle. Be diligent so that the only movement of the eyes is down—not left, right, or up.

Numerous sessions of practice on Drills A through E and extensive newspaper and magazine columnar reading will be necessary to assure conscious and deliberate control of the eyes. Do not think you can succeed overnight. Why is eye control so important? Remember: When you succeed with reducing the number of stops the eyes make on a page, you will reduce the amount of time required to read that page. As reading time is reduced, speed increases; as speed increases, comprehension improves. Accomplishing this goal requires both practice and patience.

Wider and Deeper

Developing the ability to see wider areas is one key to success with rapid reading. Developing the ability to see deeper (vertical, or up-down) areas is yet another. The five drills that follow will aid you in developing a greater depth consciousness while offering additional practice for controlling your eyes and expanding your visual width.

In Drill F, focus on the white space between the letters *Z* and *A*, and read alternately left and right from the inside out, one line at a time. However, make only one fixation to read the *two* lines; then move down to the next group of six letters, etc. Repeat the drill as necessary.

NOTE: For alternate practice, this drill, and all letter drills, can be practiced by beginning at the bottom of the page and reading up.

When practicing Drill G, focus on the *centermost* letter of each group and read from the inside out, alternately to the left and to the right, line by line, but with only *one* fixation per group. Do the same for Drills H, I, and J.

DRILL F

R	Z	M
G	*A*	M
E	*A*	H
C	*O*	M
A	*I*	T
Z	*X*	B
Z	*O*	B
W	*T*	I
Q	B	O
U	*I*	N
V	*T*	Y
S	*B*	O
J	N	A
B	*R*	K
R	M	T
Y	*D*	P
S	*I*	P
J	*B*	A
R	*T*	W
W	*C*	K
P	*I*	M
O	*I*	L
M	*K*	M
D	*O*	V
O	Z	R
J	*M*	K
I	*T*	S
E	*B*	W
T	*I*	M
R	*W*	S
		B
		V
		V

DRILL G

A	R	NQT	B	D
C	K	AKP	N	R
M	D	YRL	X	A
K	D	LPY	K	S
M	F	KTP	B	X
R	O	LDH	M	R
K	Q	DMT	A	J
M	F	LDF	M	T
Y	M	FLP	B	C
O	F	KVM	T	P
V	K	XPR	O	S
D	P	MCO	F	K
I	E	SLT	B	H
O	C	HDU	L	S
C	P	FKY	R	N
J	R	UGJ	X	I
A	B	FKT	J	K
A	K	FTU	J	S
A	I	VRP	C	I
L	D	TPB	M	T
L	R	IDF	V	G
Q	L	JML	I	X
P	F	WPG	V	K
F	J	YPL	M	R
X	O	UML	V	N
Q	B	AMR	Z	O
F	L	NML	D	B
W	P	LVR	X	V
K	R	PFJ	R	L
C	O	ELX	A	I
N	V	EXA	C	B
X	B	SUM	V	Z
I	Q	OBL	C	T

DRILL H

R	M	Z	P	N
S	K	*T*	B	N
A	J	M	W	N
J	F	K	B	M
W	O	*N*	V	J
Q	I	B	A	L
F	B	E	I	C
P	F	*M*	V	L
J	F	B	K	D
S	L	N	I	E
L	S	*M*	A	T
K	D	M	W	P
A	L	T	B	T
Z	O	*J*	M	X
W	P	K	S	M
P	T	G	N	X
K	G	*N*	C	M
P	S	L	C	M
T	O	L	D	L
E	P	*B*	X	L
S	L	U	M	C
O	F	A	K	D
S	K	*M*	T	O
I	D	L	R	P
Q	M	Z	V	Y
K	C	*Y*	L	E
M	S	J	L	T
H	C	S	M	W
K	D	J	U	T
R	J	O	L	S
B	C	M	K	L
N	B	V	C	X
Z	W	R	Q	U

DRILL I

T	E	ESN	N	O
D	L	SCB	N	E
W	P	F*H*B	S	O
A	L	FCB	G	E
X	B	WYO	P	F
Q	O	PAB	C	M
E	K	GZS	F	A
L	S	HVN	T	I
D	I	EGB	P	D
W	L	QCX	O	K
K	R	DMG	Y	N
X	O	EJQ	O	L
A	Z	FWJ	P	K
B	J	KRS	E	L
P	A	TGB	R	V
D	U	KVX	Z	M
V	J	EOP	G	M
K	R	FXB	M	I
T	M	JRD	V	J
K	A	VUT	Y	B
A	K	DUR	I	H
G	Y	WLM	U	D
D	B	X*HY*	J	N
T	N	FIV	F	L
R	P	HCW	Q	M
A	I	OMP	C	I
D	K	WQJ	K	I
L	S	F*HY*	C	O
W	G	BJY	L	W
S	N	VXE	D	P
T	V	CNW	N	S
A	B	BOM	X	T
Z	E	JIP	W	S
V	D	OTQ	R	O
D	A	QUW	I	S

DRILL J

C	S	P	URL	N	B	N
M	D	R	TYH	B	M	S
L	S	K	DTB	X	J	W
L	A	D	RYM	C	K	E
P	A	F	G*T*W	Q	M	D
T	K	F	EXB	U	M	W
T	N	D	RWS	C	I	A
R	J	E	P*Q*T	X	P	M
L	E	G	JWQ	U	I	N
S	J	D	VBN	Z	Q	T
M	E	O	I*U*K	L	A	P
L	B	W	SFB	C	X	C
F	T	Q	HLS	C	V	M
C	M	E	S*BC*	D	H	E
M	R	W	QUM	L	D	J
A	D	Q	GXB	M	K	L
R	E	S	SCN	F	S	D
L	B	D	TYZ	V	S	L
B	R	S	QUI	E	P	W
W	L	T	H*KX*	A	T	H
K	L	T	BZS	W	W	L
C	B	S	NBC	F	T	H
K	L	R	UZA	M	F	E
H	P	U	QUT	V	E	B
C	T	G	BMD	R	M	A
E	X	B	C*DJ*	F	H	Q
B	N	J	FWQ	T	P	M
M	S	F	ACH	R	M	S
P	Q	K	LSG	A	W	E
R	S	L	BSQ	T	Y	A

When you have mastered Drills A through J with vocal and/or subvocal practice, repeat them all several times *without* vocalization. Focus on the center letter of each line just as before, but do not read aloud or "say" the letters to yourself.

If you persist with a tendency to either vocalize or subvocalize what you see, try counting aloud repeatedly from one to ten, or recite a simple poem or the lyrics to a song you know well as your eyes visually "comprehend" each line. This practice in "sight-reading" will help to overcome subvocalization and an innate tendency to resist accelerated reading—a tendency that is akin to the fear that something may be missed if you cover material rapidly.

It cannot be said too many times: Mastery of these drills is of paramount importance if you have a serious desire to succeed as an Accelerated Reader. They *cannot* be practiced too much; however, avoid overdoing during any single drill session.

Learn Pacing and Block Reading

Even after having developed better eye control and a wider, deeper, and more effective vision span, would-be rapid readers often are hindered from achieving really impressive rates because of a failure to maintain an accelerated rate throughout a longer reading. Oftentimes they tend to get bogged down or frustrated and lose hold of the word-per-minute rate of which they are capable. In short, the pace is lost, and the rate of visual coverage of the pages being read fluctuates from too fast to too slow.

The primary purpose of the following drills is to give you some needed practice with pacing—maintaining a regular and steady rate over a page. They are to be practiced without concerning yourself about comprehension. Try to become used to the visual stop-start pattern as you count yourself down and then up the page.

Drill K contains 30 five-letter lines. The focal point for each line is just slightly above the *center* letter; your eyes should move down one line at a time, one fixation per line. Aloud or subvocally, count from 1 to 30—once for each line and fixation. At first, attempt to "sight read" only the three inner columns; "graduate" to the other two.

Remember that your eyes can see accurately enough to read *only* when they are stopped completely. If you experience blurs as the eyes are moved down the page, you are scanning or sweeping in a more or less continuous pattern. As a result, no reading or recognition with certainty can take place. You must, therefore, stop the eyes—briefly, but totally—on every line.

DRILL K

D	B	A	C	E
K	T	L	Y	C
C	V	I	J	F
V	F	K	R	K
B	R	K	T	V
X	B	J	T	T
G	U	K	V	F
H	R	J	F	H
H	Y	G	T	G
G	Y	T	R	I
J	S	C	B	W
R	B	C	N	X
G	B	M	N	S
R	B	C	N	X
J	S	C	B	W
G	Y	T	R	I
H	Y	G	T	G
A	R	J	F	H
G	U	K	V	F
X	B	J	T	O
B	R	K	T	V
V	F	K	R	K
C	V	I	J	F
K	T	L	Y	C
Z	U	B	R	L
Q	L	D	G	K
L	W	A	F	K
M	Z	V	G	P
L	S	G	Y	T
K	A	U	J	O

Now, repeat Drill K taking two lines with each fixation and move down the page for a count of 15. The focal point will be between the center letters of each pair of lines. If you come out "uneven," continue to practice until you finish easily on the count of 15.

Then, repeat Drill K taking three lines with each fixation to a count of 10. You may need to take this count a bit slower at first. Work until you can cover the whole drill with just 10 distinct eye-stops. It is worth your time and effort!

The short article (Drill L) which follows is to be "sight read" in essentially the same manner as you practiced Drill K. Focus in the center of the column, move the eyes down *one* line at a time while counting aloud (or to yourself) as you cover the entire passage. *Do not vocalize or subvocalize any words printed in the selection*. Continue repeating your visual coverage one line at a time while counting. Do so as many times as necessary until you have acquired satisfactory comprehension of the article's content.

DRILL L

The Basic Idea

The basic idea of social security is a simple one: During working years, employees, their employers, and self-employed people pay social security contributions, which go into special funds; and when earnings stop or are reduced because the worker retires, dies, or becomes disabled, monthly cash benefits are paid from the funds to replace part of the earnings the family has lost.

Part of the contributions made during the working years go into a separate hospital insurance trust fund so that when workers or their dependents reach 65 they will have paid-up hospital insurance to help pay their hospital bills.

A program of supplementary medical insurance, which is available to people 65 or over, helps them pay doctors' bills and other medical expenses. This program is voluntary and, instead of being paid for out of social security contributions, is financed out of premiums shared half-and-half by the older people who sign up and the Federal Government.

Nine out of ten working people in the United States are now building protection for themselves and their families under the social security program.

Now, practice visual coverage of Drill L at *two* lines per focus. Then repeat at *three* lines per fixation. Do each procedure several times. Do not be concerned that you are repeating the same reading so many times. You are learning and practicing a technique essential to success with accelerated reading. Later you will apply what you are perfecting now to actual reading requirements, but first, you must practice, practice, practice!

The successful Accelerated Reader is able to read larger than normal "blocks" or "bites" of the printed page with each eye-stop. He has accepted, without reservation, the philosophy that the most important benefit of reading is the gaining of information, ideas, mental "pictures," and entertainment—not the fretting over words. He has come to a realization that words in and of themselves are for the most part insignificant—except to compilers of dictionaries. He knows that it is only when an author combines them with other words to form ideas that they assume any real air of importance. The very successful Accelerated Reader realizes that the skillful author shares much in common with the skillful painter. Instead of using brushes and oils to transmit an idea or image from his mind to the mind of another, the author uses words.

Are you, too, starting to think this way? If so, continue practice with the next drill.

Block read Drill M with a single fixation in the visual center of each two-line "block," or group of words. Hold each fixation for a normal vocal (or subvocal) count of 1-2-3, then move down to the center of the next "block" until you complete the entire drill. Using the same procedure, go through the selection several times until you are satisfied with your comprehension of its content.

DRILL M

The doctor was puzzled.
He again looked at the moan-

ing patient, and once again
shook his knowledgeable old

head. "Looks bad," he said.
"Temperature: 103; the pulse:

10; dark rings under the red
eyes; irregular breathing . . ."

"Another case, doctor?"
asked the worried nurse.

"Afraid so," he replied
unhappily. "Third one admit-

ted today!"
"Is there a cure for it,

doctor?" the nurse asked in
her most sympathetic voice.

The doctor, half choking
with emotional anxiety, an-

swered, "We can cure falling hair, broken spinal cords,

ingrown toenails, leprosy,
and tired blood, but there is

just no known cure for that
dreaded summerschoolitis!"

You have just witnessed
a frightening scene now en-

acted again and again on our
college campuses every year.

Isn't it terrible! And to
think some people actually

have the nerve to say that
summer school *is* wonderful!

There is a society for the
prevention of cruelty to our

dumb animal friends, or so
they say anyhow. Well, if

there is, I don't see why
they can't do something to

help the poor dumb animals
who have to go to summer

school. The least they
could do is to put all the

professors in another state
institution and not let

them out until September.
While I am talking about

professors, let me tell you
how unreasonable and de-

manding they are in summer.
Sure, I know they are always

unreasonable and demanding,
but in the summer—boy!

You know, they have the pure
audacity to expect you to

attend nearly every class! I
guess they don't realize

that students would rather go
home on Thursday than wait

until Friday to leave. And what
is even worse, they have the

nerve to expect you to be back
in time for Monday classes!

Now I ask you, what kind of a
weekend can a person have if

he doesn't get to leave until
Friday, and then has to be back

Monday? There is simply no
justice left in this world.

If you think it is awful to
have an 8 o'clock class, you

should have to meet at 7:30! You
don't believe me? Yes, that's

what I did say, 7:30 a.m. No
wonder the poor student's

health is injured so much by
going to summer school.

Anybody knows that two hours
of sleep is not enough to main-

tain a healthy body. You ask why
I only get two hours of sleep?

Well, since you asked, I will
gladly tell you. The

reason for little sleep is those
blasted long assignments. It

seems that the professors think
there are 48 hours in a

day. Why, some of the teachers
expect their students to go to

the library and do (excuse these
horrible words) outside

reading. How is that for crust?
But I think the worst thing

about summer school is the last
week. No kidding, you have to

work and study 60 hours a day
to catch up on all that work you

didn't do before. What? You ask
why I didn't do some of it

before? That's easy . . . well, I
mean, after all . . . you know, "all

work and no play" . . . You know
the old saying.

Summer school is wonder-
ful? Well, so was the bubonic

plague!
Would you mind calling a

doctor? I am coming down with
a very, very bad case of that

dreadful disease, summer
schoolitis!

Drill M was printed deliberately with an average column width
of approximately 2¼ inches, about an inch less than the width of
most paperback titles. If you have practiced all the vision span
and eye control drills faithfully, you should have increased your
vision acuity to such a degree that seeing and reading up to 2¼
inches with a single fixation in the vertical center of the lines
was entirely possible without too much difficulty.

If you did experience problems with reading the 2¼ inch-lines,
this would tend to indicate that you need additional practice,
especially on Drills A through E. Go back now and practice if
necessary.

Assuming you had little if any difficulty with mastery of Drill M, you are ready to proceed with learning and practicing the Two-Stop Method which, in effect, visually splits each page into two vertical halves. This "split" technique, when mastered, requires that you read line lengths of only slightly over 1½ inches with each fixation—a width adequate for success with paperbacks and one you certainly should have mastered by now.

Above all else, be honest with yourself. If you feel you need more practice, go back and do it now. If not, proceed.

Master the Two-Stop Method

After careful observation of countless rapid readers, it was found that each one had a slightly different manner for covering a printed page visually. However, most utilized some form of a pattern closely akin to an "S" or a "Z."

You will also, in time, develop a unique pattern for covering a page in the fastest, easiest, and most effective way; but for now, you are well-advised to begin that development by learning the dependable and reliable Two-Stop Method, or visual pattern.

The most important exercise (Drill N), which follows, is designed to help you learn a technique for reading most printed line lengths with only two eye-stops or fixations, regardless of the number of words. If you wish to triple your reading speed and become an Accelerated Reader, it is imperative that you master what follows.

As you read, try to imagine that your eyes are "sponges." You are to set them firmly in the middle of the left half-line and "soak up" all you possibly can; then you are to move your "sponges" quickly to the center of the right half-line, hold briefly but firmly, and once again "soak up" all you can. The pattern is repeated.

Repeat Drill N—paragraph by paragraph—several times on a 1-2 count. Focus left on the count of 1, and right on the count of 2. Resist any temptation to stop more than twice on each line, or to scan or sweep visually. If you do make more than two stops, you will see mainly blurs as your eyes hurry along over the words, in which case your comprehension will not be satisfactory.

You will need to practice this entire drill many times. Keep working until the Two-Stop Method becomes smooth and natural. After you master the Two-Stop Method reading one line at a time, practice reading two lines at a time.

DRILL N

The alert
student observed
as he
read in
Triple *Your*
Reading *Speed*
that the columns of
words increased somewhat in
width as he went
along. They increased, in
fact, so much that by Drill K
they were the same width as
the line of print on a novel page.
It is a true fact that some readers can
read straight down the middle of an entire novel page
and their peripheral vision will take in the entire line
without their eyes scanning either left or right. This is indeed quite
an achievement for anyone to make in his reading improvement.

Of course,
this would be ideal.
But most of us find it
necessary to have some eye movement,
and that's surely all right provided it's
the proper left-right pattern, consciously controlled
until it becomes an automatic habit. As you read this exercise,
you note that it began with one word to the left and the next to
the right. It is quite obvious that printing a book in this manner,
even a small one, would require thousands of pages, and cost a
great amount of money for the paper and the printing, to say
nothing of the extra labor to set the type.

So   to
save   paper
and printing   costs, we
began printing two   words to the
left and two words   to the right. We
increased the number on each   side until soon we had an
entire line printed as you find   in all books which you read.

As you read this exercise, allow your vision to take in half the words on each printed line, whether there are two or twenty. But make certain that you make only two stops on each line—never make any more than two.

Your focal point on the left should be the center of the word or the group of words. The same type focus is made to the right. In making the

focal change, do be certain   that your eyes make only one
stop to the left and   one stop to the right.
When you master   this One-Line,
Two-Stop   pattern,
wild horses can-   not hold you back
from increased speed   and improved comprehension. Notice how we   alternate back and forth

with different line lengths to remind you again and again how your eye movement pattern should be controlled. Remember that your speed is controlled to a great extent by the deviations of fixations you make on each line of print. Reduce the number of stops and increase speed.

If you maintain only two deviations or focuses per line, you cannot "word hop"—a very tiring and wasteful habit. It works much the same way as travel time varies on a trip. If you stop at every town along the way, your arrival time will doubtless be much later, and you will likely be much more fatigued than if you travel straight through stopping only when it is necessary. Not only will you arrive sooner, you will not be nearly so weary and probably not as tired.

"For Real" Practice

After you fully master the Two-Stop Method illustrated in Drill N, you will wish to gain additional confidence and further perfect your new skills by reading and rereading the seven selections that follow.

Since the number of words in each selection is given, all you will need to determine is the rate at which you are going to read each one. Your rate will be, of course, largely a matter of the progress you have made to date. Some students of the Accele*read* Method will be reading three times their beginning rate; others who have dedicated themselves more seriously, and diligently practiced all of the drills may be able to read at rates even more impressive than three times their original speed.

On the other hand, those who have been in such a hurry that they have neglected to practice most or all of the drills may not have improved upon their less than impressive beginning rate. If this is your sad plight, go back now and start over. Going further at this time will not help you to increase your reading speed— that is, if you fully aspire to be a bona fide Accelerated Reader.

To illustrate how to determine the average reading time and rate, and the approximate amount of time to spend per page, it will be assumed that you are going to read the first selection at either two or three times your beginning rate.

If your starting rate was 200 words per minute, you would set either 400 (to double rate) or 600 (to triple rate) as your goal. Then, how long will you have to read this first selection, which contains approximately 2,400 words?

To find out, divide 400 into 2,400. The answer is 6 minutes— the time allowed to double a beginning rate of 200. Or, divide 600 into 2,400. The answer is 4, which means you are required to read the selection in only 4 minutes in order to achieve an average of 600 wpm or three times the beginning speed of 200. And so on.

Next, count the pages of text to be covered so as to determine how much time you can afford to allot to each whole page. However, keep in mind that some pages will require more time to read than others. This means you must push harder over light, descriptive matter, and slow down somewhat when the "plot thickens."

Since the first selection is about four pages long, you will want to allow an *average* of 1½ minutes (90 seconds) per page to finish at 400 wpm. Allow only 1 minute (60 seconds) to finish for a 600 wpm average rate.

Since this reading is one of nonfiction, you will want to follow all the steps outlined earlier in "How to Preview a Chapter." (In previewing, do not assume the selection is straight text and overlook the step that deals with graphics. There is a table in this selection.)

Now you are ready to "condition" yourself to your desired pace and the reading material as well. Using the Two-Stop pattern, read the *first* page in the time limit that you have set for one page. Of course, you will need to position a watch or clock nearby so you may observe the time easily. If you have a stop-watch available, you will find it most useful. (You might even have a friend call aloud the lapsed time at 5- or 10-second intervals.)

Get the feel of covering the printed lines at the pace necessary, even if you have to make several attempts before you finish the page exactly on time. Comprehension may not be especially good since you will be dividing attention between reading and keeping time. Do not worry; you will soon repeat this page.

When you complete this pacing process, take a few moments to assess your understanding of the reading selection. Do not be overly concerned if your recall is very fragmented. Your comprehension will improve as you gain confidence with faster rates and learn to concentrate more on *what* you are reading than *how* you are reading.

Now, go ahead and finish the entire first selection at the rate you have set. Note the time to the nearest minute when you finish. Calculate words-per-minute by dividing the total minutes into 2,400.

Measure comprehension by taking the 10-question multiple-choice test following the selection.

The Web of Life, by John H. Storer*

(approximately 2,400 words)

CHAPTER 9. THE COMMUNITY THROUGH THE SEASONS

As we look at the quiet stillness of a forest we may imagine something of the feverish activity going on within it, and some of this we may see if we have the patience to watch for it.

Throughout the ages of its existence the fortunes of the great forest community are constantly fluctuating under the influence of four fundamental forces and a host of lesser ones. The long-range cycles of weather, the cycles of disease and prosperity among member groups, and the resulting changes in the influence of these groups on each other, all play a major part in the existence of a whole community. But the changing seasons of the year have the most obvious effect.

In winter the plants of the northern climates rest from their function of producing food, and all the creatures of the forest must adjust their lives to a reduced food supply. Most of the birds go south. Many animals, such as the chipmunks, woodchucks, skunks, snakes, and frogs, and many insects, retire for a long sleep during the winter. Those that remain active must depend on food stored up from the summer's harvest.

The ruffed grouse and cardinal will find it stored in the seeds, fruits, and buds of trees and bushes. The nuthatch finds the eggs of insects hidden in the bark of trees. Woodpeckers drill through the bark to find the insect larvae that winter beneath it. The red squirrel, flying squirrel, and gray squirrel live on stored seeds and nuts. Perhaps the most active and numerous animals of the forest are the white-footed mice and the shrews, and in them we see a good example of interdependence. The mice live on their stores of seeds and on what insects they can find hidden in winter retreats, while the shrews hunt day and night, digging tunnels through soil and humus and through rotting logs to capture the mice, as well as great numbers of insects.

These mammals and birds in their turn offer food to the fox, the weasel, and the barred owl, which of course can exist only in smaller numbers, since for their support they require so many of the lesser creatures.

*Copyright 1953, by John Storer. Published by The New American Library, Inc.

As the snow melts and the suns of March and April warm the ground, a change comes over the forest. The low plants on the earth's surface come to life. The early insects come out of hiding and many more hatch to take advantage of the new supply of food. The skunk, the chipmunk, and several kinds of snakes, toads, and frogs wake from their winter sleep, and all include in their varied diets great numbers of insects. Now the ground grows bright with spring flowers—spring beauties, yellow adder's-tongue, hepatica, trillium, and many others. The flower buds of the elms and red maples offer food for gray squirrels. Frogs add their music to the notes of birds returning from their winter in the south. For now nature's food factory has begun again to build new life from sunlight, air, and water. The green algae in the pools, the forest plants, shrubs, and trees are all doing their share, offering their stores of energy to the creatures that come to feed on them. And the creatures respond. Insects of different kinds attack every part of every tree and plant—buds and blossoms, leaves and bark and wood. Spiders and predatory insects feed on these plant eaters, and all are in turn preyed on by the larger animals, including snakes and frogs, and by waves of migrating birds that spread up from the South to find nesting sites and hunting grounds to support their hungry young.

Many of these birds stop merely for a rest and a meal, and hurry on to find summer homes farther north. Others stay to fill every available niche in the forest and, as the leaves unfold, the branches that yesterday were bare and inhospitable, now offer shelter from weather and predators.

Dr. Arthur B. Williams of Cleveland made an interesting four-year study of the relationships of the nesting birds in a 65-acre tract of climax beech maple forest near his city. During these four years the number of pairs of nesting birds present on the tract were 136, 174, 176, and 134. This gave a yearly average of 2.3 pairs of nesting birds per acre. When one thinks of the enormous number of insects needed by a growing family of young birds, each one requiring nearly its own weight in them every day, this seems like a very small territory to supply the needs of each family. But actually the territory includes more living space than might appear, for it reaches upward to the tree tops and above, as well as along the ground. Within this territory, as we have already seen, there are many different kinds of hunting grounds. Each different kind of bird is specially adapted to hunt in its own niche, and each, having selected its own hunting territory, will defend that territory against all competitors of its own species. But many different kinds of birds may nest close together without competing, because each species occupies a different niche, while others that might compete are so scattered as to cause little trouble.

For example, Dr. Williams found four different kinds of woodpeckers nesting in the area, the pileated, hairy, downy, and red-bellied. But since each species is so specialized as to confine its hunting to a different part of the larger trees, there was apparently little competition among them. Three pairs of white-breasted nuthatches in the area might have competed with the downy woodpeckers in hunting among the bark crevices, but as their nests were widely separated, there was probably no serious competition. The chickadees and tufted titmice perhaps competed with the nuthatches, but their nests also were well scattered, so that the area allowed about 3.6 acres for each pair.

The flycatchers, living on flying insects, divided the territory, each pair of Acadian flycatchers having staked out its own separate nesting and hunting ground in a little glen by a stream. The crested flycatcher used a different part of the woods, and the wood pewees used widely separated territories in the higher areas of the forest.

On the ground and among the lower bushes, the Louisiana water thrush, wood thrush, cardinal, ovenbird, and towhee shared the territory, which totaled about two acres of hunting ground for each nesting pair. The hooded warblers and redstarts hunted chiefly at a higher level. In the leafy foliage of the taller trees the tanagers, vireos, and cerulean warblers were the chief hunters, while the black-throated green warblers confined themselves chiefly to the upper branches of hemlocks.

Thus, every part of every tree, bush, and plant in the forest received its regular protection from its own special guardian.

As the young birds grew and left their nests, the hunting territories were less strictly guarded by their parents and finally were abandoned altogether as great numbers of young searched for their own food. In the process of growing up, many young died of accident and exposure to weather and by predator.

By summer's end, conditions began to change again for our forest community. Much of the tree and plant growth had stopped, providing less appetizing food for insects. Their own time of greatest multiplication had passed. The birds begin to move south again. The redstarts are among the first to go, followed closely by the ovenbirds. By the end of August the red-eyed vireos and wood thrushes have gone. Purple martins and chimney swifts busily hunt flying insects that seek sunshine above the dark canopy of the forest.

By the beginning of October the scarlet tanagers and hooded warblers, last of the summer birds, have gone, and now the forest is filled by great waves of southward-bound migrants coming down from the north. Hundreds of robins, thrushes of several kinds—first the hermits, then the olive-backs, veeries, and gray-cheeks—stop to feed on wild grapes and on the fruits and berries of many trees and bushes. They vary this diet with beetles, grubs, and other insects, which they dig out from under dead leaves.

By early November most of the leaves have fallen and the bare tree tops again admit light to the forest floor. The robins and thrushes continue southward. Bobwhites may come in from the fields to gather beechnuts in the woods. Tracks in the early snows of late November tell of the search for food by squirrels, cottontail rabbits, red fox, white-footed mouse, and short-tailed shrew.

So the population of the forest fluctuates greatly throughout the seasons. Dr. Williams estimated the average bird population for the 65 acres that he studied to be as follows:

Permanent residents	March	May	July	Sept.	Oct.	Dec.	Jan.
woodpeckers							
barred owls							
titmice, chickadees							
cardinals, nuthatches							
towhees, etc.							
total 11 species	100	69	52	78	86	106	102

Summer residents							
vireos, thrushes							
warblers, robins							
flycatchers, tanagers, etc.							
total 10 species	0	365	184	195	510	2	2

Autumn and winter
 visitors and transients
red-breasted nuthatches
juncoes, thrushes
warblers, sparrows, etc.

total 56 species	200	505	3	295	465	218	50
Grand total	300	939	239	568	1,061	326	154

All this great company of birds, mammals, and insects in Dr. Williams's study must adapt itself to the environment established and controlled by three kinds of trees—the beech, the sugar maple, and the hemlock. The tulip, red oak, red maple, and white ash play important, but secondary, roles. The chestnut once shared a dominant position until it was wiped out by blight.

With these seven trees there are 20 other lesser kinds that grow in the forest openings or borders or under the shade of the dominant trees. With them are seven species of vines, 45 common herbs and shrubs, together with 24 other rare or uncommon species; 14 ferns, 10 mosses, and six miscellaneous algae, lichen, liverwort, and sedge. Besides these, it is estimated there are between 1,200 and 1,500 different species of large fungi and other plants that live on dead organic matter from trees and plants.

Dr. Williams concluded after his study that the existence of this great forest depends on the birds, mammals, and predatory insects that protect it from its enormous population of plant-eating insects. On the other hand, the insectivorous creatures must have insects to feed them, and many of the insects, as we have seen, play an important role in preparing the forest soil and pollinating plants.

Thus, in every forest the living creatures that make up the community are actually selected by the dominant trees and the lesser plants that determine the environment in which they must live.

From all this we see that the forest is a great organization made up of many separate and indispensable parts. Some of these parts may appear to be harmful to its life. But in most cases the degree of harm or value will depend on the perfection of the control or balance that the different members achieve among themselves.

Owing to the hazards of climate and disease, this balance is never quite achieved, and its fluctuations play an important part in forest life. And on the degree of its attainment will depend the amount of life that the land can support, in other words its carrying capacity.

It is interesting to note how this principle is applied by nesting birds in the forest where, as we have just seen, each pair selects and defends enough territory to support its family. But this defense is exerted only against members of the same species, while nests of other, noncompeting species might be tolerated in the same tree.

COMPREHENSION TEST

THE WEB OF LIFE, CHAPTER 9

(Circle the letter preceding the most correct answer)

1. Which of the following plays the major and most obvious role in the existence of the forest community?

    (A) Long-range cycles of weather
    (B) Cycles of disease and prosperity
    (C) Resulting changes of groups on each other
    (D) The changing seasons

2. Which of the following does not occur when plants in the northern climates rest for winter?

    (A) Most birds go south.
    (B) Snakes retire for a long sleep.
    (C) Chipmunks go south.
    (D) Bears hibernate.

3. In the winter, squirrels live mainly on

    (A) stored seeds and nuts.
    (B) small tree buds.
    (C) unharvested grain.
    (D) honey stolen from bears.

4. A very vicious small animal frequently mentioned in the chapter is the

    (A) field mouse.
    (B) wild white rat.
    (C) ring-tail skunk.
    (D) shrew.

5. The fox, weasel, and horned owl exist in small numbers mainly because they

    (A) are very wild and vicious.
    (B) require so many lesser creatures for food.
    (C) often kill each other for food.
    (D) are so frequently trapped by man.

6. Different species of birds nested in the same area seem to give little competition to each other mainly because they

    (A) feed at different hours.
    (B) feed on different parts of plants.
    (C) eat very little.
    (D) soon migrate to other areas.

7. Among the first birds to migrate south in winter are the

   (A) eagles.
   (B) redstarts.
   (C) ovenbirds.
   (D) birds named in (B) and (C).

8. The population of the forest throughout the seasons

   (A) remains relatively stable.
   (B) fluctuates greatly.
   (C) changes twice annually.
   (D) doesn't really change.

9. Creatures which feed mainly on insects are said to be

   (A) insectivorous.
   (B) carnivorous.
   (C) herbivorous.
   (D) mantises.

10. Birds of the same species seldom nest in the same tree because

   (A) each parent pair selects and defends a territory to support its family.
   (B) birds of a feather never flock together.
   (C) birds are by nature warlike.
   (D) the young offspring would be fighting constantly.

(When finished answering the questions, check the answers below.)

Correct Answers for Test

THE WEB OF LIFE

(Value: 10 points each)

Approximately 2,400 words

1. The correct answer is (D).   6. The correct answer is (B).

2. The correct answer is (C).   7. The correct answer is (D).

3. The correct answer is (A).   8. The correct answer is (B).

4. The correct answer is (D).   9. The correct answer is (A).

5. The correct answer is (B).   10. The correct answer is (A).

"Go For More" Practice

No matter what your test results were in the previous test, you can do better. Prove this to yourself! (There is "method in this madness.")

Repeat the selection *five* times as per the following suggestions.

1. Repeat at the same rate as your initial coverage

2. Repeat at a rate of at least 100 words per minute faster than your initial coverage

3. Repeat at a rate of at least 200 words per minute faster than your initial coverage

4. Repeat at a rate of at least 300 words per minute faster than your initial coverage

5. Repeat at the same rate as your initial coverage (Note, by comparison, how slow this coverage seems.)

Pause to assess your overall understanding of what you have read several times. If you wish, retake the test on scratch paper. Remember that you are learning and practicing techniques to improve reading speed and comprehension. You will not have to read everything six times from now on in order to have satisfactory comprehension—that is why you are being advised to do so *now*.

Follow the same general procedure as outlined above with each of the selections that follow. Later, you will be pleased that you did!

"The Cask of Amontillado," by Edgar Allan Poe

(approximately 2,600 words)

The thousand injuries of Fortunato I had borne as I best could; but when he ventured upon insult, I vowed revenge. You, who so well know the nature of my soul, will not suppose, however, that I gave utterance to a threat. At *length* I would be avenged; this was a point definitely settled—but the very definitiveness with which it was resolved, precluded the idea of risk. I must not only punish, but punish with impunity. A wrong is unredressed when retribution overtakes its redresser. It is equally unredressed when the avenger fails to make himself felt as such to him who has done the wrong.

It must be understood, that neither by word nor deed had I given Fortunato cause to doubt my good-will. I continued, as was my wont, to smile in his face, and he did not perceive that my smile *now* was at the thought of his immolation.

He had a weak point—this Fortunato—although in other regards he was a man to be respected and even feared. He prided himself on his connoisseurship in wine. Few Italians have the true virtuoso spirit. For the most part their enthusiasm is adopted to suit the time and opportunity—to practise imposture upon the British and Austrian *millionaires*. In painting and gemmary Fortunato, like his countrymen, was a quack—but in the matter of old wines he was sincere. In this respect I did not differ from him materially: I was skillful in the Italian vintages myself, and bought largely whenever I could.

It was about dusk, one evening during the supreme madness of the carnival season, that I encountered my friend. He accosted me with excessive warmth, for he had been drinking much. The man wore motley. He had on a tight-fitting parti-striped dress, and his head was surmounted by the conical cap and bells. I was so pleased to see him, that I thought I should never have done wringing his hand.

I said to him: "My dear Fortunato, you are luckily met. How remarkably well you are looking to-day! But I have received a pipe of what passes for Amontillado, and I have my doubts."

"How?" said he. "Amontillado? A pipe? Impossible! And in the middle of the carnival!"

"I have my doubts," I replied; "and I was silly enough to pay the full Amontillado price without consulting you in the matter. You were not to be found, and I was fearful of losing a bargain."

"Amontillado!"

"I have my doubts."

"Amontillado!"

"And I must satisfy them."

"Amontillado!"

"As you are engaged, I am on my way to Luchesi. If any one has a critical turn, it is he. He will tell me—"

"Luchesi cannot tell Amontillado from Sherry."

"And yet some fools will have it that his tastes are a match for your own."

"Come, let us go."

"Whither?"

"To your vaults."

"My friend, no; I will not impose upon your good nature. I perceive you have an engagement. Luchesi—"

"I have no engagement;—come."

"My friend, no. It is not the engagements, but the severe cold with which I perceive you are afflicted. The vaults are insufferably damp. They are encrusted with nitre."

"Let us go, nevertheless. The cold is merely nothing. Amontillado! You have been imposed upon. And as for Luchesi, he cannot distinguish Sherry from Amontillado."

Thus speaking, Fortunato possessed himself of my arm. Putting on a mask of black silk, and drawing a *roquelaire* closely about my person, I suffered him to hurry me to my palazzo.

There were no attendants at home; they had absconded to make merry in honor of the time. I had told them that I should not return until the morning, and had given them explicit orders not to stir from the house. These orders were sufficient, I well knew, to insure their immediate disappearance, one and all, as soon as my back was turned.

I took from their sconces two flambeaux, and giving one to Fortunato, bowed him through several suites of rooms to the archway that led into the vaults. I passed down a long and wind-ing staircase, requesting him to be cautious as he followed. We came at length to the foot of the descent, and stood together on the damp ground of the catacombs of the Montresors.

The gait of my friend was unsteady, and the bells upon his cap jingled as he strode.

"The pipe?" said he.

"It is farther on," said I; "but observe the white webwork which gleams from these cavern walls."

He turned toward me, and looked into my eyes with two filmy orbs that distilled the rheum of intoxication.

"Nitre?" he asked, at length.

"Nitre," I replied. "How long have you had that cough?"

"Ugh! ugh! ugh!—ugh! ugh! ugh!—ugh! ugh! ugh!—ugh! ugh! ugh!—ugh! ugh! ugh!"

My poor friend found it impossible to reply for many minutes.

"It is nothing," he said at last.

"Come," I said, with decision, "we will go back; your health is precious. You are rich, respected, admired, beloved; you are happy, as once I was. You are a man to be missed. For me it is no matter. We will go back; you will be ill, and I cannot be respon-sible. Besides, there is Luchesi—"

"Enough," he said; "the cough is a mere nothing; it will not kill me. I shall not die of a cough."

"True—true," I replied; "and, indeed, I had no intention of alarming you unnecessarily; but you should use all proper cau-tion. A draught of this Medoc will defend us from the damps."

Here I knocked off the necks of a bottle which I drew from a long row of its fellows that lay upon the mould.

"Drink," I said, presenting him the wine.

He raised it to his lips with a leer. He paused and nodded to me familiarly, while his bells jingled.

"I drink," he said, "to the buried that repose around us."

"And I to your long life."

He again took my arm and we proceeded.

"These vaults," he said, "are extensive."

"The Montresors," I replied, "were a great and numerous family."

"I forget your arms."

"A huge human foot d'or, in a field azure; the foot crushes a serpent rampant whose fangs are imbedded in the heel."

"And the motto?"

"Nemo me impune lacessit."

"Good!" he said.

The wine sparkled in his eyes and the bells jingled. My own fancy grew warm with the Medoc. We had passed through walls of piled bones, with casks and puncheons intermingling, into the inmost recesses of the catacombs. I paused again, and this time I made bold to seize Fortunato by an arm above the elbow.

"The nitre!" I said; "see, it increases. It hangs like moss upon the vaults. We are below the river's bed. The drops of moisture trickle among the bones. Come, we will go back ere it is too late. Your cough—"

"It is nothing," he said; "let us go on. But first, another draught of the Medoc."

I broke and reached him a flagon of De Grave. He emptied it at a breath. His eyes flashed with a fierce light. He laughed and threw the bottle upward with a gesticulation I did not understand.

I looked at him in surprise. He repeated the movement—a grotesque one.

"You do not comprehend?" he said.

"Not I," I replied.

"Then you are not of the brotherhood."

"How?"

"You are not of the masons."

"Yes, yes," I said; "yes, yes."

"You? Impossible! A mason?"

"A mason," I replied.

"A sign," he said.

"It is this," I answered, producing a trowel from beneath the folds of my *roquelaire*.

"You jest," he exclaimed, recoiling a few paces. "But let us proceed to the Amontillado."

"Be it so," I said, replacing the tool beneath the cloak, and again offering him my arm. He leaned upon it heavily. We continued our route in search of the Amontillado. We passed through a range of low arches, descended, passed on, and descending again, arrived at a deep crypt, in which the foulness of the air caused our flambeaux rather to glow than flame.

At the most remote end of the crypt there appeared another less spacious. Its walls had been lined with human remains, piled to the vault overhead, in the fashion of the great catacombs of Paris. Three sides of this interior crypt were still ornamented in this manner. From the fourth the bones had been thrown down, and lay promiscuously upon the earth, forming at one point a mound of some size. Within the wall thus exposed by the displacing of the bones, we perceived a still interior recess, in depth about four feet, in width three, in height six or seven. It seemed to have been constructed for no especial use within itself, but formed merely the interval between two of the colossal supports of the roof of the catacombs, and was backed by one of their circumscribing walls of solid granite.

It was in vain that Fortunato, uplifting his dull torch, endeavored to pry into the depth of the recess. Its termination the feeble light did not enable us to see.

"Proceed," I said; "herein is the Amontillado. As for Luchesi—"

"He is an ignoramus," interrupted my friend, as he stepped unsteadily forward, while I followed immediately at his heels. In an instant he had reached the extremity of the niche, and finding his progress arrested by the rock, stood stupidly bewildered. A moment more and I had fettered him to the granite. In its surface were two iron staples, distant from each other about two feet, horizontally. From one of these depended a short chain, from the other a padlock. Throwing the links about his waist, it was but the work of a few seconds to secure it. He was too much astounded to resist. Withdrawing the key I stepped back from the recess.

"Pass your hand," I said, "over the wall; you cannot help feeling the nitre. Indeed it is very damp. Once more let me *implore* you to return. No? Then I must positively leave you. But I must first render you all the little attentions in my power."

"The Amontillado!" ejaculated my friend, not yet recovered from his astonishment.

"True," I replied; "the Amontillado."

As I said these words I busied myself among the pile of bones of which I have before spoken. Throwing them aside, I soon uncovered a quantity of building stone and mortar. With these materials and with the aid of my trowel, I began vigorously to wall up the entrance of the niche.

I had scarcely laid the first tier of the masonry when I discovered that the intoxication of Fortunato had in a great measure worn off. The earliest indication I had of this was a low moaning cry from the depth of the recess. It was not the cry of a drunken man. There was then a long and obstinate silence. I laid the second tier, and the third, and the fourth; and then I heard the furious vibrations of the chain. The noise lasted for several minutes, during which, that I might hearken to it with the more satisfaction, I ceased my labors and sat down upon the bones. When at last the clanking subsided, I resumed the trowel, and finished without interruption the fifth, the sixth, and the seventh tier. The wall was now nearly upon a level with my breast. I again paused, and holding the flambeaux over the mason-work, threw a few feeble rays upon the figure within.

A succession of loud and shrill screams, bursting suddenly from the throat of the chained form, seemed to thrust me violently back. For a brief moment I hesitated—I trembled. Unsheathing my rapier, I began to grope with it about the recess; but the thought of an instant reassured me. I placed my hand upon the solid fabric of the catacombs, and felt satisfied. I reapproached the wall. I replied to the yells of him who clamored. I re-echoed—I aided—I surpassed them in volume and in strength. I did this, and the clamorer grew still.

It was now midnight, and my task was drawing to a close. I had completed the eighth, the ninth, and the tenth tier. I had finished a portion of the last and the eleventh; there remained but a single stone to be fitted and plastered in. I struggled with its weight; I placed it partially in its destined position. But now there came from out the niche a low laugh that erected the hairs upon my head. It was succeeded by a sad voice, which I had difficulty in recognizing as that of the noble Fortunato. The voice said—

"Ha! ha! ha!—he! he!—a very good joke indeed—an excellent jest. We will have many a rich laugh about it at the palazzo—he! he! he!—over our wine—he! he! he!

"The Amontillado!" I said.

"He! he! he!—he! he! he!—yes, the Amontillado. But is it not getting late? Will not they be awaiting us at the palazzo, the Lady Fortunato and the rest? Let us be gone."

"Yes," I said, "let us be gone."

"For the love of God, Montresor!"

"Yes," I said, "for the love of God!"

But to these words I hearkened in vain for a reply. I grew impatient. I called aloud:

"Fortunato!"

No answer. I called again:

"Fortunato!"

No answer still. I thrust a torch through the remaining aperture and let it fall within. There came forth in return only a jingling of the bells. My heart grew sick—on account of the dampness of the catacombs. I hastened to make an end of my labor. I forced the last stone into its position; I plastered it up. Against the new masonry I re-erected the old rampart of bones. For the half of a century no mortal has disturbed them. *In pace requiescat!*

COMPREHENSION TEST

"THE CASK OF AMONTILLADO"

(Circle the letter preceding the most correct answer)

1. The villain desired Fortunato's death because

    (A)   Fortunato drank to excess.
    (B)   Fortunato had frequently forced injuries and insults.
    (C)   Fortunato was a bungling businessman.
    (D)   Fortunato was unclean.

2. Obviously the murder was

    (A)   carefully thought out and planned.
    (B)   totally unplanned.
    (C)   partially premeditated.
    (D)   done on the spur of the moment.

3. Fortunato's fatally weak point was that he

    (A)   drank too heavily.
    (B)   was overweight, which caused him to limp.
    (C)   prided himself as a connoisseur of wines.
    (D)   had a weak heart.

4. The fatal meeting of the two occurred during the

    (A)   winter season.
    (B)   rainy season.
    (C)   carnival season.
    (D)   summer season.

5. The ruse used to lure Fortunato to the vaults was that he was to taste for proof

    (A)   a cask of sherry.
    (B)   a pipe of amontillado.
    (C)   a keg of dark spirits.
    (D)   a foreign champagne.

6. The soon-to-be murderer pretended to be going to get which person to taste his recent purchase?

    (A)   Lombard.
    (B)   Luchesi.
    (C)   Montresor.
    (D)   Lady Fortunato.

7. When they met, Fortunato obviously

    (A) was drunk.
    (B) was drunk, wore motley, and was dressed in a cap with bells.
    (C) was in a tight-fitting parti-striped dress.
    (D) was drunk and wore motley.

8. Fortunato was plagued by

    (A) a severe cough.
    (B) rheumatism.
    (C) astigmatism.
    (D) a limp.

9. The vaults contained mainly

    (A) cobwebs.
    (B) nitre.
    (C) bones.
    (D) clay.

10. The murderer sealed the tomb with how many tiers of stones?

    (A) six.
    (B) sixteen.
    (C) thirty.
    (D) eleven.

(When finished answering the questions, check the answers below.)

Correct Answers for Test

"THE CASK OF AMONTILLADO"

(Value: 10 points each)

Approximately 2,600 words

1. The correct answer is (B).

2. The correct answer is (A).

3. The correct answer is (C).

4. The correct answer is (C).

5. The correct answer is (B).

6. The correct answer is (B).

7. The correct answer is (B).

8. The correct answer is (A).

9. The correct answer is (C).

10. The correct answer is (D).

A Short History of the Civil War, by Bruce Catton*

(approximately 4,300 words)

CHAPTER 1. A HOUSE DIVIDED

The American people in 1860 believed that they were the happiest and luckiest people in all the world, and in a way they were right. Most of them lived on farms or in very small towns, they lived better than their fathers had lived, and they knew that their children would do still better. The landscape was predominantly rural, with unending sandy roads winding leisurely across a country which was both drowsy with enjoyment of the present and vibrant with eagerness to get into the future. The average American then was in fact what he has been since only in legend, an independent small farmer, and in 1860—for the last time in American history—the products of the nation's farms were worth more than the output of its factories.

This may or may not have been the end of America's golden age, but it was at least the final, haunted moment of its age of innocence. Most Americans then, difficult as the future might appear, supposed that this or something like it would go on and on, perhaps forever. Yet infinite change was beginning, and problems left unsolved too long would presently make the change explosive, so that the old landscape would be blown to bits forever, with a bewildered people left to salvage what they could. Six hundred thousand young Americans, alive when 1860 ended, would die of this explosion in the next four years.

At bottom the coming change simply meant that the infinite ferment of the industrial revolution was about to work its way with a tremendously energetic and restless people who had a virgin continent to exploit. One difficulty was that two very different societies had developed in America, one in the North and the other in the South, which would adjust themselves to the industrial age in very different ways. Another difficulty was that the differences between these two societies were most infernally complicated by the existence in the South of the institution of chattel slavery. Without slavery, the problems between the sections could probably have been worked out by the ordinary give-and-take of politics; with slavery, they became insoluable. So

*© American Heritage, a division of Forbes Inc. Reprinted with permission from *A Short History of the Civil War,* by Bruce Catton.

in 1861 the North and the South went to war, destroying one. America and beginning the building of another which is not even yet complete.

In the beginning slavery was no great problem. It had existed all across colonial America, it died out in the North simply because it did not pay, and at the turn of the century most Americans, North and South alike, considered that eventually it would go out of existence everywhere. But in 1793 Yankee Eli Whitney had invented the cotton gin—a simple device which made it possible for textile mills to use the short-staple cotton which the Southern states could grow so abundantly—and in a very short time the whole picture changed. The world just then was developing an almost limitless appetite for cotton, and in the deep South enormous quantities of cotton could be raised cheaply with slave labor. Export figures show what happened. In 1800 the United States had exported $5,000,000 worth of cotton—7 per cent of the nation's total exports. By 1810 this figure had tripled, by 1840 it had risen to $63,000,000, and by 1860 cotton exports were worth $191,000,000—57 per cent of the value of all American exports. The South had become a cotton empire, nearly four million slaves were employed, and slavery looked like an absolutely essential element in Southern prosperity.

But if slavery paid, it left men with uneasy consciences. This unease became most obvious in the North, where a man who demanded the abolition of slavery could comfort himself with the reflection that the financial loss which abolition would entail would, after all, be borne by somebody else—his neighbor to the south. In New England the fanatic William Lloyd Garrison opened a crusade, denouncing slavery as a sin and slave-owners as sinners. More effective work to organize anti-slavery sentiment was probably done by such Westerners as James G. Birney and Theodore Weld, but Garrison made the most noise—and, making it, helped to arouse most intense resentment in the South. Southerners liked being called sinners no better than anyone else. Also, they undeniably had a bear by the tail. By 1860 slave property was worth at least two billion dollars, and the abolitionists who insisted that this property be outlawed were not especially helpful in showing how this could be done without collapsing the whole Southern economy. In a natural reaction to all of this, Southerners closed ranks. It became first unhealthy and then impossible for anyone in the South to argue for the end of slavery; instead, the institution was increasingly justified as a positive good. Partly from economic pressure and partly in response to the shrill outcries of men like Garrison, the South bound itself emotionally to the institution of slavery.

Yet slavery (to repeat) was not the only source of discord. The two sections were very different, and they wanted different things from their national government.

In the North, society was passing more rapidly than most men realized to an industrial base. Immigrants were arriving by the tens of thousands, there were vast areas in the West to be opened, men who were developing new industries demanded protection from cheap European imports, systems of transportation and finance were mushrooming in a fantastic manner—and, in short, this dynamic society was beginning to clamor for all sorts of aid and protection from the Federal government at Washington.

In the South, by contrast, society was much more static. There was little immigration, there were not many cities, the factory system showed few signs of growth, and this cotton empire which sold in the world market wanted as many cheap European imports as it could get. To please the South, the national government must keep its hands off as many things as possible; for many years Southerners had feared that if the North ever won control in Washington it would pass legislation ruinous to Southern interests.

John C. Calhoun of South Carolina had seen this first and most clearly. Opposing secession, he argued that any state could protect its interests by nullifying within its own borders, any act by the Federal government which it considered unconstitutional and oppressive. Always aware that the North was the faster-growing section, the South foresaw the day when the North would control the government. Then, Southerners be-lieved, there would be legislation—a stiff high-tariff law, for instance—that would ruin the South. More and more, they developed the theory of states' rights as a matter of self-protection.

Although there were serious differences between the sections, all of them except slavery could have been settled through the democratic process. Slavery poisoned the whole situation. It was the issue that could not be compromised, the issue that made men so angry they did not want to compromise. It put a cutting edge on all arguments. It was not the only cause of the Civil War, but it was unquestionably the one cause without which the war would not have taken place. The antagonism between the sections came finally, and tragically, to express itself through the slavery issue.

Many attempts to compromise this issue had been made. All of them worked for a while; none of them lasted. Perhaps the most that can be said is that they postponed the conflict until the nation was strong enough—just barely so—to survive the shock of civil war.

There had been the Missouri Compromise, in 1820, when North and South argued whether slavery should be permitted in the land acquired by the Louisiana Purchase. Missouri was admitted as a slave state, but it was decreed that thereafter there should be no new slave states north of the parallel that marked Missouri's southern boundary. Men hoped that this would end the whole argument, although dour John Quincy Adams wrote that he considered the debate over the compromise nothing less than "a title-page to a great, tragic volume."

Then there was the Compromise of 1850, which followed the war with Mexico. Immense new territory had been acquired, and Congressman David Wilmot of Pennsylvania introduced legislation stipulating that slavery would never be permitted in any of these lands. The Wilmot Proviso failed to pass, but it was argued furiously, in Congress and out of it, for years, and immense heat was generated. In the end the aging Henry Clay engineered a new compromise. California was to be admitted as a free state, the territories of New Mexico and Utah were created without reference to the Wilmot Proviso, the slave trade in the District of Columbia was abolished, and a much stiffer act to govern the return of fugitive slaves was adopted. Neither North nor South was entirely happy with this program, but both sections accepted it in the hope that the slavery issue was now settled for good.

This hope promptly exploded. Probably nothing did more to create anti-Southern, antislavery sentiment in the North than the Fugitive Slave Act. It had an effect precisely opposite to the intent of its backers: it aroused Northern sentiment in favor of the runaway slave, and probably caused a vast expansion in the activities of the Underground Railroad, the informal and all but unorganized system whereby Northern citizens helped Negro fugitives escape across the Canadian border. With this excitement at a high pitch Harriet Beecher Stowe in 1852 brought out her novel Uncle Tom's Cabin, which sold three hundred thousand copies in its first year, won many converts to the antislavery position in the North, and, by contrast, aroused intense new resentment in the South.

On the heels of all of this, in 1854 Senator Stephen A. Douglas of Illinois introduced the fateful Kansas-Nebraska Act, which helped to put the whole controversy beyond hope of settlement.

Douglas was a Democrat, friendly to the South and well liked there. He cared little about slavery, one way or the other; what he wanted was to see the long argument settled so that the country could go about its business, which, as he saw it, included the development of the new Western country between the Missouri River and California. Specifically, Douglas wanted a transcontinental railroad, and he wanted its eastern terminus to be Chicago. Out of this desire came the Kansas-Nebraska Act.

Building the road would involve grants of public land. If the northerly route were adopted the country west of Iowa and Missouri must be surveyed and plotted, and for this a proper territorial organization of the area was needed. But the South wanted the road to go to the Pacific coast by way of Texas and New Mexico. To get Southern support for his plan, the Illinois Senator had to find powerful bait.

He found it. When he brought in a bill to create the territories of Kansas and Nebraska he put in two special provisions. One embodied the idea of "popular sovereignty"—the concept that the people of each territory would decide for themselves, when time for statehood came, whether to permit or exclude slavery—and the other specifically repealed the Missouri Compromise. The South took the bait, the bill was passed—and the country moved a long stride nearer to war.

For the Kansas-Nebraska Act raised the argument over slavery to a desperate new intensity. The moderates could no longer be heard; the stage was set for the extremists, the fire-eaters, the men who invited violence with violent words. Many Northerners, previously friendly to the South, now came to feel that the "slave power" was dangerously aggressive, trying not merely to defend slavery where it already existed but to extend it all across the national domain. Worse yet, Kansas was thrown open for settlement under conditions which practically guaranteed bloodshed.

Settlers from the North were grimly determined to make Kansas free soil; Southern settlers were equally determined to win Kansas for slavery. Missouri sent over its Border Ruffians—hardfisted drifters who crossed the line to cast illegal votes, to intimidate free-soil settlers, now and then to raid an abolitionist town. New England shipped in boxes of rifles, known as Beecher's Bibles in derisive reference to the Reverend Henry Ward Beecher, the Brooklyn clergyman whose antislavery fervor had led him to say that there might be spots where a gun was more useful than a Bible. The North also sent down certain free-lance fanatics, among them a lantern-jawed character named John Brown.

By 1855 all of this was causing a great deal of trouble. Proslavery patrols clashed with antislavery patrols, and there were barn-burnings, horse-stealings, and sporadic shootings. The free-soil settlement of Lawrence was sacked by a proslavery mob; in retaliation, John Brown and his followers murdered five Southern settlers near Pottawatomie Creek. When elections were held, one side or the other would complain that the polls were unfairly rigged, would put on a boycott, and then would hold an election of its own; presently there were two territorial legislatures, of clouded legality, and when the question of a constitution arose there were more boycotts, so that no one was quite sure what the voters had done.

Far from Kansas, extremists on both sides whipped up fresh tensions. Senator Charles Sumner, the humorless, self-righteous abolitionist from Massachusetts, addressed the Senate on "the crime against Kansas," loosing such unmeasured invective on the head of Senator Andrew Butler of South Carolina that Congressman Preston Brooks, also of South Carolina, a relative of Senator Butler, caned him into insensibility on the Senate floor a few days afterward. Senator William H. Seward of New York spoke vaguely but ominously of an "irrepressible conflict" that was germinating. Senator Robert Toombs of Georgia predicted a vast extension of slavery and said that he would one day auction salves on Boston Common itself. In Alabama the eloquent William Lowndes Yancey argued hotly that the South would never find happiness except by leaving the Union and setting up an independent nation.

Now the Supreme Court added its bit. It had before it the case of Dred Scott, a Negro slave whose master, an army surgeon, had kept him for some years in Illinois and Wisconsin, where there was no slavery. Scott sued for his freedom, and in 1857 Chief Justice Roger Taney delivered the Court's opinion. That Scott's plea for freedom was denied was no particular surprise, but the grounds on which the denial was based stirred the North afresh. A Negro of slave descent, said Taney, was an inferior sort of person who could not be a citizen of any state and hence could not sue anyone; furthermore the act by which Congress had forbidden slavery in the Northern territories was invalid because the Constitution gave slavery ironclad protection. There was no legal way in which slavery could be excluded from any territory.

An intense political ferment was working. The old Whig Party had collapsed utterly and the Democratic Party was showing signs of breaking into sectional wings. In the North there had risen the new Republican Party, an amalgamation of former Whigs, free-soilers, business leaders who wanted a central govern-ment that would protect industry, and ordinary folk who wanted a homestead act that would provide free farms in the West. The party had already polled an impressive number of votes in the Presidential campaign of 1856, and it was likely to do better in 1860. Seward of New York hoped to be its next Presidential nominee; so did Salmon P. Chase, prominent antislavery leader from Ohio; and so, also, did a lawyer and former congressman who was not nearly so well known as these two, Abraham Lincoln of Illinois.

In 1858 Lincoln ran for the Senate against Douglas. In a series of famous debates which drew national attention, the two argued the Kansas-Nebraska Act and the slavery issue up and down the state of Illinois. In the end Douglas won reelection but he won on terms that may have cost him the Presidency two years later. Lincoln had pinned him down: Was there any lawful way in which the people of a territory could exclude slavery? (In other words, could Douglas's "popular sovereignty" be made to jibe with the Supreme Court's finding in the Dred Scott case?) Dou-glas replied that the thing was easy. Slavery could not live a day unless it were supported by protective local legislation. In fact, if a territorial legislature simply refused to enact such legislation, slavery would not exist regardless of what the Supreme Court had said. The answer helped Douglas win reelection, but it mortally offended the South. The threatened split in the Democratic Party came measurably nearer, and such a split could mean nothing except victory for the Republicans.

The 1850s were the tormented decade in American history. Always the tension mounted, and no one seemed able to provide an easement. The Panic of 1857 left a severe business depression, and Northern pressure for higher tariff rates and a homestead act became stronger than ever. The depression had hardly touched the South since world demand for cotton was unabated, and Southern leaders became more than ever convinced that their society and their economy were sounder and stronger than anything the North could show. There would be no tariff revision, and although Congress did pass a homestead act President James Buchanan, a Pennsylvanian but a strong friend of the South, promptly vetoed it. The administration, indeed, seemed unable to do anything. It could not even make a state out of Kansas, in which territory it was clear, by now, that a strong majority opposed slavery. The rising antagonism between the sections had almost brought paralysis to the Federal government.

And then old John Brown came out of the shadows to add the final touch.

With a mere handful of followers, Brown undertook, on the night of October 16, 1859, to seize the Federal arsenal at Harpers Ferry and with the weapons thus obtained to start a slave insurrection in the South. He managed to get possession of an enginehouse, which he held until the morning of the eighteenth; then a detachment of U.S. marines—temporarily led by Colonel Robert E. Lee of the U.S. Army—overpowered him and snuffed out his crack-brained conspiracy with bayonets and clubbed muskets. Brown was quickly tried, was convicted of treason, and early in December he was hanged. But what he had done had a most disastrous effect on men's minds. To people in the South, it seemed that Brown confirmed their worst fears: this was what the Yankee abolitionists really wanted—a servile insurrection, with unlimited bloodshed and pillage, from one end of the South to the other! The fact that some vocal persons in the North persisted in regarding Brown as a martyr simply made matters worse. After the John Brown raid the chance that the bitter sectional argument could be harmonized faded close to the vanishing point.

It was in this atmosphere that the 1860 election was held. The Republicans nominated Lincoln, partly because he was considered less of an extremist than either Seward or Chase; he was moderate on the slavery question; and agreed that the Federal government lacked power to interfere with the peculiar institution in the states. The Republican platform, however, did represent a threat to Southern interests. It embodied the political and economic program of the North—upward revision of the tariff, free farms in the West, railroad subsidies, and all the rest.

But by now a singular fatalism gripped the nation. The campaign could not be fought on the basis of these issues; men could talk only about slavery, and on that subject they could neither talk nor, for the most part, even think, with moderation. Although it faced a purely sectional opposition, the Democratic Party promptly split into halves. The Northern wing nominated Douglas, but the Southern wing flatly refused to accept the man because of his heresy in regard to slavery in the territories; it named John C. Breckinridge of Kentucky, while a fourth party, hoping desperately for compromise and conciliation, put forward John Bell of Tennessee.

The road led steadily downhill after this. The Republicans won the election, as they were bound to do under the circumstances. Lincoln got less than a majority of the popular votes, but a solid majority in the electoral college, and on March 4, 1861, he would become President of the United States. . . but not, it quickly developed, of all of the states. Fearing the worst, the legislature of South Carolina had remained in session until after the election had been held. Once it saw the returns it summoned a state convention, and this convention, in Charleston, on December 20, voted unanimously that South Carolina should secede from the Union.

This was the final catalytic agent. It was obvious that one small state could not maintain its independence; equally obvious that if South Carolina should now be forced back into the Union no one in the South ever need talk again about secession. The cotton states, accordingly, followed suit. By February, South Carolina had been joined by Mississippi, Alabama, Georgia, Florida, Louisiana, and Texas, and on February 8 delegates from the seceding states met at Montgomery, Alabama, and set up a new nation, the Confederate States of America. A provisional constitution was adopted (to be replaced in due time by a permanent document, very much like the Constitution of the United States), and Jefferson Davis of Mississippi was elected President, with Alexander Stephens of Georgia as Vice-President.

Perhaps it still was not too late for an adjustment. A new nation had come into being, but its creation might simply be a means of forcing concessions from the Northern majority; no blood had been shed, and states which voluntarily left the old Union might voluntarily return if their terms were met. Leaders in Congress worked hard, that winter of 1861, to perfect a last-minute compromise, and a committee led by Senator John J. Crittenden of Kentucky worked one out. In effect, it would re-establish the old line of the Missouri Compromise, banning slavery in territories north of the line and protecting it south; it would let future states enter the Union on a popular sovereignty basis; it called for enforcement of the fugitive slave law, with Federal funds to compensate slaveowners whose slaves got away; and it provided that the Constitution could never be amended in such a way as to give Congress power over slavery in any of the states.

The Crittenden Compromise hung in the balance, and then collapsed when Lincoln refused to accept it. The sticking point with him was the inclusion of slavery in the territories; the rest of the program he could accept, but he wrote to a Republican associate to "entertain no proposition for a compromise in regard to the extension of slavery."

So the last chance to settle the business had gone, except for the things that might happen in the minds of two men—Abraham Lincoln and Jefferson Davis. They were strangers, very unlike each other, and yet there was an odd linkage. They were born not far apart in time or space; both came from Kentucky, near the Ohio River, and one man went south to become spokesman for the planter aristocracy, while the other went north to become representative of the best the frontier Northwest could produce. In the haunted decade that had just ended, neither man had been known as a radical. Abolitionists considered Lincoln too conservative, and Southern fire-eaters like South Carolina's Robert B. Rhett felt that Davis had been cold and unenthusiastic in regard to secession.

Now these two men faced one another, figuratively, across an ever-widening gulf, and between them they would say whether a nation already divided by mutual understanding would be torn apart physically by war.

COMPREHENSION TEST

S<small>HORT</small> H<small>ISTORY OF THE</small> C<small>IVIL</small> W<small>AR</small>, C<small>HAPTER</small> 1

(Circle the letter preceding the most correct answer)

1. Approximately how many Americans died in the Civil War?

    (A)   Six hundred thousand
    (B)   Twelve hundred thousand
    (C)   Two hundred thousand
    (D)   Nineteen hundred thousand

2. In the beginning, slavery was no great problem.

    (A)   False
    (B)   True
    (C)   Yes and no
    (D)   No one now knows.

3. The cotton gin was invented in 1793 by

    (A)   Robert Fulton.
    (B)   Theodore Weld.
    (C)   H.B. Stowe.
    (D)   Eli Whitney.

4. The title of the novel by Harriet Beecher Stowe that aroused antislavery feelings was

    (A)   *Brer Rabbit.*
    (B)   *Uncle Tom's Cabin.*
    (C)   *John Brown's Body.*
    (D)   *Snowdrift.*

5. In 1854, Senator Stephen A. Douglas of Illinois introduced the fateful

    (A)   Texas-New Mexico Act.
    (B)   Missouri Compromise.
    (C)   Kansas-Nebraska Act.
    (D)   Anti-Slavery Act.

6. One of Senator Douglas' major desires was that he wanted for America

    (A)   a transcontinental railroad.
    (B)   an end to slavery.
    (C)   equal taxation with representation.
    (D)   a lasting state of peace.

7. The idea that embodied the concept that the people of each territory would elect to permit or exclude slavery when applying for statehood was known as

   (A) "political suicide."
   (B) "states' rights."
   (C) "the big freedom."
   (D) "popular sovereignty."

8. Missouri sent over hardfisted drifters into Kansas to cast illegal votes and generally to create havoc. These groups were called

   (A) Night Raiders.
   (B) Vigilantes.
   (C) Border Ruffians.
   (D) Hardfisters.

9. John Brown and his followers murdered five Southern settlers near

   (A) Pottawatomie Creek.
   (B) the Mississippi River.
   (C) the Ozark River.
   (D) Washington Crick.

10. The Supreme Court's decision in the Dred Scott case

   (A) pleased the Yankees.
   (B) stirred the North afresh.
   (C) caused Southern animosity.
   (D) caused slavery to become unlawful.

11. In 1858, Senator Douglas won reelection over

   (A) Salmon P. Chase.
   (B) James Buchanan.
   (C) Roger Taney.
   (D) Abraham Lincoln.

12. What ten-year period is called the "tormented" decade in American history?

   (A) The 1850s
   (B) The 1840s
   (C) The 1870s
   (D) The 1860s

13. John Brown's attempt to seize the arsenal at Harper's Ferry was stopped by a detachment of U.S. Marines led by

   (A) General U. S. Grant.
   (B) Colonel Robert E. Lee.
   (C) Robert Toombs.
   (D) William L. Yancey.

14. In America in 1860, the landscape, as described by Catton, was

   (A)   partially mechanical.
   (B)   predominantly rural.
   (C)   generally unsophisticated.
   (D)   mainly urban.

15. The average American of this period was, in fact,

   (A)   an independent small farmer.
   (B)   a factory worker.
   (C)   generally well-to-do.
   (D)   an independent small businessman.

16. Slavery died out in the North because

   (A)   Northerners were more religious.
   (B)   it simply did not pay.
   (C)   Southerners wanted it to.
   (D)   the climate was too cold for Negroes.

17. By 1860, cotton exports were worth $191,000,000. This equaled what percent of total American exports?

   (A)   13 percent
   (B)   92 percent
   (C)   57 percent
   (D)   21 percent

18. Slaves employed in the South by 1860 totaled approximately

   (A)   three million.
   (B)   one million.
   (C)   ten million.
   (D)   four million.

19. Except for the slavery issue, the differences between North and South likely could have been settled through

   (A)   a later war.
   (B)   democratic processes.
   (C)   a stronger central government.
   (D)   serious peace talks.

20. After the Louisiana Purchase, what state from that territory was admitted as a slave state?

   (A)   Missouri
   (B)   Texas
   (C)   Louisiana
   (D)   Georgia

21. The system whereby Northern citizens helped Negro fugitives escape across the Canadian border was called the

    (A) Underground Railroad.
    (B) Slave Lift.
    (C) Freedom Road.
    (D) Underground System.

22. Members of the new Republican party in the North were mainly former members of which older party?

    (A) Neutral Party
    (B) States' Rights Party
    (C) Whig Party
    (D) Democratic Party

23. In the 1860 presidential election, Lincoln won as the result of having a

    (A) majority of the popular vote.
    (B) majority of the electoral votes.
    (C) tie broken by congress.
    (D) popular campaign in the South.

24. After Lincoln's election, the first state to secede from the Union was

    (A) North Carolina.
    (B) Mississippi.
    (C) South Carolina.
    (D) Missouri.

25. The man elected president of the new Confederate States of America was

    (A) Jefferson Davis.
    (B) Alexander Stephens.
    (C) Robert E. Lee.
    (D) John J. Crittenden.

(When finished answering the questions, check the answers on the following page.)

Correct Answers for Test

A SHORT HISTORY OF THE CIVIL WAR

(Value: 4 points each)

Approximately 4,300 words

1. The correct answer is (A).
2. The correct answer is (B).
3. The correct answer is (D).
4. The correct answer is (B).
5. The correct answer is (C).
6. The correct answer is (A).
7. The correct answer is (D).
8. The correct answer is (C).
9. The correct answer is (A).
10. The correct answer is (B).
11. The correct answer is (D).
12. The correct answer is (A).
13. The correct answer is (B).

14. The correct answer is (B).
15. The correct answer is (A).
16. The correct answer is (B).
17. The correct answer is (C).
18. The correct answer is (D).
19. The correct answer is (B).
20. The correct answer is (A).
21. The correct answer is (A).
22. The correct answer is (C).
23. The correct answer is (B).
24. The correct answer is (C).
25. The correct answer is (A).

Treasure Island, by Robert Louis Stevenson

(approximately 2,400 words)

CHAPTER 2. BLACK DOG APPEARS AND DISAPPEARS

It was not very long after this that there occurred the first of
the mysterious events that rid us at last of the captain, though
not, as you will see, of his affairs. It was a bitter cold winter, with
long, hard frosts and heavy gales; and it was plain from the first
that my poor father was little likely to see the spring. He sank
daily, and my mother and I had all the inn upon our hands, and
were kept busy enough without paying much regard to our
unpleasant guest.

It was one January morning, very early—a pinching, frosty
morning—the cove all grey with hoar-frost, the riplapping softly
on the stones, the sun still low and only touching the hilltops and
shining far to seaward. The captain had risen earlier than usual,
and set out down the beach, his cutlass swinging under the broad
skirts of the old blue coat, his brass telescope under his arm, his
hat tilted back upon his head. I remember his breath hanging like
smoke in his wake as he strode off, and the last sound I heard of
him, as he turned the big rock, was a loud snort of indignation, as
though his mind was still running upon Dr. Livesey.

Well, mother was upstairs with father; and I was laying the
breakfast-table against the captain's return, when the parlor door
opened, and a man stepped in on whom I had never set my eyes
before. He was a pale, tallowy creature, wanting two fingers of
the left hand; and, though he wore a cutlass, he did not look
much like a fighter. I had always my eye open for seafaring men,
with one leg or two, and I remember this one puzzled me. He
was not sailorly, and yet he had a smack of the sea about him too.

I asked him what was for his service, and he said he would
take rum; but as I was going out of the room to fetch it he sat
down upon a table, and motioned me to draw near. I paused
where I was with my napkin in my hand.

"Come here, sonny," says he. "Come nearer here."

I took a step nearer.

"Is this here table for my mate Bill?" he asked, with a kind of
leer.

I told him I did not know his mate Bill; and this was for a person who stayed in our house, whom we called the captain.

"Well," said he, "my mate Bill would be called the captain, as like as not. He has a cut on one cheek, and a mighty pleasant way with him, particularly in drink, has my mate Bill. We'll put it, for argument like, that your captain has a cut on one cheek—and we'll put it, if you like, that that cheek's the right one. Ah, well! I told you. Now, is my mate Bill in this here house?"

I told him he was out walking.

"Which way, sonny? Which way is he gone?"

And when I had pointed out the rock and told him how the captain was likely to return, and how soon, and answered a few other questions, "Ah," said he, "this'll be as good as drink to my mate Bill."

The expression of his face as he said these words was not at all pleasant, and I had my own reasons for thinking that the stranger was mistaken, even supposing he meant what he said. But it was no affair of mine, I thought; and besides, it was difficult to know what to do. The stranger kept hanging about just inside the inn door, peering round the corner like a cat waiting for a mouse. Once I stepped out myself into the road, but he immediately called me back, and as I did not obey quick enough for his fancy, a most horrible change came over his tallowy face, and he ordered me in with an oath that made me jump. As soon as I was back again he returned to his former manner, half fawning, half sneering, patted me on the shoulder, told me I was a good boy and he had taken quite a fancy to me. "I have a son of my own," said he, "as like you as two blocks, and he's all the pride of my 'art. But the great thing for boys is discipline, sonny—discipline. Now, if you had sailed along of Bill, you wouldn't have stood there to be spoke to twice—not you. That was never Bill's way, nor the way of sich as sailed with him. And here, sure enough, is my mate Bill, with a spy-glass under his arm, bless his old 'art, to be sure. You and me'll just go back into the parlour, sonny, and get behind the door, and we'll give Bill a little surprise—bless his 'art, I say again."

So saying, the stranger backed along with me into the parlour and put me behind him in the corner so that we were both hidden by the open door. I was very uneasy and alarmed, as you may fancy, and it rather added to my fears to observe that the stranger was certainly frightened himself. He cleared the hilt of his cutlass and loosened the blade in the sheath; and all the time we were waiting there he kept swallowing as if he felt what we used to call a lump in the throat.

At last in strode the captain, slammed the door behind him, without looking to the right or left, and marched straight across the room to where his breakfast awaited him.

"Bill," said the stranger in a voice that I thought he had tried to make bold and big.

The captain spun round on his heel and fronted us; all the brown had gone out of his face, and even his nose was blue; he had the look of a man who sees a ghost, or the evil one, or something worse, if anything can be; and upon my word, I felt sorry to see him all in a moment turn so old and sick.

"Come, Bill, you know me; you know an old shipmate, Bill, surely," said the stranger.

The captain made a sort of gasp.

"Black Dog!" said he.

"And who else?" returned the other, getting more at his ease. "Black Dog as ever was, come for to see his old shipmate Billy, at the Admiral Benbow inn. Ah, Bill, Bill, we have seen a sight of times, us two, since I lost them two talons," holding up his mutilated hand.

"Now, look here," said the captain; "you've run me down; here I am; well, then, speak up; what is it?"

"That's you, Bill," returned Black Dog, "you're in the right of it, Billy. I'll have a glass of rum from this dear child here, as I've took such a liking to; and we'll sit down, if you please, and talk square, like old shipmates."

When I returned with the rum, they were already seated on either side of the captain's breakfast-table—Black Dog next to the door and sitting sideways so as to have one eye on his old shipmate and one, as I thought, on his retreat.

He bade me go and leave the door wide open. "None of your keyholes for me, sonny," he said; and I left them together and retired into the bar.

For a long time, though I certainly did my best to listen, I could hear nothing but a low gabbling; but at last the voices began to grow higher, and I could pick up a word or two, mostly oaths, from the captain.

"No, no, no, no; and an end of it!" he cried once. And again, "If it comes to swinging, swing all, say I."

Then all of a sudden there was a tremendous explosion of oaths and other noises—the chair and table went over in a lump, a clash of steel followed, and then a cry of pain, and the next instant I saw Black Dog in full flight, and the captain hotly pursuing, both with drawn cutlasses, and the former streaming blood from the left shoulder. Just at the door the captain aimed at the fugitive one last tremendous cut, which would certainly have split him to the chine had it not been intercepted by our big signboard of Admiral Benbow. You may see the notch on the lower side of the frame to this day.

That blow was the last of the battle. Once out upon the road, Black Dog, in spite of his wound, showed a wonderful clean pair of heels and disappeared over the edge of the hill in half a minute. The captain, for his part, stood staring at the signboard like a bewildered man. Then he passed his hand over his eyes several times and at last turned back into the house.

"Jim," says he, "rum"; and as he spoke, he reeled a little, and caught himself with one hand against the wall.

"Are you hurt? cried I.

'Rum," he repeated. "I must get away from here. Rum! Rum!"

I ran to fetch it, but I was quite unsteadied by all that had fallen out, and I broke one glass and fouled the tap, and while I was still getting in my own way, I heard a loud fall in the parlour, and running in, beheld the captain lying full length upon the floor. At the same instant my mother, alarmed by the cries and fighting, came running downstairs to help me. Between us we raised his head. He was breathing very loud and hard, but his eyes were closed and his face a horrible colour.

"Dear, deary me," cried my mother, "what a disgrace upon the house! And your poor father sick!"

In the meantime, we had no idea what to do to help the captain, nor any other thought but that he had got his death-hurt in the scuffle with the stranger. I got the rum, to be sure, and tried to put it down his throat, but his teeth were tightly shut and his jaws as strong as iron. It was a happy relief for us when the door opened and Doctor Livesey came in, on his visit to my father.

"Oh, doctor," we cried, "what shall we do? Where is he wounded?"

"Wounded? A fiddle-stick's end!" said the doctor. "No more wounded than you or I. The man has had a stroke, as I warned him. Now, Mrs. Hawkins, just you run upstairs to your husband and tell him, if possible, nothing about it. For my part, I must do my best to save this fellow's trebly worthless life; Jim, you get me a basin."

When I got back with the basin, the doctor had already ripped up the captain's sleeve and exposed his great sinewy arm. It was tattooed in several places. "Here's luck," "A fair wind," and "Billy Bones his fancy," were very neatly and clearly executed on the forearm; and up near the shoulder there was a sketch of a gallows and a man hanging from it—done, as I thought, with great spirit.

"Prophetic," said the doctor, touching this picture with his finger. "And now, Master Billy Bones, if that be your name, we'll have a look at the colour of your blood. Jim," he said, "are you afraid of blood?"

"No, sir," said I.

"Well, then," said he, "you hold the basin"; and with that he took his lancet and opened a vein.

A great deal of blood was taken before the captain opened his eyes and looked mistily about him. First he recognized the doctor with an unmistakable frown; then his glance fell upon me, and he looked relieved. But suddenly his colour changed, and he tried to raise himself, crying, "Where's Black Dog?"

"There is no Black Dog here," said the doctor, "except what you have on your own back. You have been drinking rum; you have had a stroke, precisely as I told you; and I have just, very much against my own will, dragged you headforemost out of the grave. Now, Mr. Bones—"

"That's not my name," he interrupted.

"Much I care," returned the doctor. "It's the name of a buccaneer of my acquaintance; and I call you by it for the sake of shortness, and what I have to say to you is this: one glass of rum won't kill you, but if you take one you'll take another and another, and I stake my wig if you don't break off short, you'll die—do you understand that?—die, and go to your own place, like the man in the Bible. Come, now, make an effort. I'll help you to your bed for once."

Between us, with much trouble, we managed to hoist him upstairs, and laid him on his bed, where his head fell back on the pillow as if he were almost fainting.

"Now, mind you," said the doctor. "I clear my conscience—the name of rum for you is death."

And with that he went off to see my father, taking me with him by the arm.

"This is nothing," he said as soon as he had closed the door. "I have drawn blood enough to keep him quiet awhile; he should lie for a week where he is—that is the best thing for him and you; but another stroke would settle him."

COMPREHENSION TEST

Treasure Island, Chapter 2

(Write T for *true*, F for *false*)

__ 1. The time of year in the story was winter.

__ 2. The captain's telescope was made of pure bronze.

__ 3. There was no illness in the family at the inn.

__ 4. The stranger who entered the door had two fingers missing on one hand.

__ 5. The recently arrived guest ordered a cask of dark beer.

__ 6. The stranger called the captain "my mate, William."

__ 7. The stranger said the great thing for boys was "discipline."

__ 8. The captain called the stranger "Black Cat."

__ 9. They seated themselves in the captain's private bedroom.

__10. The stranger told the boy to leave and be sure to close the door.

__11. The boy was not at all interested in listening to the conversation.

__12. It was soon apparent that the captain and the stranger were enemies.

__13. The stranger was not even scratched in the ensuing fight.

__14. The captain's cutlass was intercepted by a signboard on the inn.

__15. The frightened captain fled rapidly from the battle scene.

__16. The young man in the story goes by the name Jim.

__17. The captain fell unconscious after suffering a stroke.

__18. The doctor did not believe in "letting blood."

__19. The doctor prescribed rum for the captain's condition.

__20. The medical man called the captain Mr. Bones.

(When finished answering the questions, check the answers below.)

Correct Answers for Test

TREASURE ISLAND

(Value: 5 points each)

Approximately 2,400 words

1. The correct answer is (T).
2. The correct answer is (F).
3. The correct answer is (F).
4. The correct answer is (T).
5. The correct answer is (F).
6. The correct answer is (F).
7. The correct answer is (T).
8. The correct answer is (F).
9. The correct answer is (F).
10. The correct answer is (F).

11. The correct answer is (F).
12. The correct answer is (T).
13. The correct answer is (F).
14. The correct answer is (T).
15. The correct answer is (F).
16. The correct answer is (T).
17. The correct answer is (T).
18. The correct answer is (F).
19. The correct answer is (F).
20. The correct answer is (T).

The Time Machine, By H. G. Wells

(approximately 6,600 words)

CHAPTER 5

As I stood there musing over this too perfect triumph of man, the full moon, yellow and gibbous, came up out of an overflow of silver light in the north-east. The bright little figures ceased to move about below, a noiseless owl flitted by, and I shivered with the chill of the night. I determined to descend and find where I could sleep.

I looked for the building I knew. Then my eye travelled along to the figure of the White Sphinx upon the pedestal of bronze, growing distinct as the light of the rising moon grew brighter. I could see the silver birch against it. There was the tangle of rhododendron bushes, black in the pale light, and there was the little lawn. I looked at the lawn again. A queer doubt chilled my complacency. "No," said I stoutly to myself, "that was not the lawn."

But it *was* the lawn. For the white leprous face of the sphinx was towards it. Can you imagine what I felt as this conviction came home to me? But you cannot. The Time Machine was gone!

At once, like a lash across the face, came the possibility of losing my own age, of being left helpless in this strange new world. The bare thought of it was an actual physical sensation. I could feel it grip me at the throat and stop my breathing. In another moment I was in a passion of fear and running with great leaping strides down the slope. Once I fell headlong and cut my face; I lost no time in stanching the blood, but jumped up and ran on, with a warm trickle down my cheek and chin. All the time I ran I was saying to myself: "They have moved it a little, pushed it under the bushes out of the way." Nevertheless, I ran with all my might. All the time, with the certainty that sometimes comes with excessive dread. I knew that such assurance was folly, knew instinctively that the machine was removed out of my reach. My breath came with pain. I suppose I covered the whole distance from the hill crest to the little lawn, two miles perhaps, in ten minutes. And I am not a young man. I cursed aloud, as I ran, at my confident folly in leaving the machine, wasting good breath thereby. I cried aloud, and none answered. Not a creature seemed to be stirring in that moonlit world.

When I reached the lawn my worst fears were realized. Not a trace of the thing was to be seen. I felt faint and cold when I faced the empty space among the black tangle of bushes. I ran round it furiously, as if the thing might be hidden in a corner, and then stopped abruptly, with my hands clutching my hair. Above me towered the sphinx, upon the bronze pedestal, white, shining, leprous, in the light of the rising moon. It seemed to smile in mockery of my dismay.

I might have consoled myself by imagining the little people had put the mechanism in some shelter for me, had I not felt assured of their physical and intellectual inadequacy. That is what dismayed me: the sense of some hitherto unsuspected power, through whose intervention my invention had vanished. Yet, for one thing I felt assured: unless some other age had produced its exact duplicate, the machine could not have moved in time. The attachment of the levers—I will show you the method later—prevented any one from tampering with it in that way when they were removed. It had moved, and was hid, only in space. But then, where could it be?

I think I must have had a kind of frenzy. I remember running violently in and out among the moonlit bushes all round the sphinx, and startling some white animal that, in the dim light, I took for a small deer. I remember, too, late that night, beating the bushes with my clenched fist until my knuckles were gashed and bleeding from the broken twigs. Then, sobbing and raving in my anguish of mind, I went down to the great building of stone. The big hall was dark, silent, and deserted. I slipped on the uneven floor, and fell over one of the malachite tables, almost breaking my shin. I lit a match and went on past the dusty curtains, of which I have told you.

There I found a second great hall covered with cushions, upon which, perhaps, a score or so of the little people were sleeping. I have no doubt they found my second appearance strange enough, coming suddenly out of the quiet darkness and inarticulate noises and the splutter and flare of a match. For they had forgotten about matches. "Where is my Time Machine?" I began, bawling like an angry child, laying hands upon them and shaking them up together. It must have been very queer to them. Some laughed, most of them looked sorely frightened. When I saw them standing round me, it came into my head that I was doing as foolish a thing as it was possible for me to do under the circumstances, in trying to revive the sensation of fear. For, reasoning from their daylight behavior, I thought that fear must be forgotten.

Abruptly, I dashed down the match, and, knocking one of the people over in my course, went blundering across the big dining-hall again, out under the moonlight. I heard cries of terror and their little feet running and stumbling this way and that. I do not remember all I did as the moon crept up the sky. I suppose it was the unexpected nature of my loss that maddened me. I felt hopelessly cut off from my own kind—a strange animal in an unknown world. I must have raved to and fro, screaming and crying upon God and Fate. I have a memory of horrible fatigue, as the long night of despair wore away; of looking in this impossible place and that; of groping among moon-lit ruins and touching strange creatures in the black shadows; at last, of lying on the ground near the sphinx and weeping with absolute wretchedness. I had nothing left but misery. Then I slept, and when I woke again it was full day, and a couple of sparrows were hopping round me on the turf within reach of my arm.

I sat up in the freshness of the morning, trying to remember how I had got there, and why I had such a profound sense of desertion and despair. Then things came clear in my mind. With the plain, reasonable daylight, I could look my circumstances fairly in the face. I saw the wild folly of my frenzy overnight, and I could reason with myself. "Suppose the worst?" I said. "Suppose the machine altogether lost—perhaps destroyed? It behoves me to be calm and patient, to learn the way of the people, to get a clear idea of the method of my loss, and the means of getting materials and tools; so that in the end, perhaps, I may make another." That would be my only hope, perhaps, but better than despair. And, after all, it was a beautiful and curious world.

But probably, the machine had only been taken away. Still, I must be calm and patient, find its hiding-place, and recover it by force or cunning. And with that I scrambled to my feet and looked about me, wondering where I could bathe. I felt weary, stiff, and travel-soiled. The freshness of the morning made me desire an equal freshness. I had exhausted my emotion. Indeed, as I went about my business, I found myself wondering at my intense excitement overnight. I made a careful examination of the ground about the little lawn. I wasted some time in futile questionings, conveyed, as well as I was able, to such of the little people as came by. They all failed to understand my gestures; some were simply stolid, some thought it was a jest and laughed at me. I had the hardest task in the world to keep my hands off their pretty laughing faces. It was a foolish impulse, but the devil begotten of fear and blind anger was ill curbed and still eager to take advantage of my perplexity. The turf gave better counsel. I found a groove ripped in it, about midway between the pedestal of the sphinx and the marks of my feet where, on arrival, I had struggled with the overturned machine. There were other signs of removal about, with queer narrow footprints like those I could imagine made by a sloth. This directed my closer attention to the pedestal. It was, as I think I have said, of bronze. It was not a mere block, but highly decorated with deep framed panels on either side. I went and rapped at these. The pedestal was hollow. Examining the panels with care I found them discontinuous with the frames. There were no handles or keyholes, but possibly the panels, if they were doors, as I supposed, opened from within. One thing was clear enough to my mind. It took no very great mental effort to infer that my Time Machine was inside that pedestal. But how it got there was a difficult problem.

I saw the heads of two orange-clad people coming through the bushes and under some blossom-covered apple-trees towards me. I turned smiling to them and beckoned them to me. They came, and then, pointing to the bronze pedestal, I tried to intimate my wish to open it. But at my first gesture towards this they behaved very oddly. I don't know how to convey their expression to you. Suppose you were to use a grossly improper gesture to a delicate, minded woman—it is how she would look. They went off as if they had received the last possible insult. I tried a sweet-looking little chap in white next, with exactly the same result. Somehow, this manner made me feel ashamed of myself. But, as you know, I wanted the Time Machine, and I tried him once more. As he turned off, like the others, my temper got the better of me. In three strides I was after him, had him by the loose part of his robe round the neck, and began dragging him towards the sphinx. Then I saw the horror and repugnance of his face, and all of a sudden I let him go.

But I was not beaten yet. I banged with my fist at the bronze panels, I thought I heard something stir inside—to be explicit, I thought I heard a sound like a chuckle—but I must have been mistaken. Then I got a big pebble from the river, and came and hammered till I had flattened a coil in the decorations, and the verdigris came off in powdery flakes. The delicate little people must have heard me hammering in gusty outbreaks a mile away on either hand, but nothing came of it. I saw a crowd of them upon the slopes, looking furtively at me. At last, hot and tired, I sat down to watch the place. But I was too restless to watch long; I am too Occidental for a long vigil. I could work at a problem for years, but to wait inactive for twenty-four hours—that is another matter.

I got up after a time, and began walking aimlessly through the bushes towards the hill again. "Patience," said I to myself. "If you want your machine again you must leave that sphinx alone. If they mean to take your machine away, it's little good your wrecking their bronze panels, and if they don't, you will get it back as soon as you can ask for it. To sit among all those unknown things before a puzzle like that is hopeless. That way lies monomania. Face this world. Learn its ways, watch it, be careful of too hasty guesses at its meaning. In the end you will find clues to it all." Then suddenly the humour of the situation came into my mind: the thought of the years I had spent in study and toil to get into the future age, and now my passion of anxiety to get out of it. I had made myself the most complicated and the most hopeless trap that ever a man devised. Although it was at my own expense, I could not help myself. I laughed aloud.

Going through the big palace, it seemed to me that the little people avoided me. It may have been my fancy or it may have had something to do with my hammering at the gates of bronze. Yet I felt tolerably sure of the avoidance. I was careful, however, to show no concern and to abstain from any pursuit of them, and in the course of a day or two things got back to the old footing. I made what progress I could in the language, and in addition I pushed my explorations here and there. Either I missed some subtle point, or their language was excessively simple—almost exclusively composed of concrete substantives and verbs. There seemed to be few, if any, abstract terms, or little use of figurative language. Their sentences were usually simple and of two words, and I failed to convey or understand any but the simplest propositions. I determined to put the thought of my Time Machine and the mystery of the bronze doors under the sphinx as much as possible in a corner of memory, until my growing knowledge would lead me back to them in a natural way. Yet a certain feeling, you may understand, tethered me in a circle of a few miles round the point of my arrival.

So far as I could see, all the world displayed the same exuberant richness as the Thames valley. From every hill I climbed I saw the same abundance of splendid buildings, endlessly varied in material and style, the same clustering thickets of evergreens, the same blossom-laden trees and tree-ferns. Here and there water shone like silver, and beyond, the land rose into blue undulating hills, and so faded into the serenity of the sky. A peculiar feature, which presently attracted my attention, was the presence of certain circular wells, several, as it seemed to me, of a very great depth. One lay by the path up the hill, which I had followed during my first walk. Like the others, it was rimmed with bronze, curiously wrought, and protected by a little cupola from the rain. Sitting by the side of these wells, and peering down into the shafted darkness, I could see no gleam of water, nor could I start any reflection with a lighted match. But in all of them I heard a certain sound: a thud—thud—thud, like the beating of some big engine; and I discovered, from the flaring of my matches, that a steady current of air set down the shafts. Further, I threw a scrap of paper into the throat of one, and, instead of fluttering slowly down, it was at once sucked swiftly out of sight.

After a time, too, I came to connect these wells with tall towers standing here and there upon the slopes; for above them there was often just such a flicker in the air as one sees on a hot day above a sun-scorched beach. Putting things together, I reached a strong suggestion of an extensive system of subterranean ventilation, whose true import it was difficult to imagine. I was at first inclined to associate it with the sanitary apparatus of these people. It was an obvious conclusion, but it was absolutely wrong.

And here I must admit that I learned very little of drains and bells and modes of conveyance, and the like conveniences, during my time in this real future. In some of these visions of Utopias and coming times which I have read, there is a vast amount of detail about building, and social arrangements, and so forth. But while such details are easy enough to obtain when the whole world is contained in one's imagination, they are altogether inaccessible to a real traveller amid such realities as I found here. Conceive the tale of London which a negro, fresh from Central Africa, would take back to his tribe! What would he know of railway companies, of social movements, of telephone and telegraph wires, of the Parcels Delivery Company, and postal orders and the like? Yet we, at least, should be willing enough to explain these things to him! And even of what he knew, how much could he make his untravelled friend either apprehend or believe? Then, think how narrow the gap between a negro and a white man of our own times, and how wide the interval between myself and these of the Golden Age! I was sensible of much which was unseen, and which contributed to my comfort; but save for a general impression of automatic organization, I fear I can convey very little of the difference to your mind.

In the matter of sepulture, for instance, I could see no signs of crematoria nor anything suggestive of tombs. But it occurred to me that possibly, there might be cemeteries (or crematoria) somewhere beyond the range of my explorings. This, again, was a question I deliberately put to myself, and my curiosity was at first entirely defeated upon the point. The thing puzzled me, and I was led to make a further remark, which puzzled me still more: that aged and infirm among this people there were none.

I must confess that my satisfaction with my first theories of an automatic civilization and a decadent humanity did not long endure. Yet I could think of no other. Let me put my difficulties. The several big palaces I had explored were mere living places, great dining-halls and sleeping apartments. I could find no machinery, no appliances of any kind. Yet these people were clothed in pleasant fabrics that must at times need renewal, and their sandals, though undecorated, were fairly complex specimens of metalwork. Somehow such things must be made. And the little people displayed no vestige of a creative tendency. There were no shops, no workshops, no sign of importations among them. They spent all their time in playing gently, in bathing in the river, in making love in a half-playful fashion, in eating fruit and sleeping. I could not see how things were kept going.

Then, again, about the Time Machine: something, I knew not what, had taken it into the hollow pedestal of the White Sphinx. Why? For the life of me I could not imagine. Those waterless wells, too, those flickering pillars. I felt I lacked a clue. I felt—

how shall I put it? Suppose you found an inscription, with sentences here and there in excellent plain English, and interpolated therewith, others made up of words, of letters even, absolutely unknown to you? Well, on the third day of my visit, that was how the world of Eight Hundred and Two Thousand Seven Hundred and One presented itself to me!

That day, too, I made a friend—of a sort. It happened that, as I was watching some of the little people bathing in a shallow, one of them was seized with cramp and began drifting downstream. The main current ran rather swiftly, but not too strongly for even a moderate swimmer. It will give you an idea, therefore, of the strange deficiency in these creatures, when I tell you that none made the slightest attempt to rescue the weakly crying little thing which was drowning before their eyes. When I realized this, I hurriedly slipped off my clothes, and, wading in at a point lower down, I caught the poor mite and drew her safe to land. A little rubbing of limbs soon brought her round, and I had the satisfaction of seeing she was all right before I left her. I had got to such a low estimate of her kind that I did not expect any gratitude from her. In that, however, I was wrong.

This happened in the morning. In the afternoon I met my little woman, as I believe it was, as I was returning towards my centre from an exploration, and she received me with cries of delight and presented me with a big garland of flowers—evidently made for me and me alone. The thing took my imagination. Very possibly I had been feeling desolate. At any rate I did my best to display my appreciation of the gift. We were soon seated together in a little stone arbour, engaged in conversation, chiefly of smiles. The creature's friendliness affected me exactly as a child's might have done. We passed each other flowers, and she kissed my hands. I did the same to hers. Then I tried talk, and found that her name was Weena, which though I don't know what it meant, somehow seemed appropriate enough. That was the beginning of a queer friendship which lasted a week, and ended—as I will tell you!

She was exactly like a child. She wanted to be with me always. She tried to follow me everywhere, and on my next journey out and about it went to my heart to tire her down and leave her at last, exhausted and calling after me rather plaintively. But the problems of the world had to be mastered. I had not, I said to myself, come into the future to carry on a miniature flirtation. Yet her distress when I left her was very great, her expostulations at the parting were sometimes frantic, and I think, altogether I had as much trouble as comfort from her devotion. Nevertheless she was, somehow, a very great comfort. I thought it was mere childish affection that made her cling to me. Until it was too late, I did not clearly know what I had inflicted upon her when I left her. Nor until it was too late did I clearly understand what she was to me. For, by merely seeming fond of me, and showing in her weak, futile way that she cared for me, the little doll of a creature presently gave my return to the neighbourhood of the White Sphinx almost the feeling of coming home; and I would watch for her tiny figure of white and gold so soon as I came over the hill.

It was from her, too, that I learned that fear had not yet left the world. She was fearless enough in the daylight, and she had the oddest confidence in me; for once, in a foolish moment, I made threatening grimaces at her, and she simply laughed at them. But she dreaded the dark, dreaded shadows, dreaded black things. Darkness to her was the one thing dreadful. It was a singularly passionate emotion, and it set me thinking and observing. I discovered then, among other things, that these little people gathered into the great houses after dark, and slept in droves. To enter upon them without a light was to put them into a tumult of apprehension. I never found one out of doors, or one sleeping alone within doors, after dark. Yet I was still such a blockhead that I missed the lesson of that fear, and in spite of Weena's distress I insisted upon sleeping away from these slumbering multitudes.

It troubled her greatly, but in the end her odd affection for me triumphed, and for five of the nights of our acquaintance, including the last night of all, she slept with her head pillowed on my arm. But my story slips away from me as I speak of her. It must have been the night before her rescue that I was awakened about dawn. I had been restless, dreaming most disagreeably that I was drowned, and that sea-anemones were feeling over my face with their soft palps. I woke with a start, and with an odd fancy that some greyish animal had just rushed out of the chamber. I tried to get to sleep again, but I felt restless and uncomfortable. It was that dim grey hour when things are just creeping out of darkness, when everything is colourless and clear cut, and yet unreal. I got up, and went down into the great hall, and so out upon the flagstones in front of the palace. I thought I would make a virtue of necessity, and see the sunrise.

The moon was setting, and the dying moonlight and the first pallor of dawn were mingled in a ghastly half-light. The bushes were inky black, the ground a sombre grey, the sky colourless and cheerless. And up the hill I thought I could see ghosts. There several times, as I scanned the slope, I saw white figures. Twice I fancied I saw a solitary white, ape-like creature running rather quickly up the hill, and once near the ruins I saw a leash of them carrying some dark body. They moved hastily. I did not see what became of them. It seemed that they vanished among the bushes. The dawn was still indistinct, you must understand. I was feeling that chill, uncertain early-morning feeling you may have known. I doubted my eyes.

As the eastern sky grew brighter, and the light of the day came on and its vivid colouring returned upon the world once more, I scanned the view keenly. But I saw no vestige of my white figures. They were mere creatures of the half-light. "They must have been ghosts," I said; "I wonder whence they dated." For a queer notion of Grant Allen's came into my head, and amused me. If each generation die and leave ghosts, he argued, the world at last will get overcrowded with them. On that theory they would have grown innumerable some Eight Hundred Thousand Years hence, and it was no great wonder to see four at once. But the jest was unsatisfying, and I was thinking of these figures all the morning, until Weena's rescue drove them out of my head. I associated them in some indefinite way with the white animal I had startled in my first passionate search for the Time Machine. But Weena was a pleasant substitute. Yet all the same, they were soon destined to take far deadlier possession of my mind.

I think I have said how much hotter than our own was the weather of this Golden Age. I cannot account for it. It may be the sun was hotter, or the earth nearer the sun. It is usual to assume that the sun will go on cooling steadily in the future. But people, unfamiliar with such speculations as those of the younger Darwin, forget that the planets must ultimately fall back one by one into the parent body. As these catastrophes occur, the sun will blaze with renewed energy; and it may be that some inner planet had suffered this fate. Whatever the reason, the fact remains that the sun was very much hotter than we know it.

Well, one very hot morning—my fourth, I think—as I was seeking shelter from the heat and glare in a colossal ruin near the great house where I slept and fed, there happened this strange thing: clambering among these heaps of masonry, I found a narrow gallery, whose end and side windows were blocked by fallen masses of stone. By contrast with the brilliancy outside, it seemed at first impenetrably dark to me. I entered it groping, for the change from light to blackness made spots of colour swim before me. Suddenly I halted spellbound. A pair of eyes, luminous by reflection against the daylight without, was watching me out of the darkness.

The old instinctive dread of wild beasts came upon me. I clenched my hands and steadfastly looked into the glaring eyeballs. I was afraid to turn. Then the thought of the absolute security in which humanity appeared to be living came to my mind. And then I remembered that strange terror of the dark. Overcoming my fear to some extent, I advanced a step and spoke. I will admit that my voice was harsh and ill-controlled. I put out my hand and touched something soft. At once the eyes darted sideways, and something white ran past me. I turned with my heart in my mouth, and saw a queer little ape-like figure, its head held down in a peculiar manner, running across the sunlit space behind me. It blundered against a block of granite, staggered aside, and in a moment was hidden in a black shadow beneath another pile of ruined masonry.

My impression of it is, of course, imperfect; but I know it was a dull white, and had strange large greyish-red eyes; also that there was flaxen hair on its head and down its back. But, as I say, it went too fast for me to see distinctly. I cannot even say whether it ran on all-fours, or only with its forearms held very low. After an instant's pause I followed it into the second heap of ruins. I could not find it at first; but, after a time in the profound obscurity, I came upon one of those round well-like openings of which I have told you, half closed by a fallen pillar. A sudden thought came to me. Could this Thing have vanished down the shaft? I lit a match, and, looking down, I saw a small, white, moving creature, with large bright eyes which regarded me steadfastly as it retreated. It made me shudder. It was so like a human spider! It was clambering down the wall, and now I saw for the first time a number of metal foot and hand rests forming a kind of ladder down the shaft. Then the light burned my fingers and fell out of my hand, going out as it dropped, and when I had lit another the little monster had disappeared.

I do not know how long I sat peering down that well. It was not for some time that I could succeed in persuading myself that the thing I had seen was human. But, gradually, the truth dawned on me: that Man had not remained one species, but had differentiated into two distinct animals: that my graceful children of the Upper-world were not the sole descendants of our generation, but that this bleached, obscene, nocturnal Thing, which had flashed before me, was also heir to all the ages.

I thought of the flickering pillars and of my theory of an underground ventilation. I began to suspect their true import. And what, I wondered, was this Lemur doing in my scheme of a perfectly balanced organization? How was it related to the indolent serenity of the beautiful Upper-worlders? And what was hidden down there, at the foot of that shaft? I sat upon the edge of the well telling myself that, at any rate, there was nothing to fear, and that there I must descend for the solution of my difficulties. And withal I was absolutely afraid to go! As I hesitated, two of the beautiful Upper-world people came running in their amorous sport across the daylight in the shadow. The male pursued the female, flinging flowers at her as he ran.

They seemed distressed to find me, my arm against the overturned pillar, peering down the well. Apparently it was considered bad form to remark these apertures; for when I pointed to this one, and tried to frame a question about it in their tongue, they were still more visibly distressed and turned away. But they were interested by my matches, and I struck some to amuse them. I tried them again about the well, and again I failed. So presently I left them, meaning to go back to Weena, and see what I could get from her. But my mind was already in revolution; my guesses and impressions were slipping and sliding to a new adjustment. I had now a clue to the import of these wells, to the ventilating towers, to the mystery of the ghosts; to say nothing of a hint at the meaning of the bronze gates and the fate of the Time Machine! And very vaguely there came a suggestion towards the solution of the economic problem that had puzzled me.

Here was the new view. Plainly, this second species of Man was subterranean. There were three circumstances in particular which made me think that its rare emergence above ground was the outcome of a long-continued underground look common in most animals that live largely in the dark—the white fish of the Kentucky caves, for instance. Then, those large eyes, with that capacity for reflecting light, are common features of nocturnal things—witness the owl and the cat. And last of all, that evidence confusion in the sunshine, that hasty yet fumbling awkward flight towards dark shadow, and that peculiar carriage of the head while in the light—all reinforced the theory of an extreme sensitiveness of the retina.

Beneath my feet, then, the earth must be tunnelled enormously, and these tunnellings were the habitat of the new race. The presence of ventilating shafts and wells along the hill slopes—everywhere, in fact, except along the river valley—showed how universal were its ramifications. What so natural, then, as to assume that it was in this artificial Under-world that such work as was necessary to the comfort of the daylight race was done? The notion was so plausible that I at once accepted it, and went on to assume the how of this splitting of the human species. I dare say you will anticipate the shape of my theory; though, for myself, I very soon felt that it fell far short of the truth.

At first, proceeding from the problems of our own age, it seemed clear as daylight to me that the gradual widening of the present merely temporary and social difference between the Capitalist and the Labourer, was the key to the whole position. No doubt it will seem grotesque enough to you—and wildly incredible!—and yet even now there are existing circumstances to point that way. There is a tendency to utilize underground space for the less ornamental purposes of civilization; there is the Metropolitan Railway in London, for instance, there are new electric railways, there are subways, there are underground workrooms and restaurants, and they increase and multiply. Evidently, I thought, this tendency had increased till Industry had gradually lost its birthright in the sky. I mean that it had gone deeper and deeper into larger and ever larger underground factories, spending a still-increasing amount of its time therein, till, in the end—! Even now, does not an East-end worker live in

such artificial conditions as practically to be cut off from the
natural surface of the earth?

Again, the exclusive tendency of richer people—due, no doubt,
to the increasing refinement of their education, and the widening
gulf between them and the rude violence of the poor—is already
leading to the closing, in their interest, of considerable portions
of the surface of the land. About London, for instance, perhaps
half the prettier country is shut in against intrusion. And this
same widening gulf—which is due to the length and expense of
the higher educational process and the increased facilities for
and temptations towards refined habits on the part of the rich—
will make that exchange between class and class, that promotion
by intermarriage which at present retards the splitting of our
species along lines of social stratification, less and less frequent.
So, in the end, above ground you must have the Haves, pursuing
pleasure and comfort and beauty, and below ground the
Have-nots, the Workers getting continually adapted to the conditions of their labour. Once they were there, they would no doubt
have to pay rent, and not a little of it, for the ventilation of their
caverns; and if they refused, they would starve or be suffocated
for arrears. Such of them as were so constituted as to be miser-
able and rebellious would die; and, in the end, the balance being
permanent, the survivors would become as well adapted to the
conditions of underground life, and as happy in their way, as the
Upper-world people were to theirs. As it seemed to me, the
refined beauty and the etiolated pallor followed naturally
enough.

The great triumph of Humanity I had dreamed of took a
different shape in my mind. It had been no such triumph of
moral education and general cooperation as I had imagined.
Instead, I saw a real aristocracy, armed with a perfected science
and working to a logical conclusion the industrial system of
to-day. Its triumph had not been simply a triumph over Nature,
but a triumph over Nature and the fellow-man. This, I must warn
you, was my theory at the time. I had no convenient cicerone in
the pattern of the Utopian books. My explanation may be absolutely wrong. I still think it is the most plausible one. But even on
this supposition the balanced civilization that was at last attained
must have long since passed its zenith, and was now far fallen
into decay. The too-perfect security of the Upper-worlders had

led them to a slow movement of degeneration, to a general dwindling in size, strength, and intelligence. That I could see clearly enough already. What had happened to the Under-grounders I did not yet suspect; but from what I had seen of the Morlocks—that, by the by, was the name by which these creatures were called—I could imagine that the modification of the human type was even far more profound than among the "Eloi," the beautiful race that I already knew.

Then came troublesome doubts. Why had the Morlocks taken my Time Machine? For I felt sure it was they who had taken it. Why, too, if the Eloi were masters, could they not restore the machine to me? And why were they so terribly afraid of the dark? I proceeded, as I have said, to question Weena about this Under-world, but here again I was disappointed. At first she would not understand my questions, and presently she refused to answer them. She shivered as though the topic was unendurable. And when I pressed her, perhaps a little harshly, she burst into tears. They were the only tears, except my own, I ever saw in that Golden Age. When I saw them I ceased abruptly to trouble about the Morlocks, and was only concerned in banishing these signs of the human inheritance from Weena's eyes. And very soon she was smiling and clapping her hands, while I solemnly burned a match.

COMPREHENSION TEST

Time Machine, Chapter 5

(Write T for *true*, F for *false*)

___ 1.   In the first paragraph, the moon is described as full and rising.

___ 2.   The wisteria bushes appeared black in the pale light.

___ 3.   He discovered that the Time Machine was gone.

___ 4.   The Time Traveler experienced no noticeable fear.

___ 5.   The Time Traveler states that he was not a young man.

___ 6.   The sphinx rested upon a bronze pedestal.

___ 7.   His search for the machine soon proved fruitful.

___ 8.   When he went to the great building of stone, he found some of the little people sleeping.

___ 9.   He made no inquiry about his vehicle there.

___10. After a fitful sleep he awoke to find himself surrounded by many strange creatures.

___11. He immediately set about to build another Time Machine.

___12. He discovered the pedestal under the sphinx to be hollow.

___13. The little people were very helpful in supplying complete information about the sphinx and the pedestal.

___14. He banged upon the walls of the pedestal with a big pebble.

___15. In a few days the Time Traveler completely mastered the strange but simple language of the little people.

___16. He compares the surrounding area of the strange world with the Thames valley.

___17. He soon noted certain square wells.

___18. The wells seemed to suck in air.

___19. The writer speaks of this future time as the Golden Age.

___20. He observed many cemeteries scattered about the country side.

___21. The little people were apparently not much interested in work.

___22. The year in time was 802,701 A.D.

___23. The Time Traveler rescued a small dog from the river.

___24. His young friend's name was Weena.

___25. He describes Weena as being "exactly like a child."

___26. Weena feared daylight, but had no concern for darkness.

___27. Weena insisted that they not sleep near the others.

___28. The Time Traveler describes the weather as uncomfortably cold.

___29. In a darkened narrow gallery he was confronted by a pair of glowing eyes.

___30. What he saw appeared to be a queer little apelike figure.

___31. He soon decided that the creature was a second species of Man.

___32. The Time Traveler resolved that this second species was subterranean by nature.

___33. These underground beings were called Morlocks.

(When finished answering the questions, check the answers on the following page.)

Correct Answers for Test

THE TIME MACHINE (CHAPTER 5)

(Value: 3 points each)

Approximately 6,600 words

1. The correct answer is (T).
2. The correct answer is (F).
3. The correct answer is (T).
4. The correct answer is (F).
5. The correct answer is (T).
6. The correct answer is (T).
7. The correct answer is (F).
8. The correct answer is (T).
9. The correct answer is (F).
10. The correct answer is (F).
11. The correct answer is (F).
12. The correct answer is (T).
13. The correct answer is (F).
14. The correct answer is (T).
15. The correct answer is (F).
16. The correct answer is (T).
17. The correct answer is (F).
18. The correct answer is (T).
19. The correct answer is (T).
20. The correct answer is (F).
21. The correct answer is (T).
22. The correct answer is (T).
23. The correct answer is (F).
24. The correct answer is (T).
25. The correct answer is (T).
26. The correct answer is (F).
27. The correct answer is (F).
28. The correct answer is (F).
29. The correct answer is (T).
30. The correct answer is (T).
31. The correct answer is (T).
32. The correct answer is (T).
33. The correct answer is (T).

Dr. Jekyll and Mr. Hyde,
by Robert Louis Stevenson
(approximately 7,000 words)

HENRY JEKYLL'S FULL STATEMENT OF THE CASE

I was born in the year 18— to a large fortune, endowed besides with excellent parts, inclined by nature to industry, fond of the respect of the wise and good among my fellowmen, and thus, as might have been supposed, with every guarantee of an honourable and distinguished future. And indeed the worst of my faults was a certain impatient gaiety of disposition, such as has made the happiness of many, but such as I found it hard to reconcile with my imperious desire to carry my head high, and wear a more than commonly grave countenance before the public. Hence it came about that I concealed my pleasures; and that when I reached years of reflection, and began to look round me and take stock of my progress and position in the world, I stood already committed to a profound duplicity of life. Many a man would have even blazoned such irregularities as I was guilty of; but from the high views that I had set before me, I regarded and hid them with an almost morbid sense of shame. It was thus rather the exacting nature of my aspirations that any particular degradation in my faults, that made me what I was, and, with even a deeper trench than in the majority of men, severed in me those provinces of good and ill which divide and compound man's dual nature. In this case, I was driven to reflect deeply and inveterately on that hard law of life, which lies at the root of religion and is one of the most plentiful springs of distress. Though so profound a double-dealer, I was in no sense a hypocrite; both sides of me were in dead earnest; I was no more myself when I laid aside restraint and plunged in shame, than when I laboured, in the eye of day, at the furtherance of knowledge or the relief of sorrow and suffering. And it chanced that the direction of my scientific studies, which led wholly towards the mystic and the transcendental, reacted and shed a strong light on this consciousness of the perennial war among my members. With every day, and from both sides of my intelligence, the moral and the intellectual, I thus drew steadily nearer to that truth, by whose partial discovery I have been doomed to such a dreadful shipwreck: that man is not truly one, but truly two. I say two, because the state of my own knowledge does not pass beyond that point. Others will follow, others will outstrip me on the same lines; and I hazard the guess that man will be ultimately known for a mere polity of multifarious, incongruous, and independent denizens. I for my part, from the nature of my life, advanced infallibly in one direction and in one direction only. It was on the moral side, and in my own person, that I learned to recognise the thorough and primitive duality of man; I saw that, of the two natures that contended in the field of my consciousness, even if I could rightly be said to be either, it was only because I was radically both; and from an early date, even before the course of my scientific discoveries had begun to suggest the most naked possibility of such a miracle, I had learned to dwell with pleasure, as a beloved day-dream on the thought of the separation of these elements. If each, I told myself, could but be housed in separate identities, life would be relieved of all that was unbearable; the unjust might go his way, delivered from the aspirations and remorse of his more upright twin; and the just could walk stead-fastly and securely on his upward path, doing the good things in which he found his pleasure, and no longer exposed to disgrace and penitence by the hands of this extraneous evil. It was the curse of mankind that these incongruous faggots were thus bound together—that in the agonised womb of consciousness, these polar twins should be continuously struggling. How, then, were they dissociated?

I was so far in my reflections when, as I have said, a side light began to shine upon the subject from the laboratory table. I began to perceive more deeply than it has ever yet been stated, the trembling immateriality, the mist-like transience, of this seemingly so solid body in which we walk attired. Certain agents I found to have the power to shake and to pluck back that fleshly vestment, even as a wind might toss the curtains of a pavilion. For two good reasons, I will not enter deeply into this scientific branch of my confession. First, because I have been made to learn that the doom and burthen of our life is bound for ever on man's shoulders, and when the attempt is made to cast it off, it but returns upon us with more unfamiliar and more awful pressure. Second, because, as my narrative will make, alas! too evident, my discoveries were incomplete. Enough, then, that I not only recognised my natural body for the mere aura and effulgence of certain of the powers that made up my spirit, but managed to compound a drug by which these powers should be dethroned from their supremacy, and a second form and countenance substituted, none the less natural to me because they were the expression, and bore the stamp, of lower elements in my soul.

I hesitated long before I put this theory to the test of practice. I knew well that I risked death; for any drug that so potently controlled and shook the very fortress of identity, might by the least scruple of an overdose or at the least inopportunity in the moment of exhibition, utterly blot out that immaterial tabernacle which I looked to it to change. But the temptation of a discovery so singular and profound, at last overcame the suggestions of alarm. I had long since prepared my tincture; I purchased at once, from a firm of wholesale chemists, a large quantity of a particular salt which I knew, from my experiments, to be the last ingredient required; and late one accursed night, I compounded the elements, watched them boil and smoke together in the glass, and when the ebullition had subsided, with a strong glow of courage, drank off the potion.

The most racking pangs succeeded: a grinding in the bones, deadly nausea, and a horror of the spirit that cannot be exceeded at the hour of birth or death. Then these agonies began swiftly to subside, and I came to myself as if out of a great sickness. There was something strange in my sensations, something indescribably new and, from its very novelty, incredibly sweet. I felt younger, lighter, happier in body; within I was conscious of a heady recklessness, a current of disordered sensual images running like a mill race in my fancy, a solution of the bonds of obligation, an unknown but not an innocent freedom of the soul. I knew myself, at the first breath of this new life, to be more wicked, tenfold more wicked, sold a slave to my original evil; and the thought, in that moment, braced and delighted me like wine. I stretched out my hands, exulting in the freshness of these sensations; and in the act, I was suddenly aware that I had lost in stature.

There was no mirror, at that date, in my room; that which stands beside me as I write, was brought there later on for the very purpose of these transformations. The night, however, was far gone into the morning—the morning, black as it was, was nearly ripe for the conception of the day—the inmates of my house were locked in the most rigorous hours of slumber; and I determined, flushed as I was with hope and triumph, to venture in my new shape as far as to my bedroom. I crossed the yard, wherein the constellations looked down upon me, I could have thought, with wonder, the first creature of that sort that their unsleeping vigilance had yet disclosed to them; I stole through the corridors, a stranger in my own house; and coming to my room, I saw for the first time the appearance of Edward Hyde.

I must speak by theory alone, saying not that which I know, but that which I suppose to be most probable. The evil side of my nature, to which I had now transferred the stamping efficacy, was less robust and less developed than the good which I had just deposed. Again, in the course of my life, which had been, after all, nine-tenths a life of effort, virtue, and control, it had been much less exercised and much less exhausted. And hence, as I think, it came about that Edward Hyde was so much smaller, slighter, and younger than Henry Jekyll. Even as good shone upon the countenance of the one, evil was written broadly and plainly on the face of the other. Evil besides (which I must still believe to be the lethal side of man) had left on that body an imprint of deformity and decay. And yet when I looked upon that ugly idol in the glass, I was conscious of no repugnance, rather of a leap of welcome. This, too, was myself. It seemed natural and human. In my eyes it bore a livelier image of the spirit, it seemed more express and single, than the imperfect and divided countenance I had been hitherto accustomed to call mine. And in so far I was doubtless right. I have observed that when I wore the semblance of Edward Hyde, none could come near to me at first without a visible misgiving of the flesh. This, as I take it, was because all human beings, as we meet them, are commingled out of good and evil: and Edward Hyde, alone in the ranks of mankind, was pure evil.

I lingered but a moment at the mirror: the second and conclusive experiment had yet to be attempted; it yet remained to be seen if I had lost my identity beyond redemption and must flee before daylight from a house that was no longer mine; and hurrying back to my cabinet, I once more prepared and drank the cup, once more suffered the pangs of dissolution, and came to myself once more with the character, the stature, and the face of Henry Jekyll.

That night I had come to the fatal cross roads. Had I approached my discovery in a more noble spirit, had I risked the experiment while under the empire of generous or pious aspirations, all must have been otherwise, and from these agonies of death and birth, I had come forth an angel instead of a fiend. The drug had no discriminating action; it was neither diabolical nor divine; it but shook the doors of the prison house of my disposition; and like the captives of Philippi, that which stood within ran forth. At that time my virtue slumbered; my evil, kept awake by ambition, was alert and swift to seize the occasion; and the thing that was projected was Edward Hyde. Hence, although I had now two characters as well as two appearances, one was wholly evil, and the other was still the old Henry Jekyll, that incongruous compound of whose reformation and improvement I had already learned to despair. The movement was thus wholly towards the worse.

Even at that time, I had not yet conquered my aversion to the dryness of a life of study. I would still be merrily disposed at times; and as my pleasures were (to say the least) undignified, and I was not only well known and highly considered, but growing towards the elderly man, this incoherency of my life was daily growing more unwelcome. It was on this side that my new power tempted me until I fell in slavery. I had but to drink the cup, to doff at once the body of the noted professor, and to assume, like a thick cloak, that of Edward Hyde. I smiled at the notion; it seemed to me at the time to be humourous; and I made my preparations with the most studious care. I took and furnished the house in Soho, to which Hyde was tracked by the police; and engaged as housekeeper a creature whom I well knew to be silent and unscrupulous. On the other side, I announced to my servants that a Mr. Hyde (whom I described) was to have full liberty and power about my house in the square; and to parry mishaps, I even called and made myself a familiar object, in my second character. I next drew up that will to which you so much objected; so that if anything befell me in the person of Dr. Jekyll, I could enter on that of Edward Hyde without pecuniary loss. And thus fortified, as I supposed, on every side, I began to profit by the strange immunities of my position.

Men have before hired bravos to transact their crimes, while their own person and reputation sat under shelter. I was the first that ever did so for his pleasures. I was the first that could thus plod in the public eye with a load of genial respectability, and in a moment, like a schoolboy, strip off these lendings and spring headlong into the sea of liberty. But for me, in my impenetrable mantle, the safety was complete. Think of it—I did not even exist! Let me but escape into my laboratory door, give me but a second or two to mix and swallow the draught that I had always standing ready; and whatever he had done, Edward Hyde would pass away like the stain of breath upon a mirror; and there in his stead, quietly at home, trimming the midnight lamp in his study, a man who could afford to laugh at suspicion, would be Henry Jekyll.

The pleasures which I made haste to seek in my disguise were, as I have said, undignified; I would scarce use a harder term. But in the hands of Edward Hyde, they soon began to turn towards the monstrous. When I would come back from these excursions, I was often plunged into a kind of wonder at my vicarious depravity. This familiar that I called out of my own soul, and sent forth alone to do his good pleasure, was a being inherently malign and villainous; his every act and thought centered on self; drinking pleasure with bestial avidity from any degree of torture to another; relentless like a man of stone. Henry Jekyll stood at times aghast before the acts of Edward Hyde; but the situation was apart from ordinary laws, and insidiously relaxed the grasp of conscience. It was Hyde, after all, and Hyde alone, that was guilty. Jekyll was no worse; he worked again to his good qualities seemingly unimpaired; he would even make haste, where it was possible, to undo the evil done by Hyde. And thus his conscience slumbered.

Into the details of the infamy at which I thus connived (for even now I can scarce grant that I committed it) I have no design of entering; I mean but to point out the warnings and the successive steps with which my chastisement approached. I met with one accident which, as it brought on no consequence, I shall no more than mention. An act of cruelty to a child aroused against me the anger of a passer-by, whom I recognised the other day in the person of your kinsman; the doctor and the child's family joined him; there were moments when I feared for my life; and at last, in order to pacify their too just resentment, Edward Hyde had to bring them to the door, and pay them in a cheque drawn in the name of Henry Jekyll. But this danger was easily eliminated from the future, by opening an account at another bank in the name of Edward Hyde himself; and when, by sloping my own hand backward, I had supplied my double with a signature, I thought I sat beyond the reach of fate.

Some two months before the murder of Sir Danvers, I had been out for one of my adventures, had returned at a late hour, and woke the next day in bed with somewhat odd sensations. It was in vain I looked about me; in vain I saw the decent furniture and tall proportions of my room in the square; in vain that I recognised the pattern of the bed curtains and the design of the mahogany frame; something still kept insisting that I was not where I was, that I had not wakened where I seemed to be, but in the little room in Soho where I was accustomed to sleep in the body of Edward Hyde. I smiled to myself, and, in my psychological way began lazily to inquire into the elements of this illusion, occasionally, even as I did so, dropping back into a comfortable morning doze. I was still so engaged when, in one of my more wakeful moments, my eyes fell upon my hand. Now the hand of Henry Jekyll (as you have often remarked) was professional in shape and size: it was large, firm, white, and comely. But the hand which I now saw, clearly enough, in the yellow light of a mid-London morning, lying half shut on the bed clothes, was lean, corded, knuckly, of a dusky pallor, and thickly shaded with a swart growth of hair. It was the hand of Edward Hyde.

I must have stared upon it for near half a minute, sunk as I was in the mere stupidity of wonder, before terror woke up in my breast as sudden and startling as the crash of cymbals; and bounding from my bed, I rushed to the mirror. At the sight that met my eyes, my blood was changed into something exquisitely thin and icy. Yes, I had gone to bed Henry Jekyll, I had awakened Edward Hyde. How was this to be explained? I asked myself; and then, with another bound of terror—how was it to be remedied? It was well on in the morning; the servants were up; all my drugs were in the cabinet—a long journey down two pair of stairs, through the back passage, across the open court and through the anatomical theatre, from where I was then standing horror-struck. It might indeed be possible to cover my face; but of what use was that, when I was unable to conceal the alteration in my stature? And then with an overpowering sweetness of relief, it came back upon my mind that the servants were already used to the coming and going of my second self. I had soon dressed, as well as I was able, in clothes of my own size; had soon passed through the house, where Bradshaw stared and drew back at seeing Mr. Hyde at such an hour and in such a strange array; and ten minutes later, Dr. Jekyll had returned to his own shape and was sitting down, with a darkened brow, to make a feint of breakfasting.

Small indeed was my appetite. This inexplicable incident, this reversal of my previous experience, seemed, like the Babylonian finger on the wall, to be spelling out the letters of my judgment; and I began to reflect more seriously than ever before on the issues and possibilities of my double existence. That part of me which I had the power of projecting, had lately been much exercised and nourished; it had seemed to me of late as though the body of Edward Hyde had grown in stature, as though (when I wore that form) I were conscious of a more generous tide of blood; and I began to spy a danger that, if this were much pro-longed, the balance of my nature might be permanently over-thrown, the power of voluntary change be forfeited, and the character of Edward Hyde become irrevocably mine. The power of the drug had not been always equally displayed. Once, very early in my career, it had totally failed me; since then I had been obliged on more than one occasion to double, and once, with infinite risk of death, to treble the amount; and these rare uncer-tainties had cast hitherto the sole shadow on my contentment. Now, however, and in the light of that morning's accident, I was led to remark that whereas, in the beginning, the difficulty had been to throw off the body of Jekyll, it had of late gradually but decidedly transferred itself to the other side. All things therefore seemed to point to this: that I was slowly losing hold of my original and better self, and becoming slowly incorporated with my second and worse.

Between these two, I now felt I had to choose. My two natures had memory in common, but all other faculties were most unequally shared between them. Jekyll (who was composite) now with the most sensitive apprehensions, now with a greedy gusto, projected and shared in the pleasures and adventures of Hyde; but Hyde was indifferent to Jekyll, or but remembered him as the mountain bandit remembers the cavern in which he conceals himself from pursuit. Jekyll had more than a father's interest; Hyde had more than a son's indifference. To cast in my lot with

Jekyll, was to die to those appetites which I had long secretly
indulged and had of late begun to pamper. To cast it in with
Hyde, was to die to a thousand interests and aspirations, and to
become, at a blow and for ever, despised and friendless. The
bargain might appear unequal; but there was still another consideration in the scales; for while Jekyll would suffer smartingly in
the fires of abstinence, Hyde would be not even conscious of all
that he had lost. Strange as my circumstances were, the terms of
this debate are as old and commonplace as man; much the same
inducements and alarms cast the die for any tempted and trembling sinner; and it fell out with me, as it falls with so vast a
majority of my fellows, that I chose the better part and was
found wanting in the strength to keep to it.

Yes, I preferred the elderly and discontented doctor, surrounded by friends and cherishing honest hopes; and bade a
resolute farewell to the liberty, the comparative youth, the light
step, leaping impulses and secret pleasures, that I had enjoyed in
the disguise of Hyde. I made this choice perhaps with some
unconscious reservation, for I neither gave up the house in Soho,
nor destroyed the clothes of Edward Hyde, which still lay ready
in my cabinet. For two months, however, I was true to my determination; for two months I led a life of such severity as I had
never before attained to, and enjoyed the compensations of an
approving conscience. But time began at last to obliterate the
freshness of my alarm; the praises of conscience began to grow
into a thing of course; I began to be tortured with throes and
longings, as of Hyde struggling after freedom; and at last, in an
hour of moral weakness, I once again compounded and swallowed the transforming draught.

I do not suppose that, when a drunkard reasons with himself
upon his vice, he is once out of five hundred times affected by
the dangers that he runs through his brutish, physical insensibility; neither had I, long as I had considered my position, made
enough allowance for the complete moral insensibility and
insensate readiness to evil, which were the leading characters of
Edward Hyde. Yet it was by these that I was punished. My devil
had been long caged, he came out roaring. I was conscious, even
when I took the draught, of a more unbridled, a more furious
propensity to ill. It must have been this, I suppose, that stirred in
my soul that tempest of impatience with which I listened to the

civilities of my unhappy victim; I declare, at least, before God, no man morally sane could have been guilty of that crime upon so pitiful a provocation; and that I struck in no more reasonable spirit than that in which a sick child may break a plaything. But I had voluntarily stripped myself of all those balancing instincts by which even the worst of us continues to walk with some degree of steadiness among temptations; and in my case, to be tempted, however slightly, was to fall.

Instantly the spirit of hell awoke in me and raged. With a transport of glee, I mauled the unresisting body, tasting delight from every blow; and it was not till weariness had begun to succeed, that I was suddenly, in the top fit of my delirium, struck through the heart by a cold thrill of terror. A mist dispersed; I saw my life to be forfeit; and fled from the scene of these excesses, at once glorifying and trembling, my lust of evil gratified and stimulated, my love of life screwed to the topmost peg. I ran to the house in Soho, and (to make assurance doubly sure) de- stroyed my papers; thence I set out through the lamplit streets, in the same divided ecstasy of mind, gloating on my crime, light-headedly devising others in the future, and yet still hasten- ing and still hearkening in my wake for the steps of the avenger. Hyde had a song upon his lips as he compounded the draught, and as he drank it, pledged the dead man. The pangs of transfor- mation had not done tearing him, before Henry Jekyll, with streaming tears of gratitude and remorse, had fallen upon his knees and lifted his clasped hands to God. The veil of self-indulgence was rent from head to foot. I saw my life as a whole: I followed it up from the days of childhood, when I had walked with my father's hand, and through the self-denying toils of my professional life, to arrive again and again, with the same sense of unreality, at the damned horrors of the evening. I could have screamed aloud; I sought with tears and prayers to smother down the crowd of hideous images and sounds with which my memory swarmed against me; and still, between the petitions, the ugly face of my iniquity stared into my soul. As the acuteness of this remorse began to die away, it was succeeded by a sense of joy. The problem of my conduct was solved. Hyde was thence- forth impossible; whether I would or not, I was now confined to the better part of my existence; and O, how I rejoiced to think it! with what willing humility, I embraced anew the restrictions of natural life! with what sincere renunciation, I locked the door by which I had so often gone and come, and ground the key under my heel!

The next day came the news that the murder had been over-looked, that the guilt of Hyde was patent to the world, and that the victim was a man high in public estimation. It was not only a crime, it had been a tragic folly. I think I was glad to know it; I think I was glad to have my better impulses thus buttressed and guarded by the terrors of the scaffold. Jekyll was now my city of refuge; let but Hyde peep out an instant, and the hands of all men would be raised to take and slay him.

I resolved in my future conduct to redeem the past; and I can say with honesty that my resolve was fruitful of some good. You know yourself how earnestly in the last months of last year, I laboured to relieve suffering; you know that much was done for others, and that the days passed quietly, almost happily for myself. Nor can I truly say that I wearied of this beneficent and innocent life; I think instead that I daily enjoyed it more completely; but I was still cursed with my duality of purpose; and as the first edge of my penitence wore off, the lower side of me, so long indulged, so recently chained down, began to growl for license. Not that I dreamed of resuscitating Hyde; the bare idea of that would startle me to frenzy: no, it was in my own person, that I was once more tempted to trifle with my conscience; and it was as an ordinary secret sinner, that I at last fell before the assaults of temptation.

There comes an end to all things; the most capacious measure is filled at last; and this brief condescension to my evil finally destroyed the balance of my soul. And yet I was not alarmed; the fall seemed natural, like a return to the old days before I had made my discovery. It was a fine, clear, January day, wet under-foot where the frost had melted, but cloudless overhead; and the Regent's Park was full of winter chirrupings and sweet with spring odours. I sat in the sun on a bench; the animal within me licking the chops of memory; the spiritual side a little drowsed, promising subsequent penitence, but not yet moved to begin. After all, I reflected, I was like my neighbours; and then I smiled, comparing myself with other men, comparing my active good-will with the lazy cruelty of their neglect. And at the very moment of that vain-glorious thought, a qualm came over me, a horrid nausea and the most deadly shuddering. These passed away, and left me faint; and then as in its turn the faintness subsided, I began to be aware of a change in the temper of my thoughts, a greater boldness, a contempt of danger, a solution of the bonds of obligation. I looked down; my clothes hung form-lessly on my shrunken limbs; the hand that lay on my knee was corded and hairy. I was once more Edward Hyde. A moment before I had been safe of all men's respect, wealthy, beloved—the cloth laying for me in the dining room at home; and now I was the common quarry of mankind, hunted, houseless, a known murderer, thrall to the gallows.

My reason wavered, but it did not fail me utterly. I have more than once observed that, in my second character, my faculties seemed sharpened to a point and my spirits more tensely elastic; thus it came about that, where Jekyll perhaps might have suc-cumbed, Hyde rose to the importance of the moment. My drugs were in one of the presses of my cabinet; how was I to reach them? That was the problem that (crushing my temples in my hands) I set myself to solve. The laboratory door I had closed. If I sought to enter by the house, my own servants would consign me to the gallows. I saw I must employ another hand, and thought of Lanyon. How was he to be reached? how persuaded? Supposing that I escaped capture in the streets, how was I to make my way into his presence and how should I, an unknown and displeasing visitor, prevail on the famous physician to rifle the study of his colleague, Dr. Jekyll? Then I remembered that of my original character, one part remained to me: I could write my own hand; and once I had conceived that kindling spark, the way that I must follow became lighted up from end to end.

Thereupon I arranged my clothes as best I could, and summon-ing a passing hansom, drove to an hotel in Portland Street, the name of which I chanced to remember. At my appearance (which was indeed comical enough, however tragic, a fate these gar-ments covered) the driver could not conceal his mirth. I gnashed my teeth upon him with a gust of devilish fury; and the smile withered from his face—happily for him—yet more happily for myself, for in another instant I had certainly dragged him from his perch. At the inn, as I entered, I looked about me with so black a countenance as made the attendants tremble; not a look did they exchange in my presence; but obsequiously took my orders, led me to a private room, and brought me wherewithal to write. Hyde in danger of his life was a creature new to me;

shaken with inordinant anger, strung to the pitch of murder, lusting to inflict pain. Yet the creature was astute; mastered his fury with a great effort of the will; composed his two important letters, one to Lanyon and one to Poole; and that he might receive actual evidence of their being posted, sent them out with directions that they should be registered.

Thenceforward, he sat all day over the fire in the private room, gnawing his nails; there he dined, sitting alone with his fears, the waiter visibly quailing before his eye; and thence, when the night was fully come, he set forth in the corner of a closed cab, and was driven to and fro about the streets of the city. He, I say—I cannot say, I. That child of Hell had nothing human; nothing lived in him but fear and hatred. And when at last, thinking the driver had begun to grow suspicious, he discharged the cab and ventured on foot, attired in his misfitting clothes, an object marked out for observation, into the midst of the nocturnal passengers, these two base passions raged within him like a temptest. He walked fast, hunted by his fears, chattering to himself, skulking through the less frequented thoroughfares, counting the minutes that still divided him from midnight. Once a woman spoke to him, offering, I think, a box of lights. He smote her in the face, and she fled.

When I came to myself at Lanyon's, the horror of my old friend perhaps affected me somewhat: I do not know; it was at least but a drop in the sea to the abhorrence with which I looked back upon these hours. A change had come over me. It was no longer the fear of the gallows, it was the horror of being Hyde that racked me. I received Lanyon's condemnation partly in a dream; it was partly in a dream that I came home to my own house and got into bed. I slept after the prostration of the day, with a stringent and profound slumber which not even the nightmares that wrung me could avail to break. I awoke in the morning shaken, weakened, but refreshed. I still hated and feared the thought of the brute that slept within me, and I had not of course forgotten the appalling dangers of the day before; but I was once more at home, in my own house and close to my drugs, and gratitude for my escape shone so strong in my soul that it almost rivalled the brightness of hope.

I was stepping leisurely across the court after breakfast, drinking the chill of the air with pleasure, when I was seized again with those indescribable sensations that heralded the change; and I had but the time to gain the shelter of my cabinet, before I was once again raging and freezing with the passions of Hyde. It took on this occasion a double dose to recall me to myself; and alas! six hours after, as I sat looking sadly in the fire, the pangs returned, and the drug had to be readministered. In short, from that day forth it seemed only by a great effort as of gymnastics, and only under the immediate stimulation of the drug, that I was able to wear the countenance of Jekyll. At all hours of the day and night, I would be taken with the premonitory shudder; above all, if I slept, or even dozed for a moment in my chair, it was always as Hyde that I awakened. Under the strain of this continually impending doom and by the sleeplessness to which I now condemned myself, ay, even beyond what I had thought possible to man, I became, in my own person, a creature eaten up and emptied by fever, languidly weak both in body and mind, and solely occupied by one thought: the horror of my other self. But when I slept, or when the virtue of the medicine wore off, I would leap almost without transition (for the pangs of transformation grew daily less marked) into the possession of a fancy brimming with images of terror, a soul boiling with causeless hatreds, and a body that seemed not strong enough to contain the raging energies of life. The powers of Hyde seemed to have grown with the sickliness of Jekyll. And certainly the hate that now divided them was equal on each side. With Jekyll, it was a thing of vital instinct. He had now seen the full deformity of that creature that shared with him some of the phenomena of consciousness, and was co-heir with him to death: and beyond these links of community, which in themselves made the most poignant part of his distress, he thought of Hyde, for all his energy of life, as of something not only hellish but inorganic. This was the shocking thing; that the slime of the pit seemed to utter cries and voices; that the amorphous dust gesticulated and sinned; that what was dead, and had no shape, should usurp the offices of life. And this again, that that insurgent horror was knit to him closer than a wife, closer than an eye; lay caged in his flesh, where he heard it mutter and felt it struggle to be born; and at every hour of weakness, and in the confidence of slumber, prevailed against him, and deposed him out of life. The hatred of Hyde for Jekyll, was of a different order. His terror of the gallows drove him continually to commit temporary suicide, and return to his subordinate station of a part instead of a person; but he loathed the necessity, he loathed the despondency into which Jekyll was now fallen, and he resented the dislike with which he was himself regarded. Hence the apelike tricks that he would play me, scrawling in my own hand blasphemies on the pages of my books, burning the letters and destroying the portrait of my father; and indeed, had it not been for his fear of death, he would long ago have ruined himself in order to involve me in the ruin. But his love of life is wonderful; I go further: I, who sicken and freeze at the mere thought of him, when I recall the abjection and passion of this attachment, and when I know how he fears my power to cut him off by suicide, I find it in my heart to pity him.

It is useless, and the time awfully fails me, to prolong this description; no one has ever suffered such torments, let that suffice; and yet even to these, habit brought—no, not alleviation—but a certain callousness of soul, a certain acquiescence of despair; and my punishment might have gone on for years, but for the last calamity which has now fallen, and which has finally severed me from my own face and nature. My provision of the salt, which had never been renewed since the date of the first experiment, began to run low. I sent out for a fresh supply, and mixed the draught; the ebullition followed, and the first change of colour, not the second; I drank it and it was without efficiency. You will learn from Poole how I have had London ransacked: it was in vain; and I am now persuaded that my first supply was impure, and that it was that unknown impurity which lent efficacy to the draught.

About a week has passed, and I am now finishing this statement under the influence of the last of the old powders. This, then, is the last time, short of a miracle, that Henry Jekyll can think his own thoughts or see his own face (now how sadly altered!) in the glass. Nor must I delay too long to bring my writing to an end; for if my narrative has hitherto escaped destruction, it has been by a combination of great prudence and great good luck. Should the throes of change take me in the act of writing it, Hyde will tear it in pieces; but if some time shall have elapsed after I have laid it by, his wonderful selfishness and circumscription to the moment will probably save it once again from the action of his apelike spite. And indeed the doom that is closing on us both, has already changed and crushed him. Half an hour from now, when I shall again and for ever reindue that hated personality, I know how I shall sit shuddering and weeping in my chair, or continue, with the most strained and fear-struck ecstasy of listening, to pace up and down this room (my last earthly refuge) and give ear to every sound of menace. Will Hyde die upon the scaffold? or will he find courage to release himself at the last moment? God knows; I am careless; this is my true hour of death, and what is to follow concerns another than myself. Here then, as I lay down the pen and proceed to seal up my confession, I bring the life of that unhappy Henry Jekyll to an end.

COMPREHENSION TEST

DR. JEKYLL AND MR. HYDE: "HENRY JEKYLL'S FULL STATEMENT OF THE CASE"

(Circle the letter preceding the most correct answer)

1. Henry Jekyll was born in the

    (A)   1600s.
    (B)   1700s.
    (C)   1900s.
    (D)   1800s.

2. Dr. Jekyll states that he was born

    (A)   to no fortune.
    (B)   to a large fortune.
    (C)   to a modest fortune.
    (D)   in dire poverty.

3. At an early age in his life he was quite aware of a distinct

    (A)   duplicity.
    (B)   hunger for wealth.
    (C)   need for love.
    (D)   lack of affection.

4. The direction of Jekyll's scientific studies led toward

    (A)   the mystical.
    (B)   the orthodox.
    (C)   the transcendental.
    (D)   both A and C.

5. He developed the means to separate the good and the evil in himself through

   (A) an electrical device.
   (B) a compounded drug.
   (C) an electronic device.
   (D) self-hypnosis.

6. He hesitated to experiment with the above because he feared

   (A) criticism.
   (B) God.
   (C) death.
   (D) himself.

7. The last ingredient or device needed for his experiment was

   (A) a particular salt.
   (B) a transformer.
   (C) a vial of elixir.
   (D) a voltmeter.

8. He describes his first sensations after starting the experiment as

   (A) racking pangs.
   (B) grinding in the bones.
   (C) a deadly nausea.
   (D) All of the above

9. The first visually noticeable change he observed in himself was

   (A) a loss in stature.
   (B) a loss in weight.
   (C) an increase in height.
   (D) long hair on his face.

10. He was able to view his changed form by sneaking to

    (A) the lake.
    (B) his lab.
    (C) his wife's room.
    (D) his bedroom.

11. His reflection was then that of

    (A) Edgar Hyde.
    (B) Edward Hyde.
    (C) Elbert Hyde.
    (D) Egbert Hyde.

12. Mr. Hyde is described as being

    (A)   an image of the devil.
    (B)   smaller, slighter, and younger than Jekyll.
    (C)   the image of a monster.
    (D)   larger, heavier, and older than Jekyll.

13. The ugly idol's reflection brought upon Jekyll

    (A)   no repugnance.
    (B)   only terror.
    (C)   a bitter hatred.
    (D)   total awe.

14. For Hyde, Dr. Jekyll took and furnished a house in

    (A)   London.
    (B)   Winchester.
    (C)   Hyde Park.
    (D)   Soho.

15. Mr. Hyde's pleasures, at first, are described by Jekyll as being

    (A)   monstrous.
    (B)   undignified.
    (C)   heinous.
    (D)   depraved.

16. The murder mentioned is that of

    (A)   Sir Edwards.
    (B)   Prince Prospero.
    (C)   Sir David Davis.
    (D)   Sir Danvers.

17. When Dr. Jekyll noticed that his hand had not made its accustomed change from that of Mr. Hyde, he was

    (A)   in bed at his home.
    (B)   in bed at the rented place.
    (C)   in his office.
    (D)   out on the public street.

18. The servant who was startled by Mr. Hyde, still in Jekyll's clothes, was named

    (A)   Bradshaw.
    (B)   Wellingham.
    (C)   McHenry.
    (D)   Bradley.

19. Soon Dr. Jekyll's greatest fear was that

    (A) Hyde would dominate.
    (B) Jekyll would dominate.
    (C) he was being dishonest.
    (D) the police would catch him.

20. The writer describes his Jekyll self as

    (A) saintlike.
    (B) totally evil.
    (C) totally good.
    (D) a composite.

21. Jekyll was able to resist transforming himself into Hyde for

    (A) two years.
    (B) two months.
    (C) two days.
    (D) two weeks.

22. Finally, the unwanted change to Hyde overtook Jekyll

    (A) in the park.
    (B) on a bench.
    (C) in his home.
    (D) in the park on a bench.

23. He hurriedly departed the place mentioned above

    (A) on a horse.
    (B) in a motorcar.
    (C) in a hansom.
    (D) on foot.

24. The two letters posted from the hotel were addressed to

    (A) Lanyon and Poole.
    (B) Jekyll and Portland.
    (C) Hyde and Poole.
    (D) Lanyon and Jekyll.

25. Soon he was able to wear the countenance of Jekyll only

    (A) with Lanyon's aid.
    (B) with drugs.
    (C) at night.
    (D) during the day.

(When finished answering the questions, check the answers on the following page.)

Correct Answers for Test

DR. JEKYLL AND MR. HYDE

(Value: 4 points each)

Approximately 7,000 words

1. The correct answer is (D).
2. The correct answer is (B).
3. The correct answer is (A).
4. The correct answer is (D).
5. The correct answer is (B).
6. The correct answer is (C).
7. The correct answer is (A).
8. The correct answer is (D).
9. The correct answer is (A).
10. The correct answer is (D).
11. The correct answer is (B).
12. The correct answer is (B).
13. The correct answer is (A).
14. The correct answer is (D).
15. The correct answer is (B).
16. The correct answer is (D).
17. The correct answer is (A).
18. The correct answer is (A).
19. The correct answer is (A).
20. The correct answer is (D).
21. The correct answer is (B).
22. The correct answer is (D).
23. The correct answer is (C).
24. The correct answer is (A).
25. The correct answer is (B).

Money Signs, by Elbert Wade*

(approximately 4,700 words)

CHAPTER 1—DOLLARS AND (COMMON) SENSE

Whether you call it afghani, baht, balboa, bolivar, cedi, colon, cordoba, cruzeiro, dalasi, deutsche mark, dinar, dirham, dollar, dong, drachma, escudo, florin, forint, franc, gourde, guarani, gulden, kip, koruna, krona, krone, kwacha, kyat, lek, lempira, leone, leu, lev, lira, mark, markka, naira, pa'anga, pataca, peseta, peso, piaster, pound, quetzal, rand, rial, riel, riyal, ruble, rupee, rupiah, schilingi, shilling, sol, sucre, taka, tala, tical, tugrik, won, yen, yuan, zaire, or zloty, it is the same thing. Money!

What is money? It is merely a convenient medium of exchange—nothing more and nothing less. Before its invention, mankind used the barter system of trading objects for other objects and/or services. One pig might have been worth five chickens in trade; a week's labor might have yielded one goat, and so on. Can you imagine the problems inherent in carrying around enough livestock or grain to do one's weekly shopping? The barter system worked well until man improved his modes of transportation and started to move about more and to greater distances.

Before coins were invented, such materials and items as gold, silver, small stones, seashells, gems, feathers, and other small and durable objects were used as money. Since the coinage of money, it has appeared in the form of paper and various metals ranging from gold to aluminum and lead, and in many shapes and denominations. With few exceptions, all of it is small and lightweight enough so that it can be carried in quantity in pocket or purse.

Important to remember is that with the exception of gold and silver, no money has any real value aside from its metal content. The value of any ordinary money depends almost totally upon the trust or faith individuals place in it.

In the United States, there was a time when no more paper money was in circulation than there was gold or silver to back it up. One could take paper money to a bank and demand silver or gold in exchange. This certainly is no longer the case, and is one

*Copyright, 1982, by American Federation of Astrologers, Inc.

major reason for the dollar's decrease in value. There has been a loss of trust in it mainly because there is so much more paper in circulation than gold or silver in reserve. (In 1933, the United States dropped the gold standard and went to what amounts to a "paper standard" which is called by some a "managed, floating-exchange-rate system.")

During the Civil War, the South in particular experienced severe problems with its unsecured paper money. Late in the war, it is said that it took a wagon load of Confederate money to buy a wagon load of supplies for its soldiers.

Considering that the value of money is mainly a matter of public trust, confidence, faith, and belief, it might be accurate to state that wealth is quite importantly an attitude, a state of mind. On this premise, it would be possible to state that many of you are wealthy who do not, at this moment, possess an abundance of money. Many intangibles—intelligence, talent, good health, appearance, energy, efficiency, enthusiasm, optimism, etc.—figure importantly in evaluating anyone's total worth. These positive attributes can contribute markedly to any individual's own sense or feeling of wealth and riches, but not very much to others' evaluations of that person's financial status.

Normally, others judge everyone's level of prosperity mainly by the way they dress, the automobile they drive, their residence, and their general lifestyle. Maybe it is unfair and unfortunate, but it is mainly the external trappings which cause one to be labeled as poor, average or rich.

It is common to hear that money cannot buy happiness, and this is true; however, it is also true that money can buy a lot of items and services which can quite positively contribute to happiness. Certainly there are some rich people who are not happy, but there are far more poor people who are not happy.

Some would say that a desire for wealth is purely selfish and patently wrong or sinful. These individuals judge from an incorrect point of view. They believe that money is the root of all evil. The correct quote is:

"The *love* of money is the root of all evil" (1 Timothy 6:10). One does not have to love money to have it, but a desire for it is absolutely necessary. One must have or acquire a money consciousness in order to have any more of it than is absolutely necessary to get by. People who think about money, who understand it, who know its advantages, and who appreciate it are much more likely to attract, acquire, and keep more of it than those who do not. The more one knows about money, their money consciousness, and their own money-making (earning) potentials, the better.

Having money in abundance allows the individual more time and means to help others, whether he does so or not. Those who must or do struggle just to survive seldom are able to be of much help to others or themselves for that matter. While the desire and intent to help others may no doubt be present, the ability to follow through seldom or never is. Strangely enough, there is an element in society which feels that somehow it is noble and necessary to be poor. They live in poverty, think poverty, talk poverty and seem somehow to think that doing so puts them a notch above the rich. One might hear comments such as: "Yes, we are poor and proud of it." "Rich people will never get to heaven." "Our family has always been poor and always will be." Good intentions are admirable, but one never reads a newspaper headline such as this: "John Smith Would Like To Donate A Million Dollars To Favorite Charity." It is only those who actually do such charitable acts who make these headlines.

Earning money always, directly or indirectly, involves some type of selling. In all the world only two classifications of things can be sold or bought—products and services. What precisely do you have to sell? The only accurate answer is your time. While your time may be spent utilizing or expressing a skill, talent or other special ability, you are paid only for your time. What you do while selling your time and how well you do it importantly determines the amount you are paid; please remember this: you receive no pay whatsoever for what you are capable of doing or what you might have done instead. Is your time "worthless," worth minimum wage, or is it worth hundreds or even thousands of dollars an hour?

Since you cannot create more hours in any day, two possibilities are open to you if you wish to improve your income: 1) You can enhance or increase the value of the time you now sell; or 2) You can sell more time. To help increase the value of your time you now sell, you can do such things as learn to better understand money and how to make it work; stimulate your desire for money; work to motivate yourself; increase your enthusiasm;

improve your efficiency; employ more of your skills, talents, etc. In short, you can make your time more valuable through self-motivation. To sell more time well may mean getting a second job, working overtime or starting a part-time business. Depending upon your needs and energy level, you may wish to do two or more of the above for a time.

Being rich or wealthy simply means that an individual possesses sizeable quantities of money or its equivalent. To state it another way, if you have an abundance of money you are rich. In order for one to be rich, two things must happen (and in this order): 1) you must get money and 2) you must keep it by sensibly limiting spending. This is a two-part process that too many who aspire to riches do not understand. Unfortunately, so many aspirants are not willing or do not know how to put forth enough concentrated energy to get more money, and too many who can and do attract large amounts of it seem unwilling or unable to manage and control it to the point that an "easy-come, easy-go" philosophy soon leaves them back at square one.

Where is your major difficulty with money? Is it in getting more of it or holding on to more of what you get? If you are not at the financial level you would like to be, it has to be either one or the other, or perhaps a combination of the two.

If you honestly desire greater wealth and diligently apply yourself to the goal of understanding your money and that of others, then abundance will be yours. Realistically, the only thing standing in your way is yourself. It is not the economy, the "system," your boss, your mate, your children, your upbringing, or anybody or anything else. If you sincerely desire improvement and are willing to work for it, it will come. Be absolutely assured of this.

Most of us work for someone else, and our level of income very much depends upon what the boss thinks of the value of our services. Too often we foolishly reason like the young man who sat in front of a jukebox and said, "Play me a record and then I'll put a quarter in." Or the person who stood before a cold fireplace and said, "Give me heat now and later I'll put in some wood and light it."

Consider a more realistic example as it might apply to someone you know—maybe even you. A young person was overheard complaining to a fellow worker: "I've just about had it up to here with this company. Look at this check; same as last month's! That fool boss of mine just will not give me a raise. And would you believe it, he had the gall to ask me why my efficiency had been down the last few months? If they'd give me a raise, I'd gladly show them what a valuable employee I really can be."

It would seem this poor misguided person expects the music first or the warmth in advance more or less as a bribe to do the job even satisfactorily. This employee desperately needs to review and change the present chain of thought. Chances are, and sadly so, that if it were mentioned that a raise would be forthcoming soon if he or she would begin immediately to work harder and more efficiently, and with a more positive attitude, the reply likely would be: "Nobody but a fool does something for nothing."

Perhaps that could be a correct statement, but if this employee would just look around, it might be observed that some of those "fools" he mentioned are depositing in the bank that "nothing" they received as a reward for the extra effort they put forth without being forced. And these same "fools" will be enjoying this "nothing" for months and years to come. There is not much reason for sympathy for this complaining employee so long as he persists in his mistaken beliefs. He is only refusing to see, understand, and use one of the infallible laws of the universe: "For every action there is an equal and opposite reaction."

If you push against a wall, it pushes back with an equal amount of pressure; otherwise, you would break through it. Looking at the law from a more applicable standpoint, one finds the following truism applies: We get back exactly what we send out. If we curse others, they curse in return; if we send out a smile, we get back smiles. That is the law. You do not need an elaborate laboratory in order to prove this. Kick your dog and he may bite you; pat his head and watch his tail wag with joy and gratitude. Repeating, but worth doing so: We get back exactly what we send out—often amplified. Who knows exactly why? Probably no one. All we really need to know is that is the way it works; and, from this knowledge, use it for our own and others' benefit.

Consequently, if you try harder, if you put forth more effort, if you markedly increase your efficiency, you are adding to the coffers of your employer, and more money will find its way back to you. It has to; it is the law of action and reaction.

Right away you might say your boss is the exception, that he or she is the kind of person who will selfishly keep all the added gains. This is extremely doubtful; but if this should be the case, you have something very positive going for you. That big plus in your favor is your employer's greed.

You may have some doubts; consider this. If you are making him more money than he requires or expects, he realizes that he can ill-afford to lose your services. He also will understand that you realize your value to him, and that if you are not fairly compensated for the extra effort, one of three things will happen: 1) you will soon begin to reduce your efficiency; 2) in due time you will leave; or 3) someone else will make you a better offer. In any case, he knows that ultimately he will be the greater loser.

You may have to ask for the raise in order to motivate his thinking, but his greed (fear of loss) will help him listen to reason. The odds will favor you strongly if you also are reasonable.

On the other hand, your bargaining position is severely weakened if you are of little but routine value to him. If you are one of the dime-a-dozen types of workers, he will feel the loss of your services will be no great disadvantage. This leaves you with little or no leverage to demand anything. Factually, you may be lucky if you are not fired.

Therefore, it behooves you to try in every way possible to make yourself into the type of employee who can confidently request and get more of what you deserve in your pay envelope. When you get down to facts, you will likely agree that few employers are so bad or unfair as they are sometimes made to look.

Begin immediately to recognize the fact that increased pay is naturally and normally a reward for excellent services rendered *in advance*. Remember this and it is not likely you will ever find yourself hard-pressed in need of fair compensation for your real worth to your employer.

If you are self-employed, whom do you blame if you are not making much money? Obviously and fairly, only yourself. Yes, it is very easy to say your sagging income is the fault of the economy, your competition, public whims, your location, inflation, your employees, and numerous other external factors. Unfortunately, to "pass the buck" hurts mainly you. The whole responsibility to bring about positive change is yours totally. If any of the afore-mentioned factors, or others, are having a negative influence on your income, you must change negative thinking into positive thinking and take some immediate steps to cause change and bring about improvement. In the final analysis, you will need to do one or both of the following: 1) improve or expand your service(s) or 2) offer better or more products competitively priced. General efficiency must be improved, wasteful spending must be cut, new lines of merchandise may need to be added, employees may need to be reassigned to other jobs or to be discharged, a new location may be necessary, prices may need some adjustment, and advertising might need to be changed, increased or cut back. After a careful evaluation, decide what to do and then do it. Start thinking and stop complaining or feeling sorry for yourself. Take full responsibility, for you are the one who must take initial action on changes in order to get in step with the times. Some or all of the comments above may seem overly sophomoric, but you know they are true in essence.

If you are not already rich, your concept of those who are rich or very well off financially may well be that most of them are ultraconservative, difficult to sell, even tight with money. And it is probable that your opinion is not too far from being correct. Most of the rich who have made it on their own learned very early that if one takes care of the pennies, nickels and dimes, the dollars will take care of themselves. Unfortunately, those who have a difficult time financially have not learned this simple truism, which is one of the most important prerequisites to becoming wealthy. What about you? Do you watch the small money; do you get the most for what you spend; do you know how to determine if anything is wastefully expensive; do you have as much control over the outgo as you do over the income? Look for suggestions concerning these and other related matters in the paragraphs that follow.

What makes anything too expensive? What is a good price? First, understand that the price of everything is completely relative. If the general public should come to think a regular candy bar is worth a dollar, then that would be its fair and correct price. No doubt it would be as much in demand as it is at a lower price. By the same token, if the buying public should decide that a candy bar is overpriced at say, twenty-five cents, then it would not sell at that price. If it could not be made and marketed for less than twenty-five cents, then it would rapidly disappear from the marketplace. Of course, most candy manufacturers would offer other items that would sell rather than close down their businesses.

When you are motivated to make any purchase—large or relatively small, but not necessarily mandatory—how can you ascertain if you really can afford the expenditure? The price itself is not the major consideration for deciding if the item is too expensive. The major concern is whether you can afford it. You will be able to better answer after you ask yourself this important question: "What essentials or necessities could I purchase for the same money this item costs?" Another question which might aid you in deciding is this: "How much work (time) will be required to replace the money this will cost?" After answering one or both of these questions honestly, you will know if you can afford to buy. Whether you decline or buy, you will be more willing to accept whatever the consequences might be. Many have found this an excellent and effective exercise to stop impulse buying.

Consider, if you will, the following motivations for spending and you may begin to see why the "truly rich" stay that way while the "temporarily rich" seldom or never do.

1. *A high-quality, expensive automobile is purchased.*

The truly rich person's motivation is this: Quality and comfort is desired. The automobile is a good investment with many practical applications. It will give good service for years; a replacement will not be necessary for some time.

The temporarily rich buy it in order to impress others. The major motivation is ego gratification; and because of this, it will soon be necessary to replace the automobile because, in the mind of the owner, it will no longer be impressive enough.

2. *An expensive and impressive residence is purchased.*

The truly rich want the property for the comfort and convenience it offers. Besides being an excellent investment, it will be an asset to business since it will lend itself favorably to entertaining business associates as well as friends.

The temporarily rich buy the residence with a desire to impress, perhaps even to make others jealous. This

selfishness and jealousy will cause the owner to experience much difficulty in sharing his good fortune with
others. It well may become more of a worry or liability
than a joy or asset.

3. *Pressure is applied to sell a nonessential luxury item or
    service.*

The truly rich firmly decline to purchase because the item or
service is not necessary. Period.

The temporarily rich purchase in order to "keep up with the
Joneses" and out of a fear that others will think the luxury cannot
be afforded. There is concern that others will start to suspect
they are no longer rich.

4. *Intimidation is attempted in order to elicit a large
    contribution for some civic or political cause.*

The truly rich refuse to be intimidated. Unless the cause really
appeals, no donation will be forthcoming.

The temporarily rich are intimidated into giving, often more
than is "necessary," for fear that others will suspect that he or she
is running out of money and to impress.

Enough of such examples. Allow your imagination to fill in the
many others of a similar nature. Important to note is that the
truly rich individual acts at all times to keep wealth. There is little
if any motivation or attempt solely to impress others. There is a
kind of protective selfishness ever present. For the most part, the
motivation for spending on the part of the temporarily rich is to
gratify ego and to impress.

Some further observations follow. The truly rich always keep
good records of all transactions and frequently or regularly seek
advice and guidance from professionals regarding investments,
bookkeeping and taxes, as well as other important matters. Within
reason, no corners are cut in employing the talents and expertise
of those most qualified to give sound advice in these matters.

The temporarily rich seldom bother with much
record-keeping. Important papers and records are scattered
between office, home, automobile gloveboxes, pockets, and who
knows where else. Advice and assistance in such matters may, at
the last minute, be sought from whoever is available or will work
for the least cost. Unfortunately, these are not the areas where
cost-cutting will pay good dividends.

The truly rich buy at wholesale when possible, ask for discounts, and transact business with friends (even relatives) if there is any financial advantage in doing so (but only for this reason).

The temporarily rich usually pay retail so they can boast about what something costs and impress others. Discounts are seldom asked for because of a mistaken belief that doing so is demeaning or somehow "cheap." Any business done with or through friendships just does not seem enough like the "big time."

The truly rich always count change, check bills, tickets, and statements for accuracy; tip the standard percentage regularly; frequent establishments where quality and good service is available at the best prices; shop during sales; and may even clip and use coupons!

The temporarily rich cannot be bothered with small change, assume figures are correct, tip (through vanity) excessively, frequent places where it is fashionable to be seen; buy at any time, and never, but never use coupons!

The truly rich, even though it may not be mandatory, have a budget and stick with it generally. Regardless of money windfalls, the regular, ongoing expenses are expected to stay within predetermined guidelines.

The temporarily rich seldom have a budget and dislike having to keep up with such mundane matters as the household expenses. To some degree, these expenditures fluctuate widely according to the cash flow—excessively high during good income periods; often skipped, even if important, during less favorable times.

The truly rich very seldom make personal loans to friends or cosign notes for them because it is widely known that mixing friends and personal loans (money) often means the loss of the money and the friendship as well. In the rare instances where a loan is made, it is done by regular legal contracts—with collateral and interest.

The temporarily rich are an "easy touch" mainly because of ego. Others may put them in a compromising position by suggesting that anyone with as much money as they have could not possibly miss the money necessary for a "small loan." Unfortunately, the loan usually becomes a gift.

In addition, the temporarily rich continue to say and/or believe fully in the following: "Don't bother to fill out the guarantee; I know it's going to work right." "No receipt is necessary. We both know that I paid cash in full." "I know my brother will pay me back." "Your check is in the mail." In addition, many may still believe in the Tooth Fairy.

Summary

The rich individual possesses large quantities of tangibles which can be converted to money. Money is a convenient medium of exchange, nothing more and nothing less. Money (paper, coins) has mainly replaced the barter system (trading objects for other objects and/or services). The value of money is established mainly by public trust and faith. The individual may possess personal intangibles—intelligence, talents, good health, appearance, energy, enthusiasm, and optimism—as assets and indicators of wealth. However, others judge wealth mainly by tangible external trappings. To accumulate riches, one must have or develop a money consciousness. Only products and services can be sold. All the individual has to sell is time. To demand more money, one must enhance the value of his time and/or sell more of it. To be rich, one must apply a two-part process: 1) get more money 2) keep more of it. Greater riches can be attracted with a strong determination. Whether employed by others or self-employed, the law of action-reaction applies. One must give more before more is received, but one cannot lose when giving more because the "law" always works. Anyone may become rich, but in order to remain so it may be necessary to become somewhat selfishly protective.

COMPREHENSION TEST

Money Signs, Chapter 1

(Circle the letter preceding the most correct answer)

1. The title of this selection is

 (A) "Money and (Common) Sense."
 (B) "Money and (Good) Sense."
 (C) "Cash and (Common) Sense."
 (D) "Dollars and (Common) Sense."

2. The article is reprinted from a book titled

 (A) *Money Management.*
 (B) *Money Signatures.*
 (C) *Money Signs.*
 (D) *Money Sense.*

3. The author's name is

 (A) Elbert Wade.
 (B) Wade Elbert.
 (C) Albert Wade.
 (D) A. Bert Wade.

4. This article is reprinted from the book's

 (A) Introduction.
 (B) Chapter 6.
 (C) Chapter 1.
 (D) Chapter 11.

5. The selection includes

 (A) subheadings.
 (B) graphics.
 (C) several footnotes.
 (D) a summary.

(NOTE: If you responded incorrectly to even one of these questions, you are not *previewing* adequately. Review "How to Preview a Chapter," in Part II.)

(Write T for true, F for false)

__ 6. Money is much more than a convenient medium of exchange.

__ 7. Before the invention of money, mankind used the barter system.

__ 8. It is unlikely seashells ever were used in lieu of money.

__ 9. "Coinage" is a word related only to the printing of paper money.

__10. Aluminum has never been used in the making of metal coins.

__11. The value of money depends importantly upon the trust and faith individuals place in it.

__12. For many years in the U.S., the circulation of paper money could not exceed the amount of gold or silver necessary to back it.

__13. There has never been a time in the U.S. that a citizen could actually exchange a $20 paper bill for a $20 gold coin.

__14. The U.S. gold standard was dropped in 1944.

__15. Late in the Civil War, a wagon load of Confederate paper money would purchase a train load of supplies.

__16. It might be accurate to state that wealth is primarily an attitude, a state of mind.

__17. Many intangibles—intelligence, good health, gold, optimism, and efficiency—figure in evaluating anyone's total worth.

__18. People tend to judge an individual's prosperity mainly by external trappings.

__19. Contrary to popular belief, money can buy happiness.

__20. Percentage-wise, there are more unhappy rich people than unhappy poor people.

__21. It stands to reason that a desire for money is purely selfish, wrong, and sinful.

__22. Money is the root of all evil.

___23. One cannot accumulate much money unless he loves it.

___24. Those who have money in abundance will assuredly help those less fortunate.

___25. Poverty-ridden individuals always desire to help others even if they cannot.

___26. Some poverty-stricken types may even brag about being poor.

___27. Earning money always—directly or indirectly—involves some type of selling.

___28. Altogether, four classifications of things can be sold or bought.

___29. All any person has to sell, in fact, is his time.

___30. It is common practice that employees are paid on the basis of what they are capable of doing.

___31. Employees seldom, if ever, are paid for what they might or could have done.

___32. Two ways to improve your income are: 1) enhance the value of the time you now sell and 2) create more hours in a day.

___33. Possessing sizable quantities of money or the equivalent entitles an individual to be regarded as wealthy or rich.

___34. To become wealthy, one must both get adequate amounts of money and learn to hold on to a good part of it.

___35. It is probable that what is standing in the way of the typical person's greater wealth is the economy, inflation, or competition.

___36. There is little correlation between an employee's income and the boss's opinion of the value of his services.

___37. Possibly the quickest way to get a raise is to promise the employer greater productivity once the raise is given.

___38. An employee who desires a raise would do well to maintain this philosophy: Nobody but a fool does something for nothing.

___39. One of the infallible laws of the universe is: "For every action there is an equal and opposite reaction."

__40. The concept that many self-made rich persons are conservative with money is more likely true than false.

__41. If a worker becomes more efficient and productive, the law of action and reaction can help to assure a raise.

__42. According to this selection, wealthy individuals take no particular concern about "nickel and dime" matters.

__43. The price alone determines what is too expensive for a particular individual to purchase.

__44. A truly rich individual seldom if ever purchases anything because of a primary motivation to impress others.

__45. The truly rich always contribute to good causes; the temporarily rich almost never do so.

__46. The truly rich normally regard detailed bookkeeping as not being cost-effective.

__47. Due to an innate fear of being cheated, the temporarily-rich always count change and check statements for accuracy.

__48. One seldom loses much if he makes casual loans to friends.

__49. The temporarily rich are typically generous mainly because of guilt relative to having more money than those asking for a hand-out.

__50. Sometimes the temporarily rich even believe in the Tooth Fairy.

(When finished answering the questions, check the answers on the following page.)

Correct Answers for Test

MONEY SIGNS

(Value: 2 points each)

Approximately 4,700 words

1. The correct answer is (D).
2. The correct answer is (C).
3. The correct answer is (A).
4. The correct answer is (C).
5. The correct answer is (D).
6. The correct answer is (F).
7. The correct answer is (T).
8. The correct answer is (F).
9. The correct answer is (F).
10. The correct answer is (F).
11. The correct answer is (T).
12. The correct answer is (T).
13. The correct answer is (F).
14. The correct answer is (F).
15. The correct answer is (F).
16. The correct answer is (T).
17. The correct answer is (F).
18. The correct answer is (T).
19. The correct answer is (F).
20. The correct answer is (F).
21. The correct answer is (F).
22. The correct answer is (F).
23. The correct answer is (F).
24. The correct answer is (F).
25. The correct answer is (F).
26. The correct answer is (T).
27. The correct answer is (T).
28. The correct answer is (F).
29. The correct answer is (T).
30. The correct answer is (F).
31. The correct answer is (T).
32. The correct answer is (F).
33. The correct answer is (T).
34. The correct answer is (T).
35. The correct answer is (F).
36. The correct answer is (F).
37. The correct answer is (F).
38. The correct answer is (F).
39. The correct answer is (T).
40. The correct answer is (T).
41. The correct answer is (T).
42. The correct answer is (F).
43. The correct answer is (F).
44. The correct answer is (T).
45. The correct answer is (F).
46. The correct answer is (F).
47. The correct answer is (F).
48. The correct answer is (F).
49. The correct answer is (F).
50. The correct answer is (T).

PART IV

Develop Your Skills Further

In this section you will learn...

📖 to develop your accelerated reading skills further through even more practical applications

📖 to discover an easy means to estimate the number of words in any type of publication

📖 how to set a reading rate (goal) and determine the time necessary to accomplish your desired goal successfully

📖 how to quarter and mark longer reading matter to maintain a preset pace—and assure your desired accelerated reading speed

📖 techniques for conditioning yourself to actually achieve a faster word-per-minute rate goal

📖 to use the additional advanced practice training which includes nine book-length reading exercises to help you develop reading skills further, with tests to measure comprehension

How to Estimate the Number of Words

In order to determine your words-per-minute rate for the materials you read outside this book, it is necessary that you have some quick and relatively accurate means for ascertaining the number of words in a given publication.

It is quite easy to learn the approximate word length of a book or article by employing the methods outlined below.

1. Determine the average number of words on a typical full page. You may do this by either of two means.

   a. Actually count all the words on what seems to be a typical page. Count all words as one no matter how few or how many letters. Also count all numerals, symbols, formulas, etc., as single words.

   b. A quicker means is to count the words on four full lines and then divide the total by 4 to get the average number of words per line. (For paperback titles, the average usually is between 10 and 15.) Next, count the number of lines on a full page (whether full lines or not) and multiply the number of lines (usually between 26 and 35) by the average number of words per line. This will give you a close estimate of the number of words on a page.

2. Find out how many pages there are in the entire text of the book, or the part you will read. When getting a word count for the whole book, be careful to note on what page the text actually begins. Sometimes it starts on the page numbered 1, but often it starts on page 5, 7, 9, 15, or later. Deduct these pages as well as any numbered pages that are solely graphics—maps, photographic inserts, etc.

Part IV: Develop Your Skills Further

196

3. Multiply the total number of pages of text (or the part you will read) by the average number of words per page.

4. Round this figure off to the lower thousand. For example, if you come up with 53,955, just call it an even 53,000 words. This adjusts the figure somewhat for accuracy by allowing for late starts on certain pages and early finishes at the ends of chapters or sections.

Estimating the number of words on a page of "non typical" books, magazines, and newspapers is very simple if you have a ruler handy.

Measure off a vertical inch of print. Count the words it contains. Then, measure the inches on a page and multiply by the number of words. Multiply this product by the number of pages and you will have the word count.

Set Rate; Get Total Reading Time

Once you know the approximate number of words in an assignment, it will be necessary to determine the rate at which you are going to read, which, in turn, will give the total reading time. To a large degree, the rate you set will be determined by your progress to date. Some of you will be reading only two or three times your beginning rate; others will have achieved far greater speeds.

To review how to set a pace, assume you are going to read a book at a rate three times faster than your beginning average. If that rate was 200 words per minute, you would set 600 as a goal. How long will you have to read a book containing 36,000 words?

To find out, divide the projected rate into the total number of words in the book. In this case, divide 600 into 36,000. The answer is 60. This means the entire book must be read in 60 minutes in order to maintain an average rate of 600 words per minute. Apply this formula to any book you plan to Accele*read*.

Quarter and Mark

Now that you know the total amount of time allotted for reading the whole text, it is necessary to divide the assignment into four equal parts so that you may more evenly allocate time to the entire book for better overall comprehension, and, at the same time, maintain the pace necessary to finish on time. Therefore, it is suggested that you "quarter and mark" the book. This means you will be dividing the text (excluding introductory front matter) into four equal parts.

Cut or tear a sheet of paper into four strips about 6 to 8 inches long, which will serve as bookmarks. Across the narrow end of each strip, write the number of minutes that you have allotted for each quarter. For this example, a total of 60 minutes is allowed. On the first strip write the number 15, on the second 30, on the third 45, and on the fourth 60. The strips are then inserted bookmark fashion at the pages that are one quarter, one half, and three quarters through the text. The last strip is placed at the final page. The strips may be inserted "stairstep fashion" so that the first is lowest and the others are graduated, allowing all to be clearly readable without opening the book to their places. If you "quarter and mark" in this manner, you will be able to know how well you are doing time-wise as you read. At 15 minutes, you should be at or past the 15-minute marker, and so on. These "reminders" will assure that you do not get bogged down and spend, for example, 30 minutes in the first quarter and then have to rush to complete the other quarters.

DETERMINE PACE

Next, in order to determine the pace you should maintain throughout the book (on the average), note the number of pages in one quarter. Suppose there are 30 pages. Continuing with the example mentioned earlier, this would mean you have approximately 30 seconds to cover each page, based upon the 15 minutes allotted for each quarter of text. (Of course, with each book you have a varying amount of time per page, depending on the number of words, pages, and the rate at which you want to read the particular book.)

"Condition" Yourself

Assuming that you have already previewed the book thoroughly, you are now ready to "condition" yourself for the reading of this book by covering a few pages in the amount of time you have set per page.

Using the Two-Stop Method you have practiced earlier, read several pages (perhaps the first chapter) being careful to spend the amount of time per page as planned. (Of course, a clock or stopwatch will be necessary.) Get the "feel" of covering the printed lines at this pace. Comprehension may not be as good as you would like since you will, of necessity, be dividing attention between reading and checking time. Do not worry, however, since you will repeat these pages soon.

Begin Accele*reading*

When you finish this important preparatory practice of the first chapter, question yourself to see what you did or did not comprehend. Write down the time, return to the first page, and begin reading, noting time less frequently. Rest assured that you are maintaining a satisfactory pace if you remove the first marker at approximately the time-lapse it indicates. (If you are behind, you need to speed up immediately; if you are ahead time-wise and feel satisfied with your comprehension, continue at the same pace or speed up a bit.) If you feel you are missing a few details at the pace you have set, remember that you are "saving" enough time to check back should the need arise. Also remember that "checking back" will become less and less necessary as you gain more and more confidence in your newly acquired reading methods and techniques. Did you drive as well when you first got behind the wheel as you do now after having gained both experience and confidence?

If possible, finish the entire book at one sitting; doing so will benefit overall comprehension. Note the time to the nearest minute when you complete reading. Divide the total number of whole minutes into the total number of words in the book to determine your reading speed in words-per-minute.

Repeat this process with more and more books. You will find that with practice both speed and comprehension, in particular, will improve. Be patient; do not defeat yourself with a negative attitude. With practice, you can become an Accelerated Reader.

Book-Length Assignments

The following pages include seven "outside" book-length reading exercises (including comprehension tests for each) to help you retain the reading speed you have accomplished to date, and to encourage you to push for even higher rates and better comprehension. However, you are cautioned not to try for unrealistic rates which result in very little or no real comprehension. Speed is one thing; comprehension is another. In learning to read faster, your motivation should be to "impress" yourself, not others.

These novels were selected because they are highly regarded works of literature by noteworthy authors, well written, interesting, relatively short, and widely available in libraries and bookstores, at a moderate price. (Some may be on your bookshelf already.)

While the assignments are numbered, you may read the books in whatever order is most convenient. However, you should Accele*read* all of them, even if you may have read them before. If you have read any or all of them, you were not likely reading at your present rate, and you may not have been tested for comprehension.

Before reading each, you should conduct a good preview (See "How to Preview a Book of Fiction" in Part II), and follow all of the steps outlined above, except determining word count since this is given with each assignment.

Assignment 1: *Animal Farm,* by George Orwell (Approximately 34,000 words)

Assignment 2: *The Pearl,* by John Steinbeck (Approximately 34,000 words)

Assignment 3: *The Time Machine,* by H.G. Wells (Approximately 39,000 words)

Assignment 4: *The Light In the Forest,* by Conrad Richter (Approximately 45,000 words)

Assignment 5: *The Turn of the Screw,* by Henry James (Approximately 53,000 words)

Assignment 6: *A Journey to the Center of the Earth,* by Jules Verne (Approximately 84,000 words)

Assignment 7: *Mutiny on the Bounty,* by Charles Nordhoff and James Norman Hall (Approximately 130,000 words)

Assignment 8: *Think and Grow Rich* by Napoleon Hill (Approximately 75,000 words)

Assignment 9: *The Death of Common Sense* by Philip K. Howard (Approximately 51,000 words)

For additional practice, you may wish to reread all or some of these books at somewhat higher rates than the first reading. Push both for speed and comprehension; you could be pleasantly surprised with what you can do.

To maintain and improve your faster, more effective reading techniques, it is suggested that you continue to read more and more without falling back into your slower habits.

COMPREHENSION TEST

Animal Farm, by George Orwell

Character Identification (2 points each)

___ 1. Benjamin   (A) owner of Manor Farm

___ 2. Boxer   (B) the prize Middle White boar

___ 3. Mollie   (C) a donkey, oldest farm animal

___ 4. Mr. Jones   (D) the powerful workhorse

___ 5. Muriel   (E) Napoleon's mouthpiece, hatchet man

___ 6. Napoleon   (F) the foolish, vain, white mare

___ 7. Pilkington   (G) the white goat

___ 8. Old Major   (H) owner of a nearby farm

___ 9. Snowball   (I) supreme ruler of Animal Farm

___10. Squealer   (J) one-time contender for ruler

Multiple Choice (3 points each)

(Circle the letter preceding the most correct answer)

1. George Orwell's *Animal Farm* is most accurately described as

   (A) a "fairy story".
   (B) a commentary on Marxism.
   (C) an historical novel.

2. Old Major insisted to his comrades that

   (A) whatever goes upon two legs is a friend.
   (B) whatever goes upon four legs or has wings is a friend.
   (C) whatever goes upon four legs or has wings is an enemy.

3. When Moses, the tame raven, told the animals of Sugarcandy Mountain that,

   (A) the pigs argued otherwise.
   (B) all the animals believed him.
   (C) none of the animals believed him.

4. The farmhouse was

   (A) burned to the ground.
   (B) occupied by some of the animals.
   (C) preserved as a museum by the animals.

5. The animals drew up a set of commandments by which all animals would live, but these commandments were changed when

   (A) the majority of the comrades voted to alter them.
   (B) they did not work.
   (C) the pigs gained control through their leader.

6. In harvesting the hay, the pigs

   (A) were the leaders and did no actual work.
   (B) did nearly all of the work.
   (C) did only their share of the work.

7. The Sunday ceremonies included

   (A) hoisting the horn and hoof flag.
   (B) reading the commandments.
   (C) drinking alcohol.

8. Two opposing philosophies for accomplishing the work on the farm (Committees of Education) were set forth by

   (A) Boxer and Mollie.
   (B) Moses and Squealer.
   (C) Snowball and Napoleon.

9. When Mr. Jones and his friends returned to recapture the farm, the animals' strategy was directed by

   (A) Napoleon, who was named after the Frenchman.
   (B) Snowball, who had read *Julius Caesar.*
   (C) Moses, the new Master.

10. At first mention of the windmill,

    (A) Snowball gave his support.
    (B) Napoleon gave his support.
    (C) both Snowball and Napoleon gave their support.

11. Napoleon won leadership from Snowball by

    (A) a vote of all the comrades.
    (B) killing Snowball.
    (C) driving Snowball away from the farm with the dogs he had raised from puppies.

12. After Snowball was subdued, Napoleon

    (A) refused to build the windmill.
    (B) attributed the windmill idea to Mr. Jones.
    (C) claimed the windmill idea was his own.

13. When the pigs began to sleep in beds, they argued that the fourth commandment was

    (A) against sheets only.
    (B) amended.
    (C) completely unconstitutional.

14. Napoleon blamed the destruction of the windmill on

    (A) Mr. Jones.
    (B) Snowball.
    (C) the lazy animals.

15. After the successful expulsion of Mr. Jones, the first attempt at rebellion was led by the

    (A) hens.
    (B) dogs.
    (C) birds.

16. The animal that actually modified the commandments on the side of the barn was

    (A) Napoleon.
    (B) Prince.
    (C) Squealer.

17. After the execution of some of the animals, one commandment was

    (A) noted to read, "No animal shall kill another animal without cause."
    (B) removed from the list of commandments.
    (C) disregarded completely.

18. During Frederick's attack against the farm, the animals

    (A) were defeated.
    (B) were successful, but the windmill was destroyed.
    (C) were able to save the windmill from destruction.

19. When the farm was declared a Republic, the animals elected a president and

    (A) Napoleon was the only candidate.
    (B) Squealer was elected.
    (C) Snowball became Chief Executive.

20. Later, Boxer

    (A) became disgusted and ran away from the farm.
    (B) murdered Napoleon.
    (C) was sold to the slaughterer.

21. As time passed, Squealer's figures demonstrated to the animals that

    (A) things were getting better.
    (B) things had been getting worse for them all along.
    (C) Napoleon had deceived.

22. The idea of the Animal Farm

    (A) caught on in England.
    (B) was unsuccessful in England.
    (C) spread into many countries.

23. The sheep normally cried "Four legs good, two legs bad," but they changed their tune to "Four legs good, two legs better" when

    (A) Jones recaptured the farm.
    (B) the pigs walked on their hind legs.
    (C) the hens took control of the farm.

24. When the commandments were finally removed from their normal place, they were replaced with this sign:

    (A) "All animals are equal, but some animals are more equal than others"
    (B) "Animals clearly are not equal"
    (C) "Some animals are equal to humans"

25. When the pigs finally triumphed, they

    (A) changed the name back to Manor Farm.
    (B) retained the name Animal Farm.
    (C) changed the name to Pig Co-Operative.

List (1 point each)

List any five of the seven original "commandments."

1.

2.

3.

4.

5.

(When finished answering the questions, check the answers on the following page.)

Correct Answers for Test

ANIMAL FARM

Entire book is approximately 34,000 words

Character Identification (2 points each)

1. The correct answer is (C).
2. The correct answer is (D).
3. The correct answer is (F).
4. The correct answer is (A).
5. The correct answer is (G).
6. The correct answer is (I).
7. The correct answer is (H).
8. The correct answer is (B).
9. The correct answer is (J).
10. The correct answer is (E).

Multiple Choice (3 points each)

1. The correct answer is (B).
2. The correct answer is (B).
3. The correct answer is (A).
4. The correct answer is (B).
5. The correct answer is (C).
6. The correct answer is (A).

7. The correct answer is (A).
8. The correct answer is (C).
9. The correct answer is (B).
10. The correct answer is (A).
11. The correct answer is (C).
12. The correct answer is (C).
13. The correct answer is (A).
14. The correct answer is (B).
15. The correct answer is (A).
16. The correct answer is (C).
17. The correct answer is (A).
18. The correct answer is (B).
19. The correct answer is (A).
20. The correct answer is (C).
21. The correct answer is (A).
22. The correct answer is (B).
23. The correct answer is (B).
24. The correct answer is (A).
25. The correct answer is (A).

List (1 point each)

Any five of the following answers are correct: Two legs, an enemy/Four legs or wings, a friend/No clothes/No sleeping in beds/No alcohol/No killing other animals/All animals equal.

COMPREHENSION TEST

The Pearl, by John Steinbeck

Character Identification (2 points each)

__1. Kino   (A) Kino's wife

__2. Apolina   (B) Kino's son

__3. Coyotito   (C) Juana's brother-in-law

__4. Juana   (D) a fisherman

__5. Juan Tomas   (E) Juan Tomas's fat wife

True or False (Write T for true, F for false) (2 points each)

__ 1. Kino was probably of the Catholic faith.

__ 2. It is obvious their home was made of mud or brick.

__ 3. Coyotito was, unfortunately, stung by a giant centipede.

__ 4. Their residence apparently was on or near the beach.

__ 5. Kino's ancestors had once been great composers of songs.

__ 6. The little baby slept in a hanging animal skin.

__ 7. Juana prepared corncakes for the morning repast.

__ 8. Kino was about fifty years old, strong, and had black hair.

__ 9. The setting of the book is in a Latin country.

__10. Pulque is a delicious sauce to be poured over corncakes.

__11. When his young son was stung, Kino went into a rage but as, nevertheless, most helpful.

__12. The villagers all knew that the sting of a scorpion meant certain death.

__13. Obviously, the doctor was very professional and ethical.

__14. Kino and his wife were completely alone when they first went for the doctor.

__15. There were six beggars in front of the church who seemed to know everything in town.

__16. It is obvious that the doctor was a poor man of modest tastes.

__17. Kino offered eight small "seed pearls" as payment to get the doctor to come.

__18. Kino had obtained a canoe (his sole possession) in a trade.

__19. Pearls tend to grow around grains of sand in the folds of the flesh inside oysters.

__20. Juana prayed they would find a large pearl so they could afford some new, more impressive furniture.

__21. The approximate size of the prize pearl was that of a sea gull's egg.

__22. Very few inhabitants of the village actually learned of Kino's find.

__23. His special pearl was called "the Pearl of the Universe."

__24. The doctor's eyes were described as "resting in ham mocks."

__25. There were many agents who bought pearls but, in fact, only one real buyer.

__26. Kino's wonderful find brought much good fortune to his village.

__27. Juana and Kino had been married in the church.

__28. From the pearl's sale, the one thing Kino wanted most was a good shotgun.

__29. Kino's fondest dreams of wealth centered only around the material and tangible.

__30. The doctor came later to treat the child mainly because of a deep-seated feeling of duty.

__31. The good doctor gave the child a treatment that was sorely needed.

__32. At first, Kino buried the large pearl in the corner of the room.

__33. The good doctor made no attempt to trick Kino into revealing the location of the valuable pearl.

__34. Some time later, Kino concealed the pearl in the baby's bed.

__35. Absolutely no attempt was made to steal the pearl the first night.

__36. According to the book, La Paz was Kino's home village.

__37. Less-than-honest dealers called the pearl "fool's gold."

__38. Kino was offered 1,000, then 500, and finally 20,000 pesos.

__39. Juana's attempt to dispose of the pearl failed as did an attempt to steal it.

__40. After Kino killed one man, he and his family fled into the mountains for safety following the destruction of their boat and home.

__41. In their escape, they were followed by four trackers.

__42. Kino eventually killed all his pursuers; his wife and baby remained unharmed.

__43. The remaining family members returned to La Paz after burying the baby in the mountains.

__44. Upon returning home, Kino threw the large pearl back into the gulf.

__45. The moral of this story is: "Wealth is the key to happiness."

(When finished answering the questions, check the answers on the following page.)

Correct Answers for Test

THE PEARL

(Value: 2 points each)

Entire book is approximately 34,000 words

Character Identification

1. The correct answer is (D).
2. The correct answer is (E).
3. The correct answer is (B).
4. The correct answer is (A).
5. The correct answer is (C).

True or False

1. The correct answer is (T).
2. The correct answer is (F).
3. The correct answer is (F).
4. The correct answer is (T).
5. The correct answer is (T).
6. The correct answer is (F).
7. The correct answer is (T).
8. The correct answer is (F).
9. The correct answer is (T).
10. The correct answer is (F).
11. The correct answer is (F).
12. The correct answer is (F).
13. The correct answer is (F).
14. The correct answer is (F).
15. The correct answer is (F).
16. The correct answer is (F).
17. The correct answer is (T).
18. The correct answer is (F).
19. The correct answer is (T).

20. The correct answer is (F).
21. The correct answer is (T).
22. The correct answer is (F).
23. The correct answer is (F).
24. The correct answer is (T).
25. The correct answer is (T).
26. The correct answer is (F).
27. The correct answer is (F).
28. The correct answer is (F).
29. The correct answer is (F).
30. The correct answer is (F).
31. The correct answer is (F).
32. The correct answer is (T).
33. The correct answer is (F).
34. The correct answer is (F).
35. The correct answer is (F).
36. The correct answer is (T).
37. The correct answer is (T).
38. The correct answer is (F).
39. The correct answer is (T).
40. The correct answer is (T).
41. The correct answer is (F).
42. The correct answer is (F).
43. The correct answer is (F).
44. The correct answer is (T).
45. The correct answer is (F).

COMPREHENSION TEST

THE TIME MACHINE, BY H.G. WELLS

Multiple Choice (2 points each)

(Circle the letter preceding the most correct answer)

1. The Time Traveler spent a great deal of time in what century?

    (A) 802,701 A.D.
    (B) 802,701 B.C.
    (C) 1,000,000 B.C.
    (D) 1,000,000 A.D.

2. He first demonstrated his Time Machine by

    (A) bringing back two flowers.
    (B) making it roar.
    (C) making a model of it disappear.
    (D) discussing its merits at length.

3. His fantastic machine worked in the

    (A) first dimension.
    (B) second dimension.
    (C) third dimension.
    (D) fourth dimension.

4. The dimension mentioned above is defined as the dimension of

    (A) length.
    (B) breadth.
    (C) depth.
    (D) time.

5. His first Time Machine was in the making for almost

    (A) 20 years.
    (B) 10 years.
    (C) 2 years.
    (D) 1 year.

6. The Time Traveler invited some of his guests to return the following

    (A) Monday.
    (B) Thursday.
    (C) Sunday.
    (D) Tuesday.

7. When the guests arrived for dinner, the host was

    (A) ill.
    (B) absent.
    (C) intoxicated.
    (D) present to greet them.

8. The host appeared

    (A) happy.
    (B) disheveled.
    (C) unfriendly.
    (D) most content.

9. The Time Traveler had just returned from

    (A) a vacation.
    (B) a trip in his machine.
    (C) a trip into time.
    (D) both (B) and (C).

10. The Time Traveler agreed to relate his fantastic story if there were no

    (A) skeptics present.
    (B) time restrictions.
    (C) interruptions.
    (D) questions asked.

11. Since the hour of 4 in the afternoon, he had lived the following number of days:

    (A) 16
    (B) 8
    (C) 20
    (D) 100

12. He called the seat of his machine a

    (A) seat.
    (B) saddle.
    (C) chair.
    (D) platform.

13. He operated his machine by means of control

    (A) knobs.
    (B) sticks.
    (C) levers.
    (D) wires.

14. He described the sensations of time traveling as

    (A)   unpleasant.
    (B)   boring.
    (C)   pleasant.
    (D)   monotonous.

15. On completely stopping his machine, he found himself

    (A)   in a hailstorm.
    (B)   in a vacuum.
    (C)   in a trance.
    (D)   very ill.

16. The first beings he met were described as

    (A)   tall, beautiful, and dark.
    (B)   short, frail, and very exquisite.
    (C)   evil, harsh, and unkind.
    (D)   tall, frail, and quite sensitive.

17. To safeguard his machine against tampering, the Time Traveler

    (A)   removed the keys.
    (B)   unscrewed the levers.
    (C)   frightened the onlookers away.
    (D)   electrified the controls.

18. The upper-world creatures were called

    (A)   Morlocks.
    (B)   the Eloi.
    (C)   Utopians.
    (D)   humanoids.

19. These upper-world creatures ate mainly

    (A)   fresh fruit.
    (B)   canned fruit.
    (C)   bitter fruit.
    (D)   frozen fruit.

20. The upper-world creatures sat mainly on

    (A)   the floor.
    (B)   cushions.
    (C)   stones.
    (D)   both (A) and (B)

21. They demonstrated a pronounced

    (A)   lack of education.
    (B)   lack of fear.
    (C)   lack of interest.
    (D)   lack of energy.

22. There were no boundary lines or fences. In fact, the whole earth seemingly had become

    (A) a pasture.
    (B) a field.
    (C) a garden.
    (D) a meadow.

23. The Time Traveler was in this strange world for

    (A) two weeks.
    (B) eight days.
    (C) one day.
    (D) two days.

24. The green porcelain building at one time had been

    (A) a museum.
    (B) a laboratory.
    (C) a meeting hall.
    (D) a library.

25. The three useful items which he found in the building mentioned above were

    (A) wire, dynamite, and matches.
    (B) camphor, matches, and books.
    (C) matches, camphor, and an iron bar.
    (D) an iron bar, camphor, and olive oil.

26. At first he thought the government of this place to be a form of

    (A) democracy.
    (B) socialism.
    (C) communism.
    (D) monarchism.

27. The Time Traveler first met Weena when he

    (A) saved her from drowning.
    (B) arrived on the scene.
    (C) was about to depart.
    (D) saved her from the enemy.

28. Weena is described as being

    (A) about 21 years old.
    (B) a little goddess.
    (C) exactly like a child in her actions.
    (D) most unhappy.

29. Weena and her people seemed to

    (A) fear the daylight.
    (B) fear the darkness.
    (C) be afraid constantly.
    (D) be unafraid.

30. The weather of this "Golden Age" as compared to that of the Time Traveler's Age was

    (A) much hotter.
    (B) much colder.
    (C) much the same.
    (D) much more unsettled.

31. He first encountered the underground beings

    (A) in a well.
    (B) in a darkened gallery.
    (C) on a hillside.
    (D) in the White Sphinx.

32. The round, well-like openings probably were

    (A) part of a ventilation system.
    (B) mineral wells.
    (C) water wells.
    (D) oil wells.

33. The underworld creatures were called

    (A) the Eloi.
    (B) Weenians.
    (C) Morlocks.
    (D) Creektians.

34. Apparently these creatures feared only

    (A) matches.
    (B) electricity.
    (C) darkness.
    (D) light in any form.

35. The only supplies the Time Traveler had brought with him included

    (A) a camera.
    (B) a jar of camphor.
    (C) matches.
    (D) pipe tobacco.

36. Weena regarded the Time Traveler's pockets as

    (A)   a puzzle.
    (B)   unnecessary.
    (C)   vases for floral decorations.
    (D)   both (A) and (C).

37. The Time Traveler reasoned that in relation to the Morlocks the Eloi were only

    (A)   slaves.
    (B)   fatted cattle.
    (C)   servants.
    (D)   fools.

38. He had planned for Weena

    (A)   a trip to his time.
    (B)   freedom from fear.
    (C)   better living conditions.
    (D)   a new wardrobe.

39. The Green Palace primarily was constructed of

    (A)   lead.
    (B)   glass.
    (C)   stone.
    (D)   porcelain.

40. From one of the machines in the museum, he secured

    (A)   a lever.
    (B)   a mace.
    (C)   a weapon.
    (D)   a tool that functioned like all of the above.

41. He found the books in the library

    (A)   very useful.
    (B)   old and torn.
    (C)   outdated.
    (D)   in excellent condition.

42. Other useful items found in the Green Palace included

    (A)   dynamite and caps.
    (B)   matches and camphor.
    (C)   matches and dynamite.
    (D)   caps and matches.

43. The Time Traveler was saved from the hordes of Morlocks by

    (A)   a thunderstorm.
    (B)   a falling star.
    (C)   a forest fire.
    (D)   an earthquake.

44. Weena apparently

    (A)   ran away.
    (B)   was captured by the Morlocks.
    (C)   was left in the woods.
    (D)   experienced both (B) and (C).

45. When the Time Traveler returned to the Sphinx, he discovered

    (A)   Weena waiting for him.
    (B)   the bronze doors open.
    (C)   his machine had vanished.
    (D)   both (A) and (B).

46. When the Morlocks attacked again, he found

    (A)   he could not strike his matches.
    (B)   he could not fix the levers.
    (C)   the iron bar useful.
    (D)   both (A) and (B).

47. Fixing the levers finally, he traveled in time to

    (A)   the immediate past.
    (B)   the distant future.
    (C)   the near future.
    (D)   the far past.

48. His first stop then was on

    (A)   a hillside.
    (B)   an island.
    (C)   a desolate beach.
    (D)   a desert.

49. The creature he saw there resembled a

    (A)   giant crab.
    (B)   giant fish.
    (C)   large serpent.
    (D)   large falcon.

50. In the Epilogue, the Time Traveler is

    (A)   in a mental hospital.
    (B)   again traveling in time.
    (C)   seated in his home.
    (D)   building another machine.

(When finished answering the questions, check the answers on the following page.)

Correct Answers for Test

THE TIME MACHINE

(Value: 2 points each)

Entire book is approximately 39,000 words

1. The correct answer is (A).
2. The correct answer is (C).
3. The correct answer is (D).
4. The correct answer is (D).
5. The correct answer is (C).
6. The correct answer is (B).
7. The correct answer is (B).
8. The correct answer is (B).
9. The correct answer is (D).
10. The correct answer is (C).
11. The correct answer is (B).
12. The correct answer is (B).
13. The correct answer is (C).
14. The correct answer is (A).
15. The correct answer is (A).
16. The correct answer is (B).
17. The correct answer is (B).
18. The correct answer is (B).
19. The correct answer is (A).
20. The correct answer is (D).
21. The correct answer is (C).
22. The correct answer is (C).
23. The correct answer is (B).
24. The correct answer is (A).
25. The correct answer is (C).
26. The correct answer is (C).
27. The correct answer is (A).
28. The correct answer is (C).
29. The correct answer is (B).
30. The correct answer is (A).
31. The correct answer is (B).
32. The correct answer is (A).
33. The correct answer is (C).
34. The correct answer is (D).
35. The correct answer is (C).
36. The correct answer is (D).
37. The correct answer is (B).
38. The correct answer is (A).
39. The correct answer is (D).
40. The correct answer is (D).
41. The correct answer is (B).
42. The correct answer is (B).
43. The correct answer is (C).
44. The correct answer is (D).
45. The correct answer is (B).
46. The correct answer is (D).
47. The correct answer is (B).
48. The correct answer is (C).
49. The correct answer is (A).
50. The correct answer is (B).

COMPREHENSION TEST

THE LIGHT IN THE FOREST, BY CONRAD RICHTER

Character Identification (2 points each)

1.	Harry Butler	(A)	True Son's cousin and friend
2.	Little Crane	(B)	red-haired army sergeant
3.	Bejance	(C)	Indian who adopted Johnny
4.	Myra Butler	(D)	Indian-hater
5.	Del Hardy	(E)	younger brother of Johnny
6.	Gordie	(F)	loaned clothes to True Son
7.	Uncle Wilse	(G)	Indian married to white girl
8.	Cuyloga	(H)	mother of kidnapped son
9.	Half Arrow	(I)	Johnny's real father
10.	Alec	(J)	Negro slave

Multiple Choice (4 points each)

(Circle the letter preceding the most correct answer)

1. True Son had lived with the Indians for

    (A) five years.
    (B) four years.
    (C) seven years.
    (D) twelve years.

2. The rescue party, sent into the wilderness to bring back the white captives, was led by Colonel

    (A) Bouquet.
    (B) Sullivan.
    (C) Elder.
    (D) Broadhead.

3. Rather than be handed over to his white parents, True Son attempted to take his own life by

    (A) drowning.
    (B) cutting his wrists.
    (C) eating deadly roots.
    (D) jumping off a cliff.

4. When True Son first saw his white father,

   (A) he was impressed with his red hair.
   (B) he felt contempt for this insignificant man.
   (C) he laughed inwardly at this fat, jolly farmer.
   (D) he desired very much to embrace him.

5. In Paxton, the "Paxton Boys" had massacred a group of friendly Indians from the

   (A) Tuscarawa tribe.
   (B) Mohican tribe.
   (C) Delaware tribe.
   (D) Conestoga tribe.

6. True Son first took a bath in his white home in accordance with the strong advice of

   (A) Del Hardy.
   (B) his father.
   (C) his mother.
   (D) his Aunt Kate.

7. True Son's new boots

   (A) were like half-hollowed logs.
   (B) wedged his toes and cramped his ankles.
   (C) made him feel as if he stood on millstones.
   (D) were all of the above.

8. If a white man killed an Indian in Paxton, he

   (A) stood trial in Paxton and was acquitted.
   (B) was taken to Philadelphia where he was tried and acquitted.
   (C) was taken to Philadelphia where he was convicted and hanged.
   (D) stood trial in Paxton, was convicted and hanged.

9. The Negro slave

   (A) was a sharecropper.
   (B) spent much of his time hunting and fishing.
   (C) weaved baskets for a living.
   (D) at one time lived with the Delawares.

10. The old Indian, Corn Blade, lived on

   (A) First Mountain.
   (B) Second Mountain.
   (C) Kittaniny Mountain.
   (D) Third Mountain.

11. Myra Butler had first taken to her bed when

    (A)   the savages kidnapped her child.
    (B)   the savages killed and scalped her husband.
    (C)   True Son ran away, taking Gordie with him.
    (D)   she came down with flu.

12. The Lancaster County doctor thought Johnny's illness was

    (A)   nothing but spring fever.
    (B)   an allergy.
    (C)   due to some mysterious forest miasma.
    (D)   a common cold.

13. In order to settle his troubled mind, Johnny's father found it helpful to

    (A)   write in his business ledger.
    (B)   ride in his fields.
    (C)   count his money.
    (D)   both (A) and (C).

14. True Son compared his white mother to

    (A)   a tall willow bending in the wind.
    (B)   a sleek white rat in a cage.
    (C)   a white mare in a meadow.
    (D)   a weak bird in a barren tree.

15. True Son recovered from his illness when

    (A)   his white father gave him a horse.
    (B)   the trees began to bud anew.
    (C)   he heard that some Indians had arrived in town.
    (D)   he took the doctor's medicine.

16. True Son hid the gun, knife, and food

    (A)   in a corn crib.
    (B)   beneath some logs.
    (C)   in a hay mow.
    (D)   in none of these places.

17. After he told some "happy stories," who was killed and scalped?

    (A)   Little Crane
    (B)   Half Arrow
    (C)   Blue Cloud
    (D)   Rain Tree

18. True Son's only regret upon leaving his white home was that

    (A) he would not see Gordie again.
    (B) he had to leave his horse behind.
    (C) he did not get to scalp his uncle.
    (D) he had to leave his real mother.

19. The two Indian boys knew they were nearing the Tuscarawas when

    (A) they passed an old Indian camp.
    (B) they had seen no whites for five days.
    (C) they spotted a stone as high as three men.
    (D) they smelled smoke.

20. The reason the two boys were unable to get more than one boat at the trading post was that

    (A) the white trader would sell only one.
    (B) the dogs chased them away too soon.
    (C) one of the boats was chained.
    (D) they were much too expensive.

(When finished answering the questions, check the answers below.)

Correct Answers for Test

The Light in the Forest

Entire book is approximately 45,000 words

Character Identification (2 points each)

1. The correct answer is (I).
2. The correct answer is (G).
3. The correct answer is (J).
4. The correct answer is (H).
5. The correct answer is (B).
6. The correct answer is (E).
7. The correct answer is (D).
8. The correct answer is (C).
9. The correct answer is (A).
10. The correct answer is (F).

Multiple Choice (4 points each)

1. The correct answer is (D).
2. The correct answer is (A).
3. The correct answer is (C).
4. The correct answer is (B).
5. The correct answer is (D).
6. The correct answer is (D).
7. The correct answer is (D).
8. The correct answer is (C).
9. The correct answer is (C).
10. The correct answer is (D).
11. The correct answer is (A).
12. The correct answer is (C).

13. The correct answer is (D).	17. The correct answer is (A).
14. The correct answer is (B).	18. The correct answer is (A).
15. The correct answer is (C).	19. The correct answer is (C).
16. The correct answer is (C).	20. The correct answer is (C).

COMPREHENSION TEST

THE TURN OF THE SCREW, BY HENRY JAMES

Character/Place Identification (2 points each)

___ 1. Mrs. Grose   (A) a ten-year-old boy

___ 2. Flora   (B) the housekeeper

___ 3. Master Miles   (C) a young girl

___ 4. Bly   (D) a lake

___ 5. Peter Quint   (E) reader of the story

___ 6. Miss Jessel   (F) governess

___ 7. "Miss"   (G) a country estate

___ 8. Harley Street   (H) former man's man

___ 9. Douglas   (I) a former governess

___10. Azof   (J) employer's address

Multiple Choice and True or False (4 points each)

(Circle the letter preceding the most correct answer)

1. This book clearly is a tale of the

    (A) natural.
    (B) unnatural.
    (C) future.
    (D) times.

2. Some of the characters frequently saw

    (A) a lost soul.
    (B) an apparition.
    (C) a bright light.
    (D) dark shadows.

3. The former governess was said to have

   (A) been fired.
   (B) died.
   (C) been re-hired.
   (D) gotten married.

4. The housekeeper was an unusually intelligent person.

   (A) True
   (B) False

5. Peter Quint always appeared wearing well-fitted clothes.

   (A) True
   (B) False

6. Upon the arrival of the new governess, the housekeeper seemed

   (A) pleased.
   (B) displeased.
   (C) angry.
   (D) indifferent.

7. The young boy frequently was referred to as "the little gentleman."

   (A) True
   (B) False

8. The first apparition appeared

   (A) late at night.
   (B) at noon.
   (C) just before nightfall.
   (D) early in the day.

9. The employer had become responsible for

   (A) a small cousin.
   (B) two small cousins.
   (C) a small nephew and a niece.
   (D) a younger brother and a sister.

10. The housekeeper and the governess were the only persons employed in the household.

    (A) True
    (B) False

11. The one unusual condition of the governess's employment was that

    (A) she never trouble her employer.
    (B) she wear white uniforms only.

(C)   she obey the housekeeper.

(D)   she would have no days off.

12. The new governess was shown through the large house by

(A)   Mrs. Grose.

(B)   Flora.

(C)   Quint.

(D)   the maid.

13. There was a total absence of towers on the country house.

(A)   True

(B)   False

14. Bly is described as being

(A)   big, ugly, old, but convenient.

(B)   small, ugly, old, but convenient.

(C)   convenient, but quite uncomfortable.

(D)   big, beautiful, old, but convenient.

15. The strange apparitions were seen by the housekeeper and the governess alike.

(A)   True

(B)   False

16. The letter from Miles' school headmaster

(A)   gave a good report.

(B)   denied his reentry into the school.

(C)   was uncomplimentary.

(D)   both (B) and (C).

17. The youngsters often were poor students.

(A)   True

(B)   False

18. Little Flora was taken away from the country house by

(A)   Quint.

(B)   Mrs. Grose.

(C)   Douglas.

(D)   Miles.

19. "Miss" was completely sane.

(A)   True

(B)   False

(C)   Reader does not know

20. As the story ends, Miles is quite well and safe.

(A)   True

(B)   False

Correct Answers for Test

THE TURN OF THE SCREW

Entire book is approximately 53,000 words

Character/Place Identification
(2 points each)

1. The correct answer is (B).
2. The correct answer is (C).
3. The correct answer is (A).
4. The correct answer is (G).
5. The correct answer is (H).
6. The correct answer is (I).
7. The correct answer is (F).
8. The correct answer is (J).
9. The correct answer is (E).
10. The correct answer is (D).

5. The correct answer is (B).
6. The correct answer is (A).
7. The correct answer is (B).
8. The correct answer is (C).
9. The correct answer is (C).
10. The correct answer is (B).
11. The correct answer is (A).
12. The correct answer is (B).
13. The correct answer is (B).
14. The correct answer is (A).
15. The correct answer is (B).
16. The correct answer is (D).
17. The correct answer is (B).
18. The correct answer is (B).
19. The correct answer is (C).
20. The correct answer is (B).

Multiple Choice and True or False
(4 points each)

1. The correct answer is (B).
2. The correct answer is (B).
3. The correct answer is (B).
4. The correct answer is (B).

COMPREHENSION TEST

A JOURNEY TO THE CENTER OF THE EARTH, BY JULES VERNE

Multiple Choice (2 points each)

(Circle the letter preceding the most correct answer)

1. Professor Hardwigg was attracted to the habit of

    (A) smoking large smelly cigars.
    (B) smoking a pipe with a large tobacco bowl.
    (C) sniffing powdered tobacco (snuff).
    (D) chewing tobacco

2. The voyagers began their dangerous journey in the month of

    (A) May.
    (B) October.
    (C) June.
    (D) August.

3. The Professor's age was reported as being

    (A) 30 years.
    (B) 50 years.
    (C) 39 years.
    (D) 63 years.

4. The total book is divided into

    (A) 13 sections.
    (B) 7 distinct parts.
    (C) 44 chapters.
    (D) 63 subparts and an epilogue.

5. The Professor, uncle of the storyteller, was, by birth,

    (A) an Englishman of noble ancestry.
    (B) a Dutchman.
    (C) a German.
    (D) an Icelander.

6. The Professor had a slight speech impediment. On certain difficult words he would often

    (A) stammer.
    (B) expel excessive air in short, rapid pants.
    (C) lisp markedly.
    (D) purse his lips in a most peculiar fashion.

7. Harry's girlfriend was the Professor's

   (A) granddaughter.
   (B) goddaughter.
   (C) younger sister.
   (D) cousin, twice removed.

8. The "mysterious parchment" fell unexpectedly from

   (A) a tall bookcase in the Professor's study.
   (B) an antique table's center drawer.
   (C) the leaves of an old bound manuscript.
   (D) a centuries-old urn, which the housekeeper dropped and broke.

9. The message written on the old slip of paper was very hard to figure out mainly because it had been written

   (A) upside down.
   (B) in several different languages.
   (C) backwards.
   (D) by a semi-illiterate person.

10. It is probable that the author of this novel had more-than-average knowledge of the science(s) of

    (A) mineralogy.
    (B) geology.
    (C) astrology.
    (D) both (A) and (B).

11. The primary puzzle of the "mysterious document" was, in fact, solved by

    (A) Professor Hardwigg.
    (B) Hans.
    (C) Adolph Reykjavik.
    (D) Harry, the nephew.

12. The loyal guide is often referred to as being

    (A) a heartless bounty hunter.
    (B) an unreliable and dull person.
    (C) the eiderdown hunter.
    (D) None of the above

13. The guide is described as having several outstanding features, including

    (A) curly blonde hair.
    (B) short black hair.
    (C) extremely red, long hair.
    (D) a heavy black beard.

14. The two Ruhmkorf's coils included among the instruments the explorers took along were used as a source of

    (A) heat for food preparation.
    (B) refrigeration to preserve foodstuffs.
    (C) light to illuminate the sunless way.
    (D) entertainment and recreation.

15. Food provisions included concentrated essence of meat and biscuit—enough to last six months. The only liquid refreshment taken along was

    (A) scheidam, a type of liquor.
    (B) water in large gourds.
    (C) fruit juices in thick glass containers.
    (D) beer in lightweight wooden casks.

16. The huge volcano which served as the entry point for the descent to the earth's center was, in height, some

    (A) 20,000 feet.
    (B) 3,000 feet.
    (C) 13,000 feet.
    (D) 5,000 feet.

17. The correct entry point (a certain pit) was ascertained by

    (A) a crude sign made by the earlier explorer.
    (B) the Professor's intuitive insight.
    (C) a shadow created by the sunshine's being interrupted by a particular mountain peak.
    (D) None of the above

18. The indication was that they should enter the

    (A) pit to the far left.
    (B) pit to the far right.
    (C) center pit.
    (D) most elevated pit.

19. The explorers began their actual inner world journey at

    (A) 13 minutes past noon.
    (B) 13 minutes after one in the afternoon.
    (C) a time not actually stated.
    (D) 13 minutes past six in the morning.

20. After descending for some seven hours, they reached the bottom of the abyss. By Harry's calculations, they had traveled downward

    (A) some 3 miles.
    (B) 5,600 feet in all.
    (C) more than an English mile.
    (D) both (B) and (C).

21. Upon checking the barometer, they discovered they were then

    (A) only at sea level.
    (B) well below the earth's actual surface.
    (C) beneath the ocean's surface.
    (D) quite within reach of the earth's center.

22. When the explorers reached a very narrow part of the tunnel, they discovered they had reached a stratum of the earth that was, in fact, a

    (A) rich granite deposit.
    (B) coal mine without miners.
    (C) good source of fresh water.
    (D) diamond mine as yet unexplored.

23. As the adventurers advanced, they were surprised to note that the underworld temperature

    (A) increased sharply and much faster than expected.
    (B) had increased only slightly.
    (C) was dropping with each mile they advanced.
    (D) had remained totally unchanged.

24. Upon retracing their steps to the point of the cross paths, Harry insisted most strongly that they all must

    (A) get a good night of rest before deciding what they should do next.
    (B) split up and explore the other passages.
    (C) go back to Sneffels to revisit the light of day.
    (D) prepare detailed and complete plans to assure reaching the center of the earth.

25. Indicating his unshakable determination to continue on the journey, Professor Hardwigg proposed that

    (A) the three of them settle down for an extended period of rest in order to renew their energies.
    (B) they search most earnestly for a water source.

(C) Harry and Hans return to the surface and he'd continue the perilous adventure alone.

(D) he'd shoot himself if they insisted on returning to Sneffels.

26. The employed guide, as usual, took up his post

    (A) in front of the procession.

    (B) in back of the others.

    (C) between the Professor and Harry.

    (D) alternating between front and rear positions.

27. In a very weakened state, Harry observed (and feared) that the guide apparently was

    (A) deserting them without notification.

    (B) unexplainably drunk and disorderly.

    (C) seemingly near death from lack of water.

    (D) about to attack him and his uncle with a pickaxe.

28. Water finally became available through a small hole made in the tunnel's thick wall by

    (A) a small charge of gunpowder set off by the Professor.

    (B) a crowbar successfully wielded by Hans.

    (C) pickaxes put to the task by all three of the adventurers.

    (D) the use of a special drill included in their supplies.

29. After journeying some 250 miles underground from the point of their departure, the adventurers calculated they were then under the

    (A) Atlantic Ocean.

    (B) Red Sea.

    (C) Pacific Ocean.

    (D) Dead Sea.

30. A most puzzling revelation for the explorers was that the innerworld temperature

    (A) dropped much faster than they had expected.

    (B) seemed to remain unexpectedly tolerable.

    (C) rose much faster than they had expected at first.

    (D) was not nearly as uncomfortable as the stifling humidity.

31. As the journey continued, an unexpected thing happened when

    (A) Harry suddenly departed from his companions

    (B) the Professor disappeared without a trace.

    (C) the guide fell head first into a very deep pit.

    (D) all three voyagers lost contact with one another.

32. In due time, the explorers were

    (A) resigned to the fact they'd never see one another again.
    (B) rescued by other adventurers.
    (C) reunited after a great deal of effort and hardship.
    (D) forced to give up their quest.

33. Discovery of the underworld sea came after the voyagers had successfully endured their tunnel "imprisonment" for a period of

    (A) 3 months and 2 days.
    (B) 47 days.
    (C) 31 days.
    (D) 53 days.

34. Near the newly discovered sea, they encountered a lofty forest of "trees" with straight trunks and tufted tops in shapes like parasols. These were, in fact, gigantic

    (A) mushrooms.
    (B) variations of a type of prehistoric oak.
    (C) petrified rock formations.
    (D) vegetations impossible to classify.

35. Calculations revealed that the innerworld explorers, upon reaching the underworld sea, had achieved a depth of slightly more than

    (A) 50 miles.
    (B) 100 miles.
    (C) 75 miles.
    (D) 200 miles.

36. The craft that they would use to travel on the large body of water was to be

    (A) a fossilized-wood raft constructed by Hans.
    (B) a very large hollowed-out log of pine.
    (C) a carved-out lightweight boat made from mineral stone.
    (D) None of the above

37. On a hook baited with meat, Hans caught a fish which the Professor said was, without question, a

    (A) sturgeon.
    (B) catfish.
    (C) member of a family extinct for ages.
    (D) large carp.

38. As the sea voyage continued, the Professor became increasingly angered and annoyed because

    (A) he felt valuable time was being wasted.
    (B) the sea was much larger than he had calculated.
    (C) he had no desire for a "party of pleasure."
    (D) of all of the above.

39. The voyagers were intensely terrified when they encountered

    (A) a very large whirlpool.
    (B) two sea monsters engaged in a fierce duel.
    (C) a king-sized whale.
    (D) an intense hailstorm.

40. As the over-water voyage continued, the rafters experienced an unbelievably severe

    (A) siege of bone-chilling temperature.
    (B) rise of temperature.
    (C) storm at sea.
    (D) attack by a large sea serpent.

41. During a pedestrian venture on the sea's north shore, Harry and the Professor perceived what they believed to be

    (A) immense animals moving about under mighty trees.
    (B) enormous elephants whose trunks tore down large boughs.
    (C) a giant human being whose height was over 12 feet.
    (D) All of the above

42. Harry hurriedly rushed to pick up an object from the sand. It was

    (A) a rusty sixteenth-century dagger.
    (B) an ancient coin made of the purest gold.
    (C) a compass fashioned of bronze metal.
    (D) a clumsy firearm of a much older vintage.

43. Laboriously carved on a square table of granite, they discovered the following:

    (A) "Arne Saknussemm."
    (B) "Arne S."
    (C) "A. Saknussemm."
    (D) "A.S."

44. Further progress to the earth's center was clearly blocked by

    (A) numerous fierce animals.
    (B) an enormous mass of granite rock.
    (C) doubts inherent within the explorers.
    (D) a narrow bottomless pit.

45. The suggestion to use gunpowder to blast away the blocking stone in the "entrance" tunnel was proposed

    (A) by the Professor.
    (B) by Harry.
    (C) by Hans.
    (D) after a group discussion and mutual decision.

46. After the explosion, a kind of earthquake resulted that opened a mighty abyss that

    (A) began to swallow the inland sea.
    (B) created a torrent, dragging the raft downward with it.
    (C) caused both (A) and (B).
    (D) created but little concern for the explorers.

47. In time, the downward movement ceased and the raft and travelers were

    (A) left awash on a rocky beach.
    (B) ascending rapidly on rising water in a narrow well.
    (C) thrown from the raft into the rushing torrent.
    (D) suddenly on the earth's surface.

48. It was soon discovered that

    (A) the temperature was increasing rapidly.
    (B) the walls were red-hot.
    (C) the water was boiling.
    (D) all of the above were realities.

49. The Professor deduced that they were about to experience

    (A) an earthquake.
    (B) a volcanic eruption.
    (C) certain death.
    (D) something other than any of the above.

50. The voyagers soon discovered that they had returned to the earth's surface in

    (A) Iceland.
    (B) Germany.
    (C) Sicily.
    (D) North America.

(When finished answering the questions, check the answers on the following page.)

Correct Answers for Test

A JOURNEY TO THE CENTER OF THE EARTH

(Value: 2 points each)

Entire book is approximately
84,000 words

1. The correct answer is (C).
2. The correct answer is (C).
3. The correct answer is (B).
4. The correct answer is (C).
5. The correct answer is (C).
6. The correct answer is (A).
7. The correct answer is (B).
8. The correct answer is (C).
9. The correct answer is (C).
10. The correct answer is (D).
11. The correct answer is (D).
12. The correct answer is (C).
13. The correct answer is (C).
14. The correct answer is (C).
15. The correct answer is (A).
16. The correct answer is (D).
17. The correct answer is (C).
18. The correct answer is (C).
19. The correct answer is (B).
20. The correct answer is (D).
21. The correct answer is (A).
22. The correct answer is (B).
23. The correct answer is (B).
24. The correct answer is (C).
25. The correct answer is (C).
26. The correct answer is (A).
27. The correct answer is (A).
28. The correct answer is (B).
29. The correct answer is (A).
30. The correct answer is (B).
31. The correct answer is (A).
32. The correct answer is (C).
33. The correct answer is (B).
34. The correct answer is (A).
35. The correct answer is (B).
36. The correct answer is (A).
37. The correct answer is (C).
38. The correct answer is (D).
39. The correct answer is (B).
40. The correct answer is (C).
41. The correct answer is (D).
42. The correct answer is (A).
43. The correct answer is (D).
44. The correct answer is (B).
45. The correct answer is (B).
46. The correct answer is (C).
47. The correct answer is (B).
48. The correct answer is (D).
49. The correct answer is (B).
50. The correct answer is (C).

COMPREHENSION TEST

Mutiny on the Bounty, by Charles Nordhoff and James Norman Hall

Multiple Choice (2 points each)

(Circle the letter preceding the most correct answer)

1. The name of the narrator's ancestral home is

   (A) Withycombe.
   (B) Quintock Hills.
   (C) Bristol Downs.
   (D) None of the above

2. Byam began his adventure at sea when he was only about

   (A) 17.
   (B) 21.
   (C) 14.
   (D) 15.

3. An earlier famous explorer who visited the South Sea area and is often mentioned in the book was

   (A) Captain Cook.
   (B) Sir Joseph Banks.
   (C) Captain Edwards.
   (D) Lord Hood.

4. The major mission of the *Bounty's* voyage to Tahiti was to gather and then transport

   (A) breadfruit plants.
   (B) slaves.
   (C) various raw precious stones.
   (D) gold and silver ore.

5. Byam's sole official assignment while in Tahiti was to

   (A) study and record the quaint native customs.
   (B) compile a native language dictionary.
   (C) enjoy the breathtaking scenery.
   (D) study the various tropical plants.

6. Before setting out to sea, Byam was one of many to witness

   (A) a cowardly murder.
   (B) the flogging of a seaman already dead from previous lashes.

    (C)   a serious violation of sea law.

    (D)   a formal change of command on a frigate.

7. The native word indicating a very close or special friend was

    (A)   *taio.*

    (B)   *parai.*

    (C)   *rahi.*

    (D)   *tuté.*

8. One of the major Indian taboos was that

    (A)   men and women must never bathe together.

    (B)   men and women must never walk side by side.

    (C)   men and women must never eat together.

    (D)   no one was allowed to drink alcohol before noon.

9. "Old Bacchus," the ship's surgeon, died unexpectedly of

    (A)   alcohol poisoning.

    (B)   a heart attack.

    (C)   eating a poisonous fish.

    (D)   an accidental drowning.

10. Byam's main host on the island of Tahiti was

    (A)   Hitihiti, a chief ruler.

    (B)   Moana, a tribal chief.

    (C)   Hura, a native dancer.

    (D)   Tetiaroa, a minor chief.

11. Of utmost importance to the initiation of the mutiny was Bligh's ridiculous interrogation concerning the missing

    (A)   pineapples.

    (B)   yams.

    (C)   coconuts.

    (D)   bananas.

12. Mr. Christian's on-deck private conversation with Byam regarded a request that if anything untoward should happen, Byam was to contact

    (A)   Christian's family in Cumberland.

    (B)   the English Admiralty in London.

    (C)   Christian's common-law wife in England.

    (D)   a lawyer to administer Christian's will.

13. Captain Bligh and several others were put adrift on the sea in

    (A)   the *Bounty's* cutter.

    (B)   a large rowboat.

    (C)   the ship's launch.

    (D)   another small sailing vessel.

14. It was profoundly clear that Byam was

    (A) a secret but integral part of the mutiny.
    (B) in no way associated with the mutiny.
    (C) a non-active supporter of the mutiny.
    (D) totally unaware of the mutiny until it ended.

15. The number of men set adrift totaled

    (A) 36.
    (B) 41.
    (C) 17.
    (D) 19.

16. One of the *Bounty's* seamen, Stewart, called his Tahitian sweetheart by a name other than her own. He called her

    (A) Sybil.
    (B) Peggy.
    (C) Helen.
    (D) Annie Cleo.

17. After taking command of the *Bounty*, the leader of the mutiny attempted a landing at Tupuai but aborted because of

    (A) unfriendly acts by Indians gathered on the shore.
    (B) unfavorable winds and tides.
    (C) fear of later discovery by an English vessel.
    (D) dangerous submerged shoals and reefs that threatened the ship.

18. Upon landing at Matavia Bay, Tahiti, the nonmutineers were

    (A) permitted to go ashore.
    (B) required to stay on board the *Bounty*.
    (C) not allowed to see their Indian friends.
    (D) treated like common slaves.

19. Byam's and his friends' hoped-for escape from the *Bounty* was foiled by prolonged unfavorable weather and the fact that

    (A) the ship's commander discovered their plan.
    (B) Peggy's sailing canoe sank in heavy waters.
    (C) they lost their nerve at the last minute.
    (D) the commander ordered the *Bounty* to sea too soon.

20. An attempt by the *Bounty's* company to establish a settlement on a part of Tupuai failed because

    (A) the Indians were dangerously hostile.
    (B) their food sources ran out.
    (C) headhunters invaded the island.
    (D) most of the ship's crew lost interest.

21. The ship's company voted concerning their future; some chose to remain with the *Bounty*, while others elected to

    (A) return to England.
    (B) be let off in Tahiti.
    (C) build their own sailing craft.
    (D) become willing prisoners of the mutineers.

22. Those choosing to remain with the *Bounty* included the commander and

    (A) 8 others.
    (B) 22 others.
    (C) 14 others.
    (D) 29 others.

23. Of all the ship's company left on Tahiti, only 7 felt no fear of the arrival, in time, of an English ship because they

    (A) planned to hide far inland.
    (B) had no hand in the mutiny.
    (C) were loyal English subjects.
    (D) fully understood their legal rights.

24. Byam formally met his Tahitian girlfriend, Tehani, while engaged in

    (A) taking a morning bath in the river.
    (B) strolling on a moonlit sandy beach.
    (C) building a hut.
    (D) a ritualistic native dance.

25. The religious part of Byam's wedding was performed by an old native priest named

    (A) Taomi.
    (B) Vehiatua.
    (C) Nui.
    (D) Robinson.

26. Morrison and certain others of the *Bounty's* former company built a small ship which they hoped to sail to Batavia. They christened it early on as the

    (A) *Freedom*.
    (B) *Resolution*.
    (C) *Liberty*.
    (D) *Bounty II*.

27. One of the mutineers shot and killed a native father and the child held in his arms just because the mother was innocently curious about his canoe. The murderer was

(A) Thompson.
(B) Burkitt.
(C) Morrison.
(D) Churchill.

28. The English ship that later docked at Matavia was a frigate named the

(A) *Pandora.*
(B) *Valencia.*
(C) *Rescue.*
(D) *Cornwall.*

29. It soon became clear that the English vessel had come to Tahiti

(A) to gather slaves.
(B) to get breadfruit plants.
(C) in search of the *Bounty* and her crew.
(D) to capture the island for England.

30. The only crew member who had participated in the mutiny and who desired to be punished for the crime was an able seaman named

(A) Richard Skinner.
(B) Michael Byrne.
(C) John Summer.
(D) William McCoy.

31. Almost immediately after boarding the newly arrived English ship, Byam was

(A) welcomed as a hero.
(B) thanked for his offer to serve as a harbor guide.
(C) arrested for mutiny/piracy.
(D) put in total command of the vessel.

32. The commmander of the newly arrived English ship was

(A) Captain Edward Edwards.
(B) Lieutenant Carl Parkin.
(C) Captain William Fletcher.
(D) Captain Samuel T. Johnson.

33. Byam and his companions were placed directly under the authority of the master-at-arms,

    (A) Lieutenant Parkin.
    (B) Seaman James Good.
    (C) Jackson, the armourer.
    (D) Mr. Hayward.

34. The demise of the *Pandora* was brought about by

    (A) damage from running aground on a reef.
    (B) a sudden and violent mutiny.
    (C) an accidental gunpowder explosion.
    (D) gunfire from another ship.

35. As a result of the unfortunate events following the end of the *Pandora*, Byam was most saddened at the loss of

    (A) his in-progress dictionary.
    (B) all of his companions.
    (C) his true friend, Stewart.
    (D) his hope to reach England.

36. Making use of certain skills learned while living in Tahiti, the prisoners were able to help all hands by providing

    (A) abundant seafood on occasion.
    (B) expert shipbuilding skills.
    (C) much needed fresh water.
    (D) improved rowing techniques.

37. The weary mariners, in their small boats, finally arrived at

    (A) Tahiti.
    (B) Timor.
    (C) Port Nelson.
    (D) Namuka.

38. On the nineteenth of June, 1792, the ship anchored in England's

    (A) London Harbour.
    (B) Portsmouth Harbour.
    (C) Cape of Good Hope Harbour.
    (D) Churchill Harbour.

39. Byam's chance for acquittal would depend almost entirely upon the testimony of one man still alive who could support his alibi, a young friend named

    (A) Robert Tinkler.
    (B) Mr. Christian.
    (C) Mr. Nelson.
    (D) Mr. Norton.

40. Sir Joseph Banks arranged that Byam was to be represented by a good lawyer familiar with courts-martial. The lawyer was

    (A) Mr. Graham.
    (B) Sir Winston.
    (C) Lord Tillery.
    (D) Mr. Devonshire.

41. On September 12, the prisoners were ordered to prepare for the start of the court-martial to be held on the

    (A) *H.M.S. Duke.*
    (B) *Hector.*
    (C) mainland.
    (D) *H.M.S. Morales.*

42. Testimony given by Thomas Hayward, Byam's former fellow midshipman, proved to be

    (A) helpful to Byam's defense.
    (B) of no particular consequence.
    (C) damaging to Byam's case.
    (D) totally doubted by every court member.

43. Byam's final comment to members of the Court was:

    (A) "I am, without a doubt, innocent."
    (B) "To the mercy of this Honourable Court I now commit myself."
    (C) "Review the testimony and you will know I am innocent."
    (D) "I rest my case with God."

44. After Byam's defense presentation, it was quite clear that

    (A) his words had favorably impressed the Court.
    (B) the Court as a whole was unimpressed.
    (C) the verdict was up in the air.
    (D) he would be found guilty as charged.

45. The Court's conclusion was that Byam was, without a doubt,

    (A) guilty of all charges.
    (B) to be hanged until dead.
    (C) completely innocent of all charges.
    (D) both (A) and (B).

46. Following the conclusion of the court-martial, Byam and the others were taken on board the

    (A) *Duke.*
    (B) *Hector.*
    (C) *Resolution.*
    (D) *Resource.*

47. The commander of this English ship was

   (A) Captain Montague.
   (B) Captain Bligh.
   (C) Captain Edwards.
   (D) Captain Engstrom.

48. Sir Joseph informed Byam that it was probable that at least one of his convicted friends would be pardoned. That man was

   (A) Mr. Christian.
   (B) William Muspratt.
   (C) William Peckover.
   (D) Thomas Ellison.

49. Byam's salvation was embodied in the fact that the only person known to still be alive and who could confirm the innocent nature of his on-deck conversation with Mr. Christian was

   (A) soon to be found in England.
   (B) willing to testify to the authorities.
   (C) still Byam's friend.
   (D) All of the above

50. After he was found innocent of the charges of mutiny and piracy, Byam decided to

   (A) return immediately to Tahiti.
   (B) make a career of sailing the sea.
   (C) write a book chronicling his adventures.
   (D) retire completely from public life.

(When finished answering the questions, check the answers on the following page.)

Correct Answers for Test

MUTINY ON THE BOUNTY

(Value: 2 points each)

Entire book is approximately
130,000 words

1. The correct answer is (A).
2. The correct answer is (A).
3. The correct answer is (A).
4. The correct answer is (A).
5. The correct answer is (B).
6. The correct answer is (B).
7. The correct answer is (A).
8. The correct answer is (C).
9. The correct answer is (C).
10. The correct answer is (A).
11. The correct answer is (C).
12. The correct answer is (A).
13. The correct answer is (C).
14. The correct answer is (B).
15. The correct answer is (D).
16. The correct answer is (B).
17. The correct answer is (A).
18. The correct answer is (B).
19. The correct answer is (D).
20. The correct answer is (A).
21. The correct answer is (B).
22. The correct answer is (A).
23. The correct answer is (B).
24. The correct answer is (A).
25. The correct answer is (A).
26. The correct answer is (B).
27. The correct answer is (A).
28. The correct answer is (A).
29. The correct answer is (C).
30. The correct answer is (A).
31. The correct answer is (C).
32. The correct answer is (A).
33. The correct answer is (A).
34. The correct answer is (A).
35. The correct answer is (C).
36. The correct answer is (A).
37. The correct answer is (B).
38. The correct answer is (B).
39. The correct answer is (A).
40. The correct answer is (A).
41. The correct answer is (A).
42. The correct answer is (C).
43. The correct answer is (B).
44. The correct answer is (C).
45. The correct answer is (D).
46. The correct answer is (B).
47. The correct answer is (A).
48. The correct answer is (B).
49. The correct answer is (D).
50. The correct answer is (B).

COMPREHENSION TEST

THINK AND GROW RICH

Multiple Choice *(2 points each)*

(Circle the letter preceding the most correct answer)

1. The book's title is

   (A) Plan and Grow Rich.
   (B) Think and Grow Wealthy.
   (C) Think and Grow Rich.
   (D) Scheme and Grow Rich.

2. The author's name is

   (A) Napoleon Bonaparte.
   (B) Napoleon Hill.
   (C) Dale Carnegie.
   (D) Thomas A. Edison.

3. The first chapter's title is

   (A) Wealth is Everything.
   (B) Money Makes the World Work.
   (C) Thoughts Are Things.
   (D) Thoughts Have Wings.

4. Of several whole-page "bill boarded" quotes, which below is not included?

   (A) There Are No Limits to the Mind Except Those We Acknowledge
   (B) Both Poverty and Riches are the Offspring of Thought
   (C) Success Requires No Explanations
   (D) Discredit Your Enemies Before They Discredit You

5. The first "impossible to do" V-8 engine was successfully built by

   (A) Chrysler Motor Company.
   (B) General Motors.
   (C) Studebaker.
   (D) Ford Motor Company.

6. The prolific American inventor dealt with in the first chapter was

   (A) Thomas A. Edison.
   (B) Bernard Thursgood.
   (C) Charles S. Randall.
   (D) Benjamin a Cooperson.

7. The "power of great dreams" is

   (A) of no importance.
   (B) mumbo-jumbo.
   (C) essential and useful.
   (D) of minor importance to success.

8. The book strongly implies that faith actually is

   (A) only for those who are deeply religious.
   (B) the head chemist of the mind.
   (C) not related to desire.
   (D) not clearly emotion-based.

9. The medium for influencing the subconscious mind is through

   (A) hypnosis.
   (B) dreaming.
   (C) autosuggestion.
   (D) controlled relaxation.

10. According to the book, the best means for acquiring the necessary "specialized knowledge" is through

   (A) a "Master Mind" group.
   (B) an advanced college degree.
   (C) deep and intense meditation.
   (D) learning yoga.

11. The Fifth Step toward riches is said to be

   (A) a good education.
   (B) concentration.
   (C) imagination.
   (D) hard work.

12. The Sixth Step toward riches is

   (A) organized planning.
   (B) getting money from pals.
   (C) crystallization of desire into action.
   (D) both (A) and (C).

13. Earning money involves the selling of

    (A) personal services.
    (B) real estate.
    (C) products.
    (D) both (A) and (C).

14. Some of the major attributes of leadership are

    (A) assuming responsibility, unwavering courage, self-
         control.
    (B) mastering details, a sense of justice, decisiveness.
    (C) planning, giving more. pleasing personality, understand-
         ing.
    (D) all of the above.

15. There are thirty-one named major causes of failure. Which
    one below is not readily correctable by an individual so
    affected?

    (A) An unfavorable hereditary background
    (B) The lack of a well-defined purpose in life
    (C) An insufficient education
    (D) The lack of self-discipline

16. A very important step in achieving success and riches relates to

    (A) going on an extended trip.
    (B) demanding a raise in pay.
    (C) taking an inventory on yourself.
    (D) getting a different job.

17. According to the author, the mastery of procrastination is best
    achieved through

    (A) personal diet improvement.
    (B) demonstrating more courage.
    (C) reaching decision.
    (D) a good exercise program.

18. The fifty-six signers of the Declaration of Independence
    understood fully that the final outcome could bring

    (A) fame and fortune.
    (B) hanging from the gallows.
    (C) exciting political futures.
    (D) worldwide recognition.

19. An important point the book emphasizes is:

    (A) If you know what you want you'll generally get it.
    (B) You waste time when trying to determine what you want.
    (C) Even if you don't know what you want you will succeed anyhow.
    (D) You have no valid way of knowing what you really want.

20. The Sixth Step (persistence) toward riches is described as

    (A) putting forth an average amount of effort.
    (B) the sustained effort necessary to induce faith.
    (C) being of only minor importance.
    (D) an impossible task for the average person.

21. Willpower and desire combined result in

    (A) a very dangerous combination.
    (B) an unworkable mix.
    (C) an irresistible pair.
    (D) little real progress to riches.

22. Developing persistence is a four-step process. Which one listed below is not one of the steps?

    (A) A definite purpose backed by a burning desire for fulfillment.
    (B) A definite plan, expressed in continuous action.
    (C) A mind closed tightly against all negative and discouraging influences.
    (D) A clever and innovative scheme that is executed properly.

23. The Ninth Step toward riches is

    (A) personal power.
    (B) the force for good.
    (C) the power of the "Master Mind."
    (D) compassion for all mankind.

24. In relation to accumulating wealth, "power" may be defined as

    (A) organized and intelligently directed knowledge.
    (B) a talent for gaining total control of others.
    (C) a clever means to manipulate others.
    (D) the effective use of some type of mass hypnosis.

25. Which of the following is not necessarily a real source of knowledge?

    (A)   "Infinite Intelligence"
    (B)   Accumulated experience
    (C)   Experiment and research
    (D)   Holding several college degrees

26. The emotion of sex has several constructive potentials. Which of the following is not necessarily constructive?

    (A)   The pleasure of sex itself.
    (B)   The perpetuation of mankind.
    (C)   Maintenance of health as a therapeutic agency.
    (D)   The transformation of mediocrity into genius through transmutation.

27. In an analysis of over 25,000 very successful individuals, it was determined that very few realized noteworthy success before the age of

    (A)   20.
    (B)   30.
    (C)   40.
    (D)   60.

28. A study of 30,000 salespersons revealed that those who were most successful were

    (A)   over 50 years of age.
    (B)   highly sexed.
    (C)   very good looking.
    (D)   slightly overweight.

29. Personal magnetism is demonstrated though the following media:

    (A)   the handshake.
    (B)   the tone of the voice.
    (C)   posture and carriage of body.
    (D)   All of the above

30. When the emotion of love is mixed with the emotion of sex the result is

    (A)   calmness and purpose.
    (B)   accuracy of judgment.
    (C)   overall balance.
    (D)   All of the above

31. The average person reaches the period of their greatest ability to create between

    (A) 40 and 60.
    (B) 40 and 50.
    (C) 30 and 40.
    (D) 20 and 30.

32. The Eleventh Step to riches is

    (A) increasing willpower.
    (B) creating a determination to win.
    (C) using the subconscious mind.
    (D) having friends in high places.

33. The author states that the subconscious mind

    (A) works day and night.
    (B) cannot be controlled entirely.
    (C) will not remain idle.
    (D) is akin to all of the above.

34. The major positive emotions (to be cultivated) number

    (A) 14.
    (B) 7.
    (C) 10.
    (D) 3.

35. The major negative emotions (to be avoided) number

    (A) 7.
    (B) 28.
    (C) 10.
    (D) 12.

36. In the book, the human brain is said to be

    (A) a mass of organized cells.
    (B) a broadcasting and receiving station for thought.
    (C) everyone's greatest asset.
    (D) None of the above

37. The "sixth sense" is said to be

    (A) the doorway to the temple of wisdom.
    (B) the apex of the author's philosophy.
    (C) the creative imagination.
    (D) All of the above

38. Fears are described as being

    (A) nothing more than a state of mind.
    (B) impossible to overcome.
    (C) best dealt with by ignoring them.
    (D) nothing to be concerned about.

39. Symptoms of the fear of poverty include (in part)

    (A) indifference.
    (B) indecision.
    (C) doubt.
    (D) All of the above

40. Symptoms of the fear of criticism include (in part)

    (A) self-consciousness.
    (B) lack of poise.
    (C) extravagance.
    (D) All of the above

41. The fear of ill health includes (in part)

    (A) all the below.
    (B) autosuggestion.
    (C) hypochondria.
    (D) self coddling.

42. Symptoms of the fear of the loss of lover are (in part)

    (A) jealousy.
    (B) fault-finding.
    (C) gambling (taking chances).
    (D) all of the above.

43. Symptoms of the fear of old age include (in part)

    (A) slowing down and developing an inferiority complex.
    (B) speaking of self as being old.
    (C) killing off initiative, imagination, self-reliance.
    (D) all of the above.

44. In addition to the basic fears, there is a very harmful evil the author calls

    (A) susceptibility to negative, harmful influences.
    (B) procrastination.
    (C) living alone.
    (D) eating too much.

45. Without doubt the most common weakness of all human beings is the habit of

    (A) becoming too lazy to exercise properly.
    (B) leaving the mind open to the negative input from others.
    (C) retiring too early.
    (D) not keeping up with the times.

46. You have absolute control over but one thing, and that is

    (A) your diet.
    (B) your finances.
    (C) your thoughts.
    (D) your spouse.

47. People who do not succeed have one distinct trait in common—they know

    (A) all the reasons for failure.
    (B) their bosses were to blame.
    (C) they never got a fair chance.
    (D) they chose the wrong career.

48. The author states that the "Master Key" that unlocks the door to life's bountiful riches is

    (A) intangible but powerful.
    (B) only for a select few.
    (C) unbelievably easy to find.
    (D) useful only for material gain.

49. This book could accurately be classified as

    (A) a self-help publication.
    (B) a how-to book.
    (C) a formula for success.
    (D) all of the above.

50. In the final paragraph, the writer borrows the words "we shall meet" from what well-known writer?

    (A) Plato
    (B) Longfellow
    (C) Emerson
    (D) Frost

(When finished answering the questions, check the answers on the following page.)

Correct Answers for Test

THINK AND GROW RICH

(Value: 2 points each)

Entire book is approximately
75,000 words.

1. The correct answer is (C).	26. The correct answer is (A).
2. The correct answer is (B).	27. The correct answer is (C).
3. The correct answer is (C).	28. The correct answer is (B).
4. The correct answer is (D).	29. The correct answer is (D).
5. The correct answer is (D).	30. The correct answer is (D).
6. The correct answer is (A).	31. The correct answer is (A).
7. The correct answer is (C).	32. The correct answer is (C).
8. The correct answer is (B).	33. The correct answer is (D).
9. The correct answer is (C).	34. The correct answer is (B).
10. The correct answer is (A).	35. The correct answer is (A).
11. The correct answer is (C).	36. The correct answer is (B).
12. The correct answer is (D).	37. The correct answer is (D).
13. The correct answer is (D).	38. The correct answer is (A).
14. The correct answer is (D).	39. The correct answer is (D).
15. The correct answer is (A).	40. The correct answer is (D).
16. The correct answer is (C).	41. The correct answer is (A).
17. The correct answer is (C).	42. The correct answer is (D).
18. The correct answer is (B).	43. The correct answer is (D).
19. The correct answer is (A).	44. The correct answer is (A).
20. The correct answer is (B).	45. The correct answer is (B).
21. The correct answer is (C).	46. The correct answer is (C).
22. The correct answer is (D).	47. The correct answer is (A).
23. The correct answer is (C).	48. The correct answer is (A).
24. The correct answer is (A).	49. The correct answer is (D).
25. The correct answer is (D).	50. The correct answer is (C).

COMPREHENSION TEST

THE DEATH OF COMMON SENSE

Multiple Choice *(4 points each)*

(Circle the letter preceding the most correct answer)

1. The book's title is

    (A) Death of Common Courtesy.
    (B) The Demise of Common Sense.
    (C) The Death of Common Sense.
    (D) none of the above.

2. The book's subtitle is

    (A) How Law is Suffocating America.
    (B) Is Everyone Just Plain Foolish?
    (C) The Buck Never Stops.
    (D) Good Laws for America.

3. Which of the following is a chapter title?

    (A) A Nation of Enemies
    (B) More Laws, More Progress
    (C) Political Correctness is Good
    (D) Good Laws for America

4. The author's name is

    (A) Howard K. Phillips.
    (B) K. Howard Philip.
    (C) Philip K. Howard.
    (D) none of the above.

5. How many chapters are in the book?

    (A) 12
    (B) 14
    (C) 6
    (D) 4

6. The author grew up in small towns in eastern

    (A) Texas.
    (B) Kentucky.
    (C) Florida.
    (D) North Carolina

7. The author is a professional in the field of

 (A) law.
 (B) medicine.
 (C) finance.
 (D) economics.

8. In the "selected bibliography" in the back of the book, there are

 (A) three pages.
 (B) 10 pages.
 (C) four pages.
 (D) six pages.

9. Which two widely known persons are mentioned on the first page of the first chapter?

 (A) Mother Teresa
 (B) Ed Koch
 (C) neither
 (D) both

10. The planned-for renovation of the two fire-gutted buildings was eventually abandoned primarily because city building codes required an unnecessary $100,000

 (A) firewall.
 (B) elevator.
 (C) paved parking lot.
 (D) sprinkler system.

11. Following to the letter EPA's (Environmental Protection Agency) detailed regulations, a major oil company spent $31 million installing benzene filters in smokestacks. The result was

 (A) little benzene filters was filtered.
 (B) $31 million was wasted.
 (C) EPA was wrong.
 (D) all of the above.

12. According to the author, the laws of government controls affects

 (A) little of anyone's private life.
 (B) almost every activity of common interest.
 (C) only what is really necessary.
 (D) only activities related to national / international matters.

13. "The characteristic complaint of our time seems to be not that government provides no reasons, but that its reasons often seem remote from human beings who must live with their consequences." This was state by

    (A) former Supreme Court Justice William Brennan.
    (B) Jimmy Carter.
    (C) Al Gore.
    (D) none of the above.

14. According to the author, laws inevitably result in rules, some of which are

    (A) ridiculous.
    (B) often impossible to understand fully.
    (C) typically very expensive to implement / obey.
    (D) all of the above.

15. The opposite of ironclad rules formulated as the result of legislative laws is

    (A) common law.
    (B) common sense.
    (C) the creating of more laws.
    (D) none of the above.

16. When government rules-enforcement inspectors visit a business to inspect, the owner is all but guaranteed that

    (A) all will go smoothly.
    (B) inspectors will be very reasonable.
    (C) fines will not be imposed.
    (D) violations will be found.

17. History proves the more precise and detailed laws are made,

    (A) the more loopholes are created.
    (B) the less they will be broken.
    (C) the less money lawyers will make.
    (D) the less power the government is given.

18. In 1962, Rachel Carson helped to give birth to the environmental movement by writing a book exposing the effects of DDT and other pesticides. It was titled

    (A) Our Poisoned Food.
    (B) The Sad Truth.
    (C) Silent Spring.
    (D) Where the Birds Are.

19. In the bureaucratic world it is not that things are approached sensibly but that

    (A) everything loves up to the precepts of universal fairness and objectivity.
    (B) every form is filled out.
    (C) there is total honesty about everything.
    (D) everything be done quickly.

20. The author states "...our bureaucratic crew is so busy playing procedural hymns that, like the band on the deck of the Titanic, it

    (A) knows what's really at stake.
    (B) does an excellent job.
    (C) has given up trying to go anywhere.
    (D) actually seeks real progress.

21. Trying to get rid of an inept federal employee is

    (A) so difficult that most supervisors don't try.
    (B) very easy to do.
    (C) very time-consuming.
    (D) encouraged by the bureaucratic process.

22. "Process" was intended to make sure everything was done responsibly but has become

    (A) a device for manipulation.
    (B) a device for extortion.
    (C) a near-total farce.
    (D) all of the above.

23. John F. Kennedy's "Ask not what your country can do for you, what you can do for your country seems now to have disintegrated into

    (A) a preoccupation with our "due," not what we can do.
    (B) a part of everyone's acts.
    (C) the nation's philosophy.
    (D) none of the above.

24. Because of the ever-increasing mountain of rules, Americans in general are feeling a sort of

    (A) collective powerlessness.
    (B) euphoria.
    (C) greater freedom.
    (D) growing satisfaction.

25. The overall tone of the book seems to suggest the author is

    (A)   in favor of the status quo.
    (B)   neutral about the status quo.
    (C)   is not in favor of the status quo.
    (D)   is overjoyed by the status quo.

(When finished answering the questions, check the answers below.)

Correct Answers for Test

THE DEATH OF COMMON SENSE

(Value: 4 points each)

Entire Book is approximately
51,000 words

1. The correct answer is (C).	14. The correct answer is (D).
2. The correct answer is (A).	15. The correct answer is (A).
3. The correct answer is (A).	16. The correct answer is (D).
4. The correct answer is (C).	17. The correct answer is (A).
5. The correct answer is (D).	18. The correct answer is (C).
6. The correct answer is (B).	19. The correct answer is (A).
7. The correct answer is (A).	20. The correct answer is (C).
8. The correct answer is (B).	21. The correct answer is (A).
9. The correct answer is (D).	22. The correct answer is (D).
10. The correct answer is (B).	23. The correct answer is (A).
11. The correct answer is (D).	24. The correct answer is (A).
12. The correct answer is (B).	25. The correct answer is (C).
13. The correct answer is (A).	

APPENDIX 1

Techniques of Better Study

In this section you will learn...

📖 worthwhile techniques for achieving better, more effective and productive study skills

📖 how to select the better (and avoid the worse) times to study productively

📖 which are the better—and less desirable—places to study and learn

📖 what "props" can aid or detract from the value of your study time

📖 how long you can study effectively, and when and how best to take breaks

A Definite Time

Do you know how to regulate and control your study time? Do you know how to squeeze the last drop of advantage from the time you spend attempting to learn what you need or desire to know? This section contains many worthwhile suggestions, guidelines, and hints relative to the "how" and "why" of effective study. Why not give them a look?

Set aside a specific period of time in your daily schedule that shall be known by you (and others!) as your "Official Study Period." Set a minimum and a maximum amount of time to be spent; observe these limits faithfully—even if you think you have "nothing to study."

Truthfully and fairly, you cannot say, "The instructor did not make a specific assignment for the next class, so there is nothing to study." If there is no specific assignment for the following class meeting, use your study period for a good review. This will practically guarantee that you will never need to stay up all night to "cram" for the next all-important test.

Once you establish your "Official Study Period," never allow a non-study activity to take priority over it. Tell your friends not to telephone or to come by for a visit. Do not answer the phone or the door and instruct others in the house to say that you are "out."

How much study time will you need? Of course, this will vary, but if you are a student, you should be able to determine this soon after courses begin. College catalogs generally suggest that a student should spend two hours of outside study/preparation per week for each semester credit. This means a three-credit course deserves six outside study hours each week.

A DEFINITE PLACE

Where exactly should you study? Any place—a desk in your room, the kitchen table—where you can be reasonably comfortable and as far away as possible from the mainstream of activity in your home, dormitory, library, or office. Stay far afield from the television set, your little sister, your friends and other potential attention grabbers!

It is most important that the spot you select be one that you normally do not use for any other purpose but study. If it is the table where you often play cards, it is too easy to begin thinking about the last game there rather than about what you are trying to study.

STUDY PROPS

In a stage production, you need certain props—a knife, umbrella, candle, etc.—to enhance your performance and make it successful. Similarly, when studying, certain props can contribute to the effectiveness of your comprehension.

Use a desk or table of adequate size and height, and clear it of everything except the book or materials you actually require to study the particular subject on which you are working at the moment. You cannot concentrate fully on writing a theme for English class if an algebra book is in front of you with 20 problems to be solved, together with a half-dozen other tasks and assignments vying for your attention. The other tasks can be each addressed in turn after you have completely finished the first assignment. You will accomplish more and do better if you devote full attention to one subject at a time.

As far as chairs are concerned, sit in one that is not too cushy and comfortable, since these seem to conspire against effective study, and too often result in an unexpected snooze!

Light and Temperature

Concentrate adequate but not glaring light on the desk or table. The rest of the room should be lighted only very softly. With soft light in the background, distant objects—paintings, wallpaper, art objects, etc.—will have less of a chance of interfering with your attention and concentration.

The temperature should be a little cooler than "normal." It is practically certain you will, sooner or later, become sleepy if the area is warmer than it should be. Open a window for some fresh air if possible.

DURATION OF STUDY

How long can you study effectively at one sitting? Of course, this depends on several factors, but it is relatively safe to estimate that approximately 30 to 45 minutes is the maximum time you can study with real efficiency without taking a break. Therefore, it is both wise and reasonable to plan to take a five-minute break every half to three-quarter hour.

When you do break, get completely away from your work, both physically and mentally. Take a walk through or around the house. Stretch. Do a few physical exercises. Get a drink of water or a glass of juice or milk. Reward yourself.

After five minutes, you can resume studying, mentally and physically refreshed, and ready to learn at an optimum level. This study-break technique will enable you to study for longer periods of time with minimum fatigue and maximum efficiency. Try it and see; you will not be sorry.

APPENDIX 2

Better Test Scores

In this section you will learn...

📖 how to assure better results with those all-important test scores

📖 methods and techniques to prepare yourself both mentally and psychologically for any test or exam

📖 common sense ways to assure you score higher on any true or false quiz

📖 helpful information to achieve better grades on multiple choice tests

📖 how to make essay-type tests easier, and how to improve your chances for a more positive outcome—and a better mark

Prepare Mentally and Psychologically

To make high scores on tests and examinations, you must: 1) know the subject matter well; and 2) know how to take tests. (In effect, you need to be a "testologist.")

Suggestions to help you know the subject well have been discussed at length in various other portions of this book. Thus, the purpose of this chapter is to divulge the techniques and "secrets" of the art of test-taking.

Test scores are exceedingly important even though they may not fully (or even accurately) measure or reflect what you really know—unfortunately, they measure only what you put on paper. Imperfect as they may be, it is a fact of life that more often than not individuals, in both education and industry, either succeed or fail because of what they do or do not "put on paper."

Too often, low scores on examinations are caused by lack of skill in test-taking rather than any real lack of study or knowledge of the subject matter.

Is there anything you can do to help get those scores up and keep them up? Fortunately, there is.

First and foremost, make certain that you have done everything within reason to know the subject thoroughly. Keep up with all assignments and homework preceding the test. Review thoroughly, study your notes, and test yourself. This sort of thorough preparation will help to instill self-confidence—an important prerequisite for making better scores.

Secondly, after you have thoroughly prepared, and done all you can to be ready, put worry about failure aside totally. What is the very worst thing that could happen? You might fail the test. Of course you do not want this to happen, but it would not mean the end of the world. Do not worry; worry is a non-profit practice. Develop more faith and confidence in yourself; no one else can do this for you.

Know Tests Are Only Routine

When a test is given, remember that it is no different really than a daily assignment; the only real difference is that you will need to budget your time more carefully.

Once the test is in your hands, immediately and quickly preview its total content. Note the number and types of questions and the point value for each. Make quick decisions concerning the amount of time you will allow for each part or question. You will find that pencilled marginal notations of the time to be allotted will serve well to help you get through the whole test within the appointed period.

Next, place your watch where you can see it easily, or note the time on the classroom clock. This is most important since you will be, in effect, working against the clock to finish. Time will be your ongoing reminder of how well you are progressing.

Then, dive right in. Answer the first question. Concentrate all your attention on it, forgetting all other questions at the moment. When you have completed it, tackle question number 2, etc. Do not hesitate; do not sit and worry. Take action. Action helps to keep concentration-robbing fear away.

Proceed steadily through the test, noting the amount of time remaining from time to time. Don't panic if you are a little behind on the time schedule; just work a little faster. Clear the cobwebs from your mind—think, write.

If you finish early, go back through and add or, if you are sure, change any answers or statements that seem wrong or weak when you read them. Remember, the teacher must evaluate what you actually put on paper, not what you "meant."

If time permits, check through again. This time be especially alert to spot and correct any technical or grammatical errors or weaknesses—spelling, punctuation, incomplete sentences, unclear writing, etc. Also make certain that you have numbered answers and pages correctly, and that test pages are arranged in correct order.

Never turn in your paper until the teacher requests it. That important answer you are searching for in memory just could turn up suddenly, but this will not help your score if the test is already submitted. (It seems some students think finishing early and turning their tests in proves how "smart" they are. If these individuals do not receive perfect scores consistently, perhaps they should stop trying to impress others and impress themselves instead.)

In summary, you never should be concerned with the test as a whole until it is completed; conquer it question by question. If you should experience a mental block at some point, take a couple of deep breaths and relax. Then re-read the question. If the "block" persists, go immediately to the next question and, without worry, keep working until you are ready to come back to the question that stumped you earlier. Above all, realize that worrying about the outcome of the test while you are taking it is counterproductive. Just give it all you have; that is the best—and all—you can do.

TRUE OR FALSE TESTS

The real secret for success with true or false tests is extreme care in reading each and every statement. Since most statements read in textbooks and heard in lectures are "true," the true or false exam puts the test taker in the rather novel position of identifying and sifting out the false—the non-truths. It is easy for the eyes to play tricks on you mainly because of the "positive" conditioning that is incorporated into the educational experience and, to an important degree, life as well. The eyes, at least momentarily, can be "blind" to a *no, not, never* in a statement, just as the mind can think a cleverly stated near-truth is absolutely true.

Just remember, if any statement (question) is not *totally* true, it must be marked as false. There are *no* exceptions; there can be no half-truths or near-truths in this type of test.

True or false tests typically contain a relatively large number of statements (questions); therefore you must read each question with utmost care, answer it to the best of your ability, and then move promptly to the next one. Many students find that it pays to allow their intuition to help with true-false tests, especially when they have no educated notion as to which is the correct answer.

If you have time to go back to check over the test, invariably doubts about some answers will arise. These doubts can cause a change of answers that often will lower your final score.

Therefore, never change any answer unless you are convinced the first response is incorrect for one of these reasons: 1) you misread the question the first time; 2) a later question gives a definite clue to indicate an error in this response; 3) you answered in the wrong blank or were guilty of another mechanical error. Never change a response (answer) for any other reason.

Attempt to answer all questions. Since you are graded on the number of correct responses, you should try even those questions you do not know. You have a 50-50 chance of getting them correct. These odds are too good to dismiss.

MULTIPLE CHOICE TESTS

It has been said (and perhaps with good reason) that multiple choice tests are manifestations of sadistic minds. These exams can, indeed, be tricky. Very careful reading is an absolute necessity. You must give full attention to each and every question before you mark an answer. Read each question twice. Then read the question and each answer choice together. Make your choice carefully and then move to the next "challenge." If you have time to check your work, be cautious regarding answer changes unless you are sure.

Essay Type Tests

These are the bugaboo of far too many students. Essay tests call for far more originality, creativity, and organizational ability than do any of the objective tests. However, even on these tests, there are some "tricks of the trade" which will prove most helpful if utilized competently.

As with all tests, preview it carefully and make estimates of time allowances for each question or section.

When you begin writing, concern yourself with answering only one question at a time. Try to forget about all the others until you get to them individually. Start to answer only after you are certain about what is being asked. Are you to define? compare? contrast? explain? discuss? outline? list? give examples? Each of these words or terms calls for a different type of response. Be certain you know what is expected and then go ahead.

If time permits, read through all answers and make additions, changes, and routine corrections if necessary.

Since essay-type examinations typically require more time than objective tests (comparatively, at least), it is most important to begin work as soon as the test is given to you, and to work steadily and efficiently until you finish. Re-checking your work is practically mandatory.

In a Nutshell

For all tests, prepare adequately in advance. (This includes having the necessary materials—paper, calculator, writing instruments, etc.) Relax; start work immediately; budget your time; read each question carefully; be concerned with only one answer at a time; recheck your work if time permits; and never turn in your paper until the teacher asks for it.

APPENDIX 3

Why This Method Works

The Cutler Acceleread Method and the other techniques described and explained in Triple Your Reading Speed are based on the following premises:

I. The average reader can increase, by a minimum of three times, his present reading rate.

II. Reading is a skill—a developed or acquired ability.

   A. An acquired or developed ability can be developed further, refined, and improved—but only to the degree of the individual's desire and motivation.

   B. A carefully worked out and tested course or program is essential to facilitate measurable improvement.

   C. Reading rates, methods, and patterns can and do become habit.

      1. In time, it is normal for an individual, lacking supervision or specialized training, to acquire and fix, by ongoing repetition, slow, ineffective reading habits and practices.

      2. More often than not, primary instruction in both oral and "forced" silent reading tends to fix the "normal" silent reading rate at or near the oral reading (speech) rate of approximately 150 words per minute.

      3. Vocalization and subvocalization—reading aloud or "reading aloud silently"—is the practice which is usually learned by the beginning reader.

      4. Once the oral reader learns to read silently, there rarely is any further instruction in silent reading throughout the entire educational experience.

III. Reading rate may be increased by either or both of two methods.

    A. If the individual, over an extended period or time, reads voluminously.

    B. If the individual has specialized instruction relative to increasing his reading rate.

IV. Reading rate is determined primarily and importantly by the deviations of eye fixations (stops) made per line of print.

    A. It is necessary to reduce the number of eye-stops in order to achieve marked increases in reading rate.

        1. A conscious and deliberate control of eye movement must be acquired.

        2. The vision consciousness (eye span) area must be increased.

        3. A regular, systematic method for visually covering the printed page must be developed and prac ticed.

        4. Intensive and extensive practice with faster, more effective methods is necessary.

    B. As eye fixations (stops) are reduced, reading speed increases accordingly.

V. Reading rate (and comprehension) is determined further by other reasons and conditions.

    A. The reader's basic intelligence, coordination, and visual acuity.

    B. The type of material being read.

    C. The purpose(s) for which the material is read.

    D. The reader's familiarity with the field or subject.

    E. The degree or level of the reader's interest and/or motivation.

    F. The reader's attitude toward reading in general, and the subject in particular.

    G. The reader's immediate state of health, well-being, fatigue, comfort, etc.

    H. The individual's previous reading experience, or lack of same.

VI. Reading is a mental activity primarily; to a lesser degree, it is also a physical one.

   A. Any activity—mental or physical—requires the expenditure of energy.

   B. Prolonged or sustained exertion of energy will produce fatigue.

   C. Fatigue, either mental or physical, tends to lessen the individual's ability to concentrate.

   D. Reducing the total time required to read a given amount of material will aid comprehension by actually reducing fatigue—both mental and physical.

VII. The total meaning and content of a book, short story, play, letter, etc., cannot be understood or appreciated fully until the entire content has been read.

   A. Reading effectively at a faster rate will enable the individual reader to see the "whole" more quickly, thereby improving overall understanding.

   B. The normal individual's thinking rate far exceeds his speech rate of approximately 150 words per minute.

VIII. Few persons know how to study effectively; teaching them proper and effective study practices will result in more productive study time and improved comprehension.

APPENDIX 4

How to Prepare a "Time-Tape"

If you have a tape recorder, a 60-minute tape, and an hour of free time, why not prepare a special training aid that will help you become an Accelerated Reader?

Select a very quiet place where you will not be interrupted by the telephone or other distractions for at least an hour.

In addition to taping equipment, you will need a stopwatch (ideally), a regular electric clock, or another clock or watch with a sweep second hand. Set and synchronize all three hands to 12 o'clock, then unplug the clock until you are ready to begin. Before you begin, make certain everything is in working order or you may waste valuable time and end up with a useless tape.

When ready, press *record* and start the tape; then start the stopwatch or clock. Say, "Begin."

First 5 Minutes: After five seconds, say, "Five," at 10 seconds, say, "Ten," etc., "Fifty-five, *one minute.*" (Count each 5 seconds—naming *each* minute—through 5 minutes.)

Second 5 Minutes: At 10 seconds past 5 minutes, say, "Ten, twenty," etc., "Fifty, *six minutes.*" (Count each 10 seconds—naming *each* minute—through 10 minutes.)

Third 5 Minutes: At 15 seconds past 10 minutes, say, "Fifteen, thirty," etc., "*Eleven minutes.*" (Count each 15 seconds—naming *each* minute—through 15 minutes.)

Next 15 Minutes: At 20 seconds past 15 minutes, say, "Twenty, forty, *sixteen minutes.*" (Count each 20 seconds—naming *each* minute—through 30 minutes.)

Final 30 Minutes: At 30 seconds past 30 minutes, say, "Thirty seconds, *thirty-one minutes.*" (Count each 30 seconds—naming *each* minute—through 60 minutes.)

Do not use this "Time-Tape" for either "Inventory Selection 1" or "Inventory Selection 2." However, its use for all other timed reading exercises—including the seven book-length assignments—can be most beneficial.

NOTE: A "Time-Tape" is not at all mandatory since full instructions for using a regular clock or watch are given in the instructions for all readings.